In all the darkest pages of the malign

supernatural there is no more terrible

tradition than that of the Vampire, a pariah

even among demons. Foul are his ravages;

gruesome and seemingly barbaric are the

ancient and approved methods by which folk

must rid themselves of this hideous pest.

IN FESTO B.M.V. DEL DIVINO AIUTO.
MONTAGUE SUMMERS
FROM HIS BOOK *THE VAMPIRE: HIS KITH AND KIN*
1928

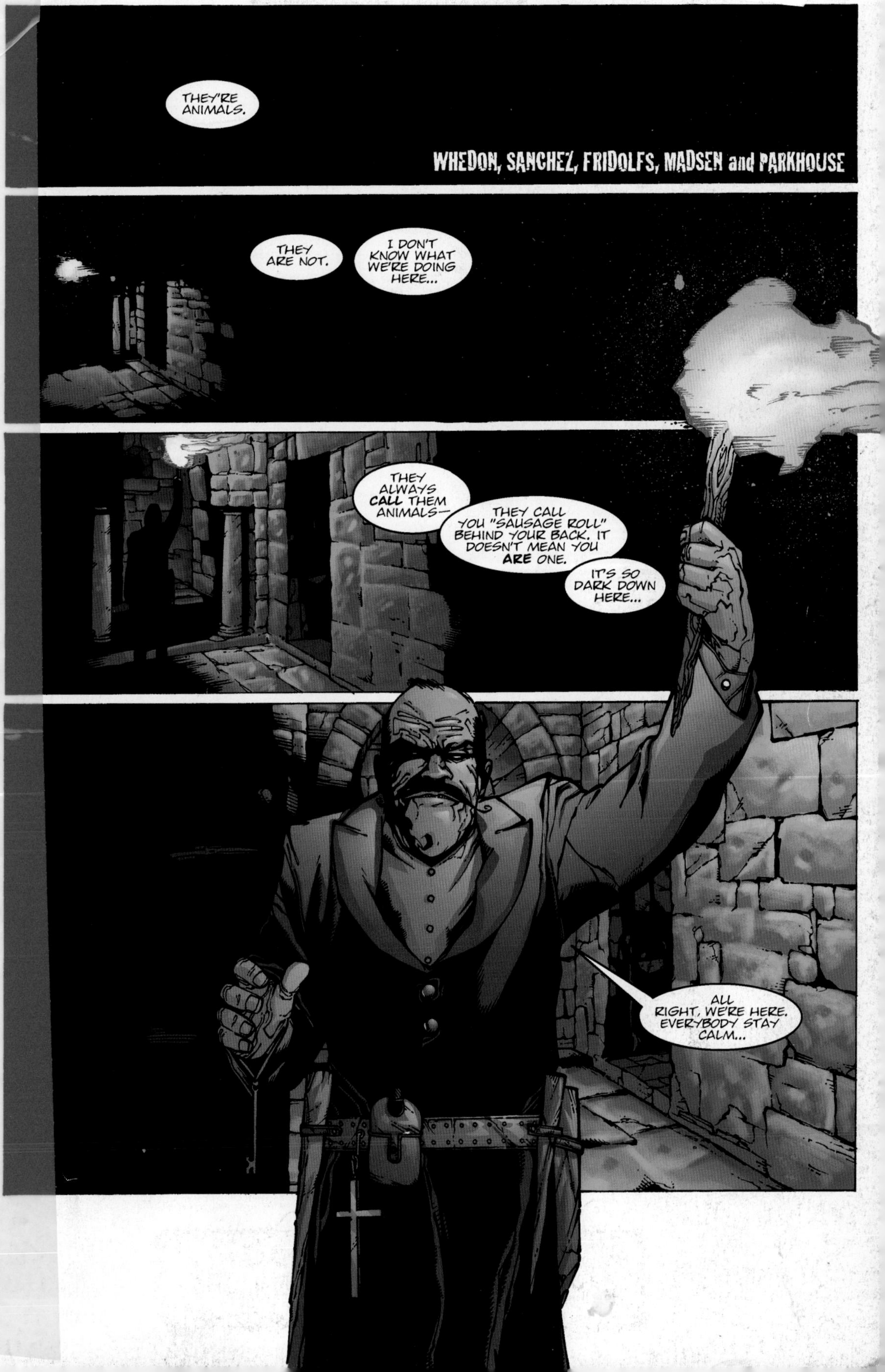
THEY'RE ANIMALS.
WHEDON, SANCHEZ, FRIDOLFS, MADSEN and PARKHOUSE
THEY ARE NOT.
I DON'T KNOW WHAT WE'RE DOING HERE...
THEY ALWAYS **CALL** THEM ANIMALS—
THEY CALL YOU "SAUSAGE ROLL" BEHIND YOUR BACK. IT DOESN'T MEAN YOU **ARE** ONE.
IT'S SO DARK DOWN HERE...
ALL RIGHT, WE'RE HERE. EVERYBODY STAY CALM...

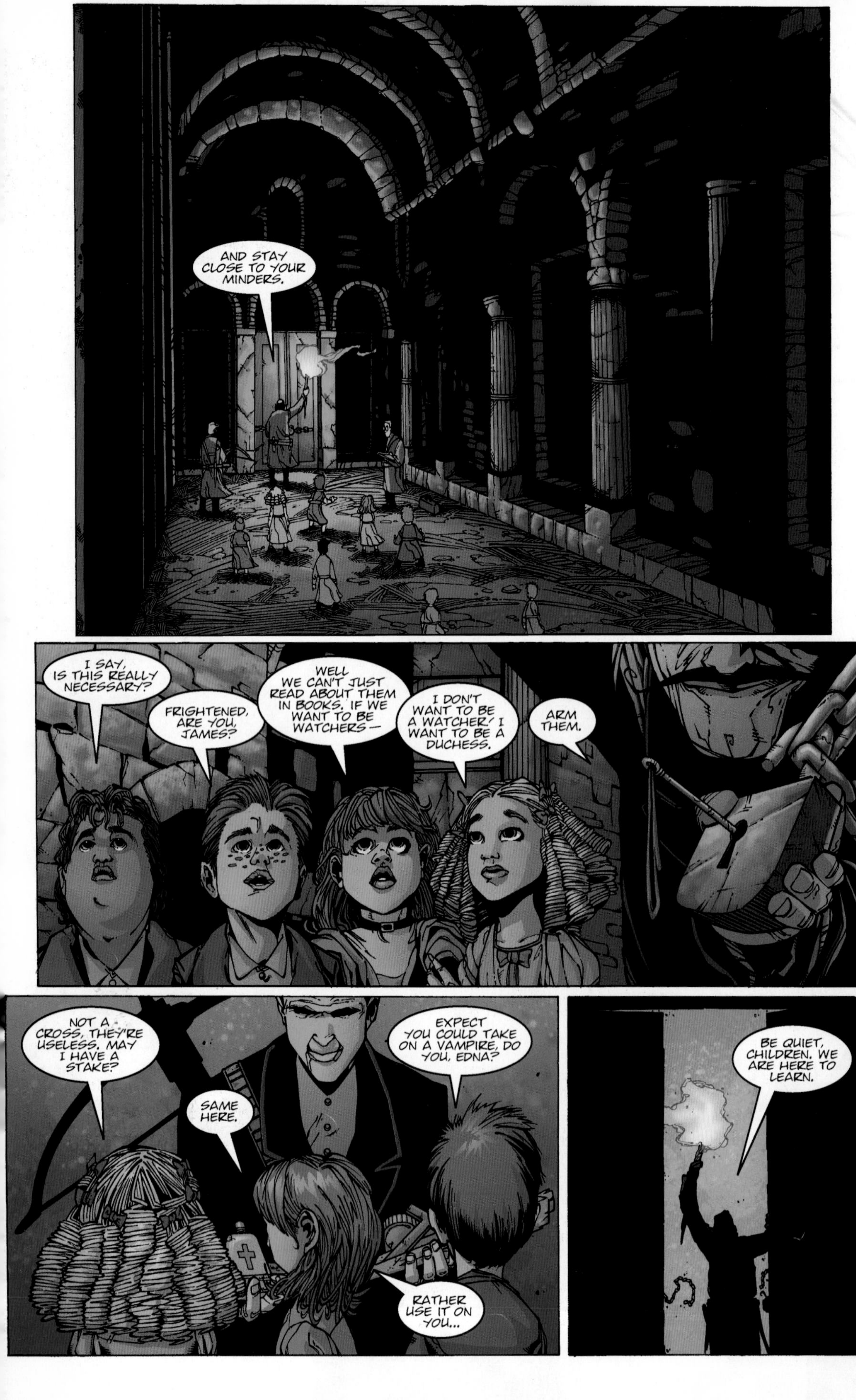
AND STAY CLOSE TO YOUR MINDERS.
I SAY, IS THIS REALLY NECESSARY?
FRIGHTENED, ARE YOU, JAMES?
WELL WE CAN'T JUST READ ABOUT THEM IN BOOKS. IF WE WANT TO BE WATCHERS—
I DON'T WANT TO BE A WATCHER! I WANT TO BE A DUCHESS.
ARM THEM.
NOT A CROSS, THEY'RE USELESS. MAY I HAVE A STAKE?
SAME HERE.
EXPECT YOU COULD TAKE ON A VAMPIRE, DO YOU, EDNA?
RATHER USE IT ON YOU...
BE QUIET, CHILDREN. WE ARE HERE TO LEARN.

BUFFY the VAMPIRE

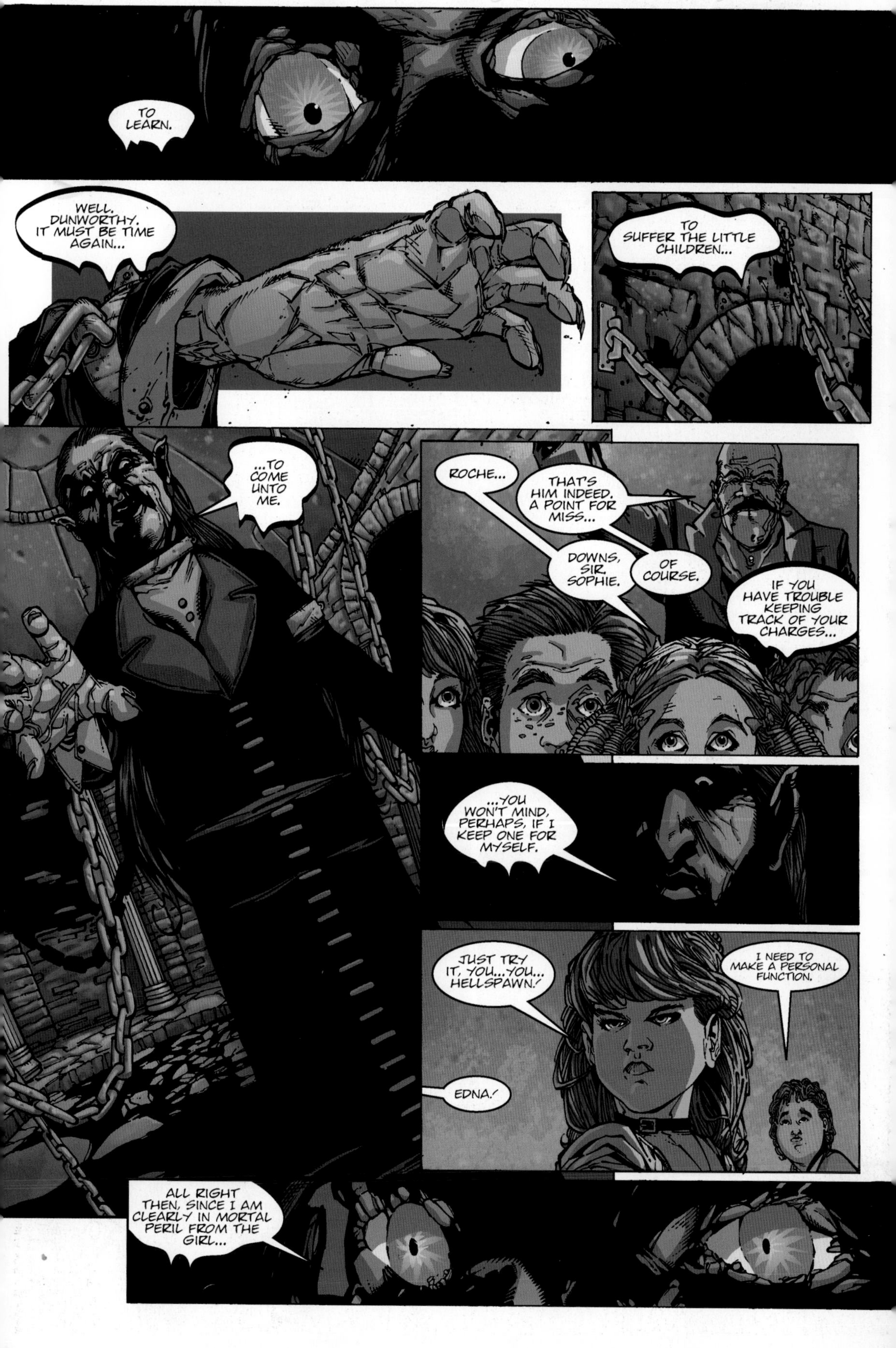

TO LEARN.
WELL, DUNWORTHY. IT MUST BE TIME AGAIN...
TO SUFFER THE LITTLE CHILDREN...
...TO COME UNTO ME.
ROCHE...
THAT'S HIM INDEED. A POINT FOR MISS...
DOWNS, SIR. SOPHIE.
OF COURSE.
IF YOU HAVE TROUBLE KEEPING TRACK OF YOUR CHARGES...
...YOU WON'T MIND, PERHAPS, IF I KEEP ONE FOR MYSELF.
JUST TRY IT, YOU...YOU... HELLSPAWN!
EDNA!
I NEED TO MAKE A PERSONAL FUNCTION.
ALL RIGHT THEN, SINCE I AM CLEARLY IN MORTAL PERIL FROM THE GIRL...

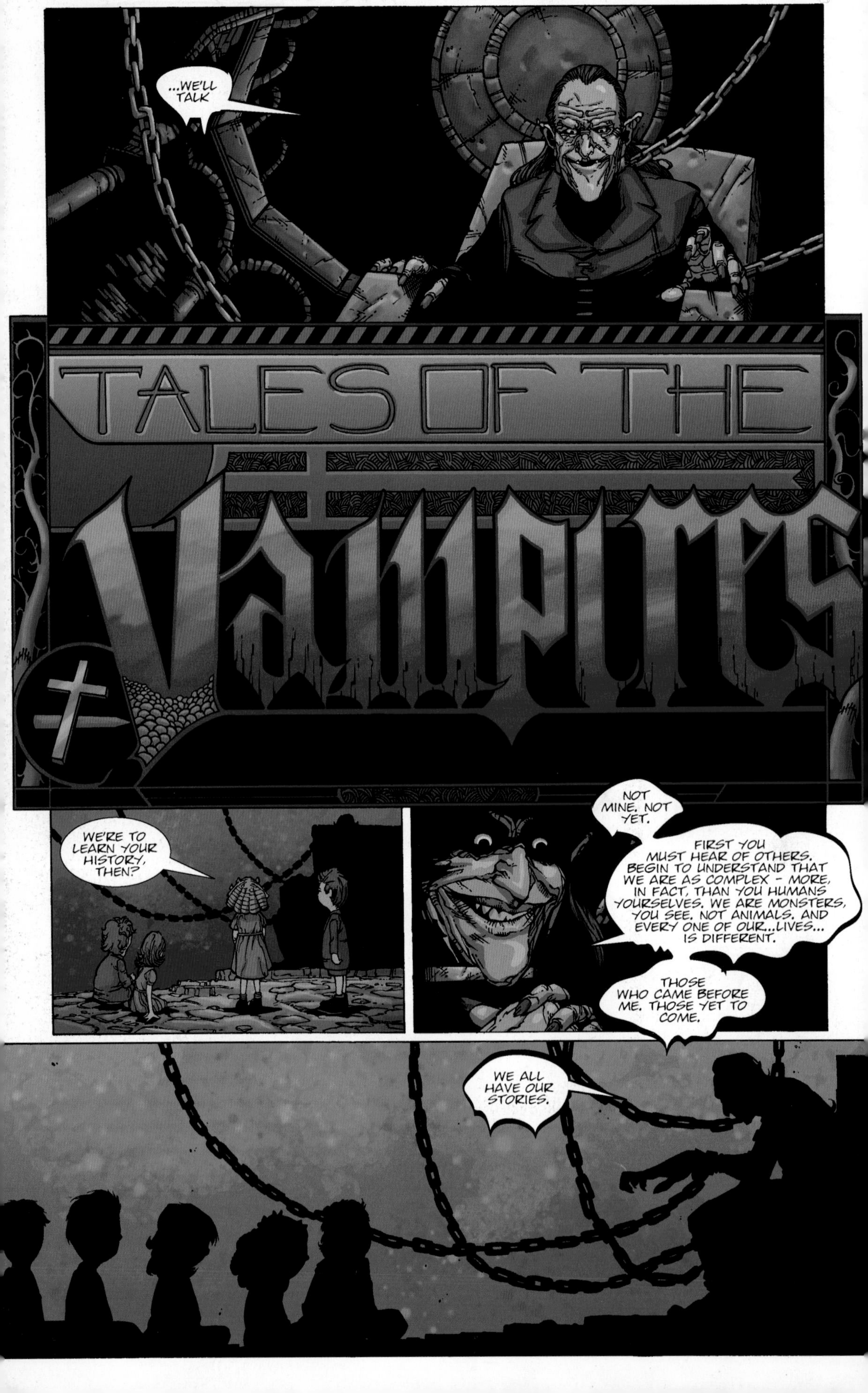
...WE'LL TALK
TALES OF THE VAMPIRES
WE'RE TO LEARN YOUR HISTORY, THEN?
NOT MINE. NOT YET.
FIRST YOU MUST HEAR OF OTHERS. BEGIN TO UNDERSTAND THAT WE ARE AS COMPLEX - MORE, IN FACT, THAN YOU HUMANS YOURSELVES. WE ARE MONSTERS, YOU SEE. NOT ANIMALS. AND EVERY ONE OF OUR...LIVES... IS DIFFERENT.
THOSE WHO CAME BEFORE ME. THOSE YET TO COME.
WE ALL HAVE OUR STORIES.

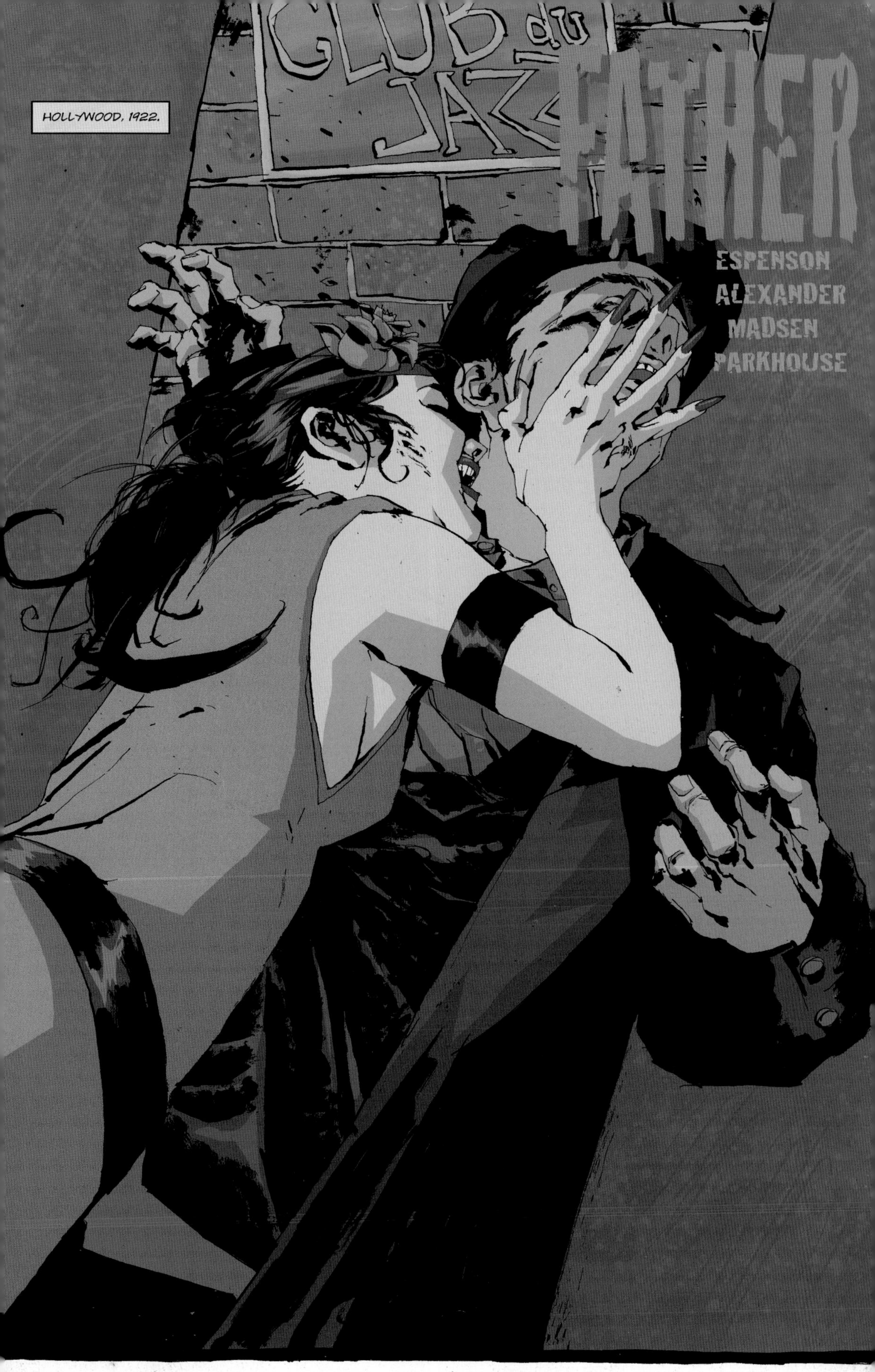
HOLLYWOOD, 1922.
CLUB du JAZZ
FATHER
ESPENSON
ALEXANDER
MADSEN
PARKHOUSE

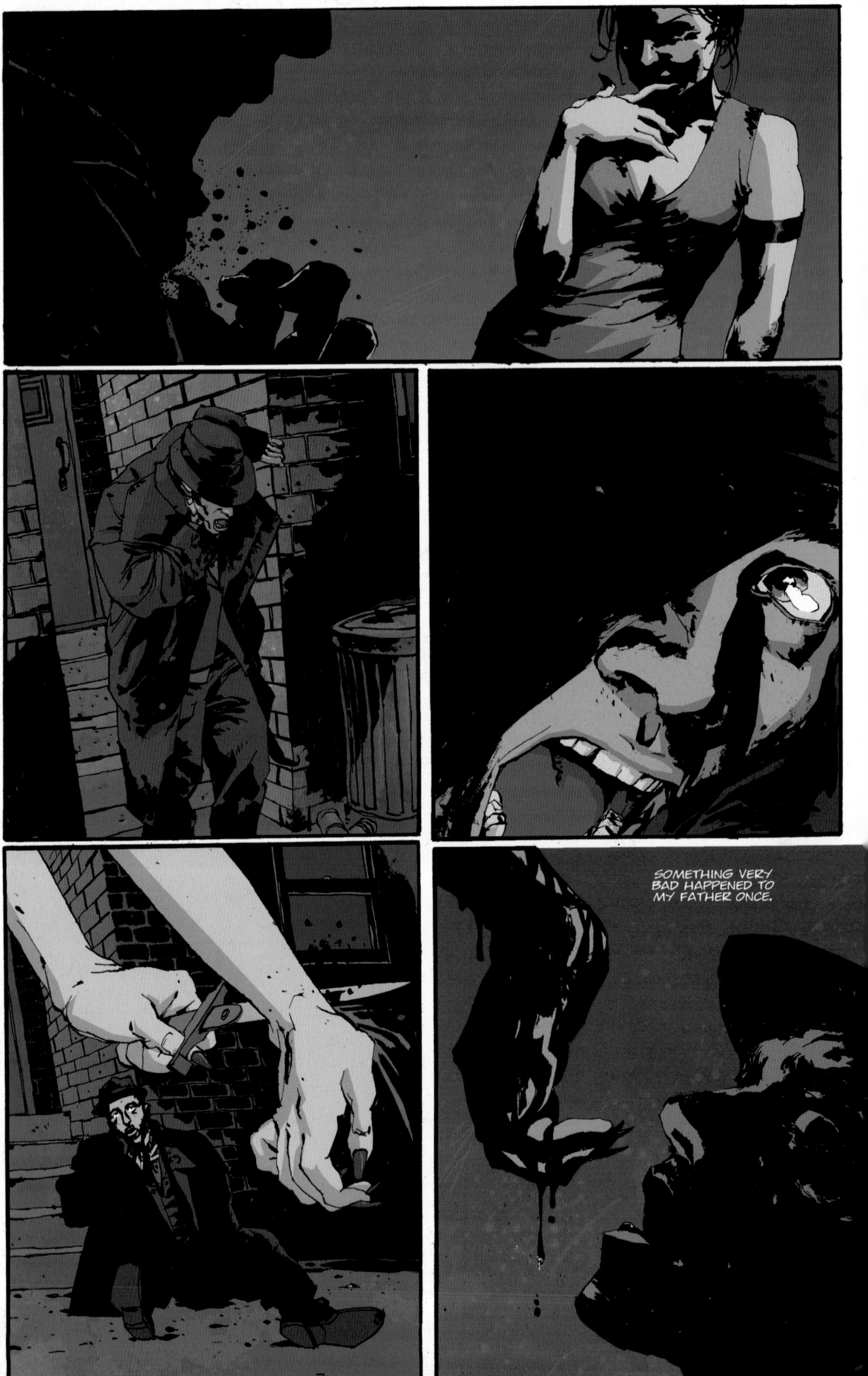
SOMETHING VERY BAD HAPPENED TO MY FATHER ONCE.

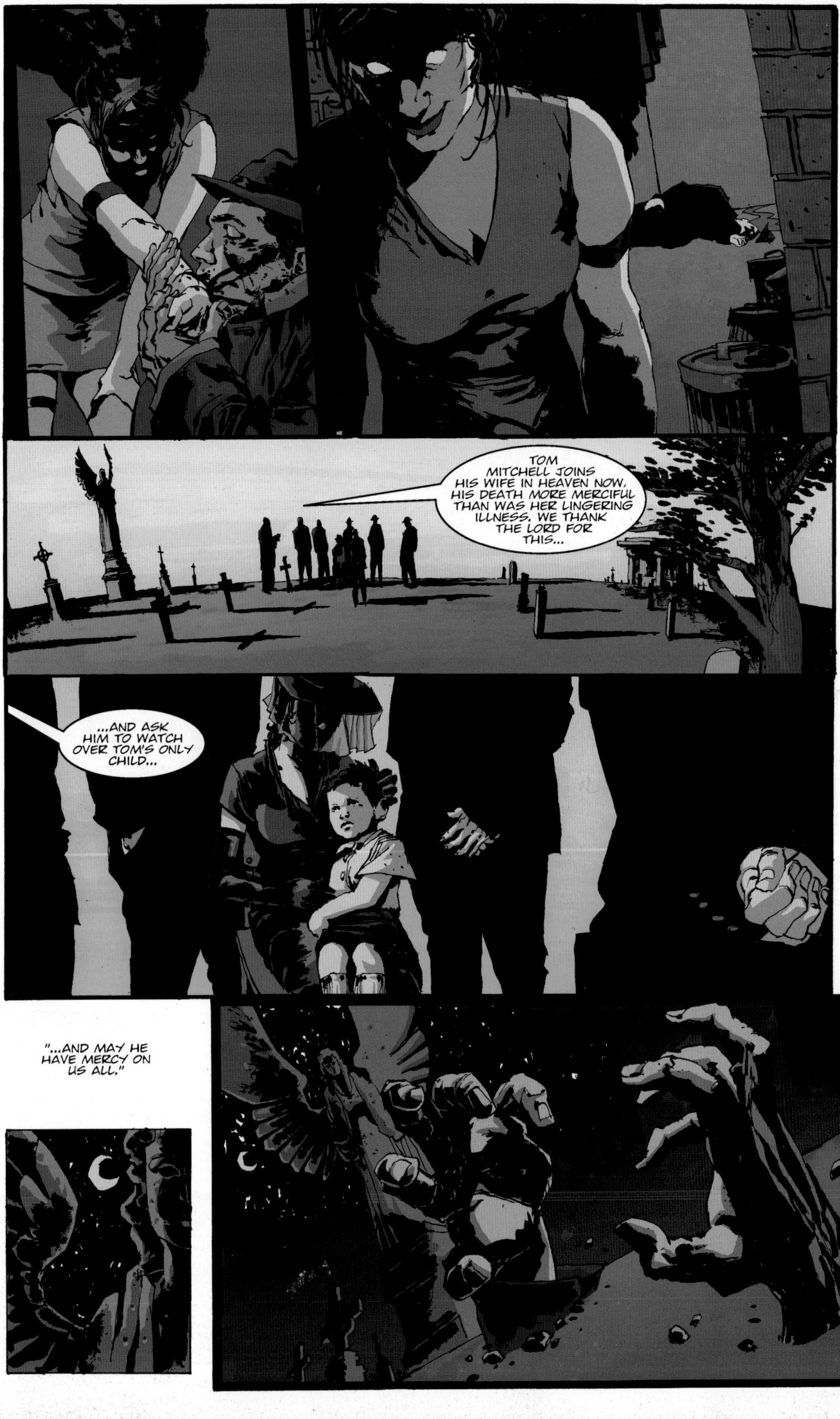
TOM MITCHELL JOINS HIS WIFE IN HEAVEN NOW, HIS DEATH MORE MERCIFUL THAN WAS HER LINGERING ILLNESS. WE THANK THE LORD FOR THIS...
...AND ASK HIM TO WATCH OVER TOM'S ONLY CHILD...
"...AND MAY HE HAVE MERCY ON US ALL."

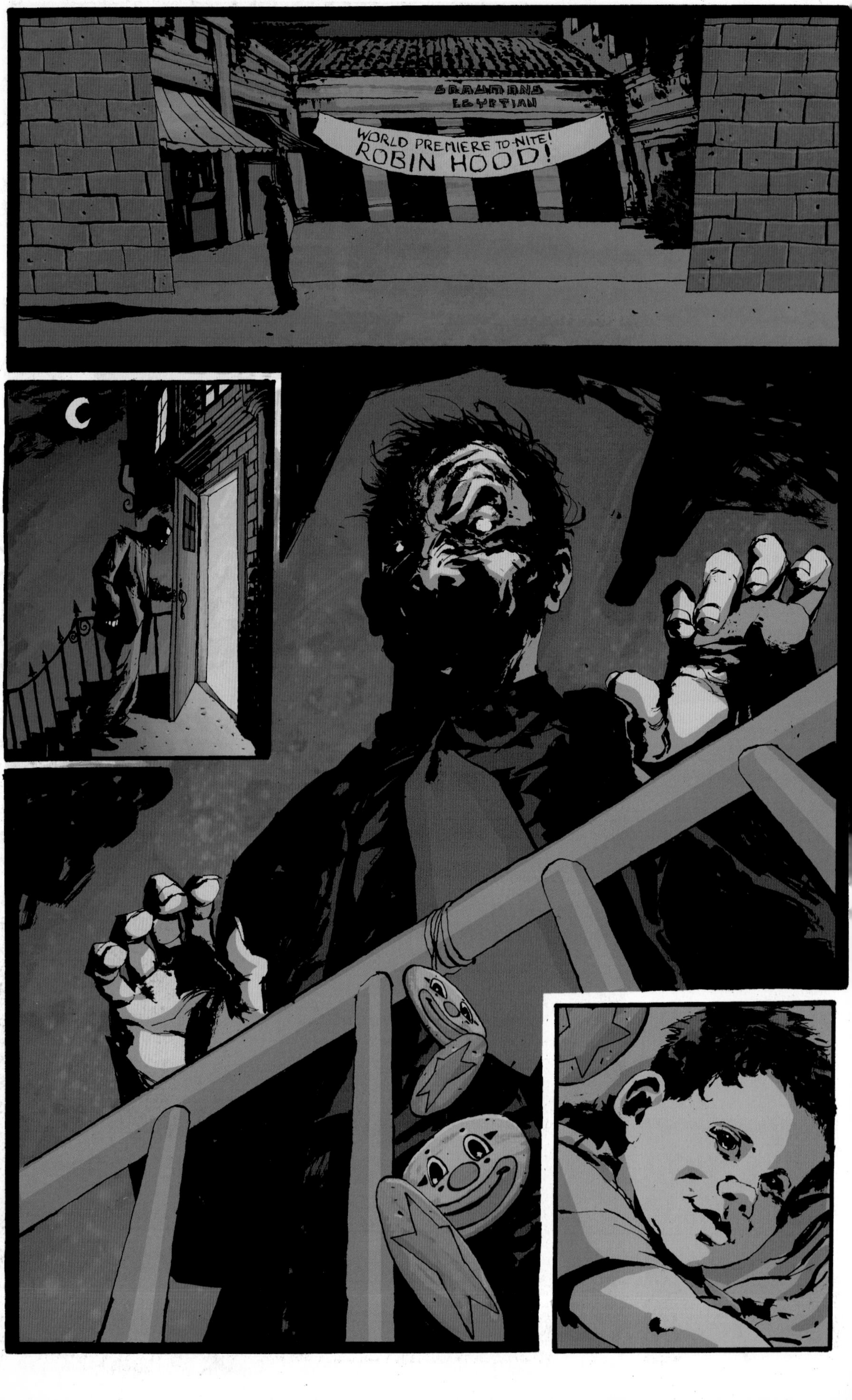
GRAUMANS
EGYPTIAN
WORLD PREMIERE TO-NITE!
ROBIN HOOD!

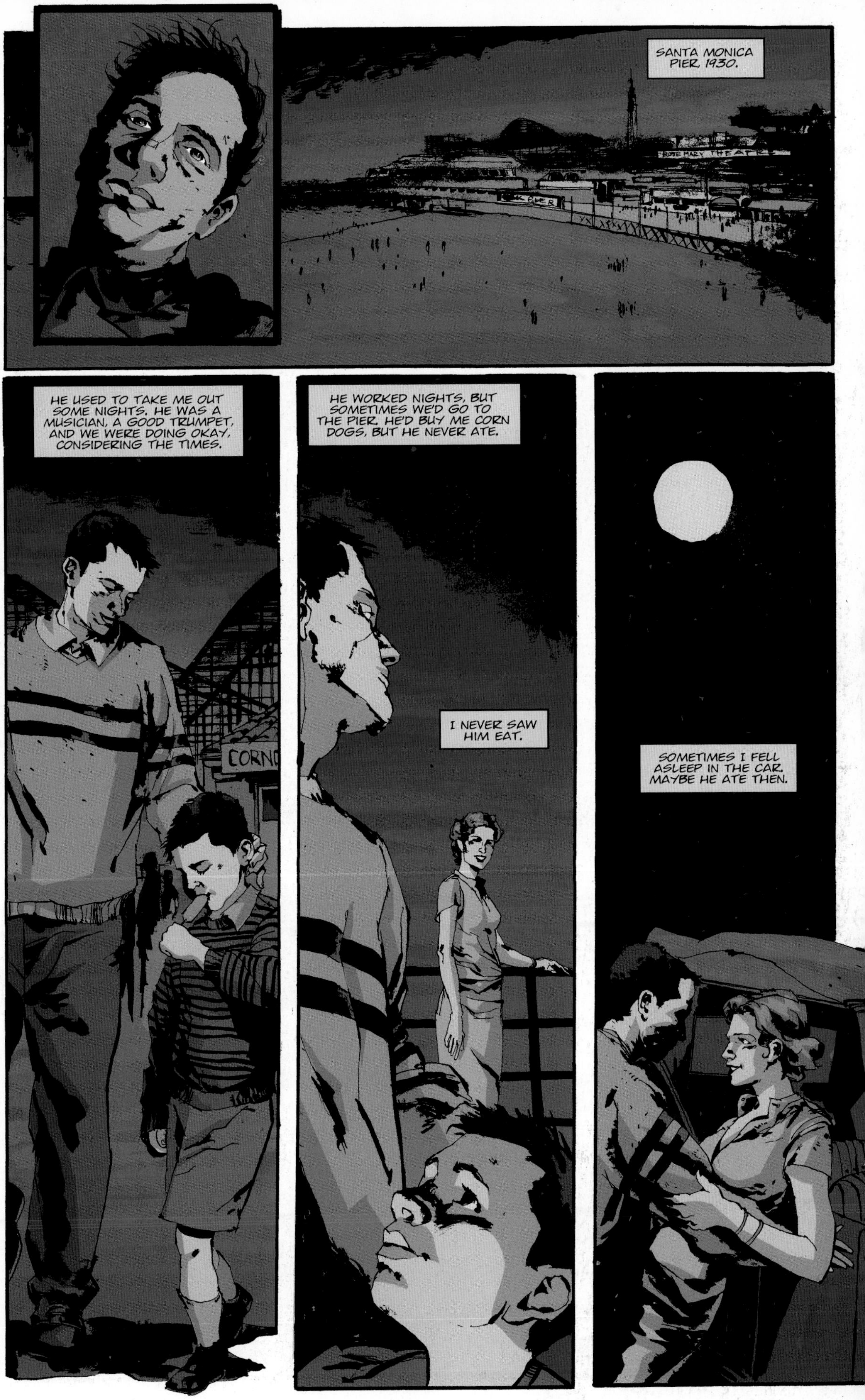
SANTA MONICA PIER, 1930.
HE USED TO TAKE ME OUT SOME NIGHTS. HE WAS A MUSICIAN, A GOOD TRUMPET, AND WE WERE DOING OKAY, CONSIDERING THE TIMES.
HE WORKED NIGHTS, BUT SOMETIMES WE'D GO TO THE PIER. HE'D BUY ME CORN DOGS, BUT HE NEVER ATE.
I NEVER SAW HIM EAT.
SOMETIMES I FELL ASLEEP IN THE CAR. MAYBE HE ATE THEN.

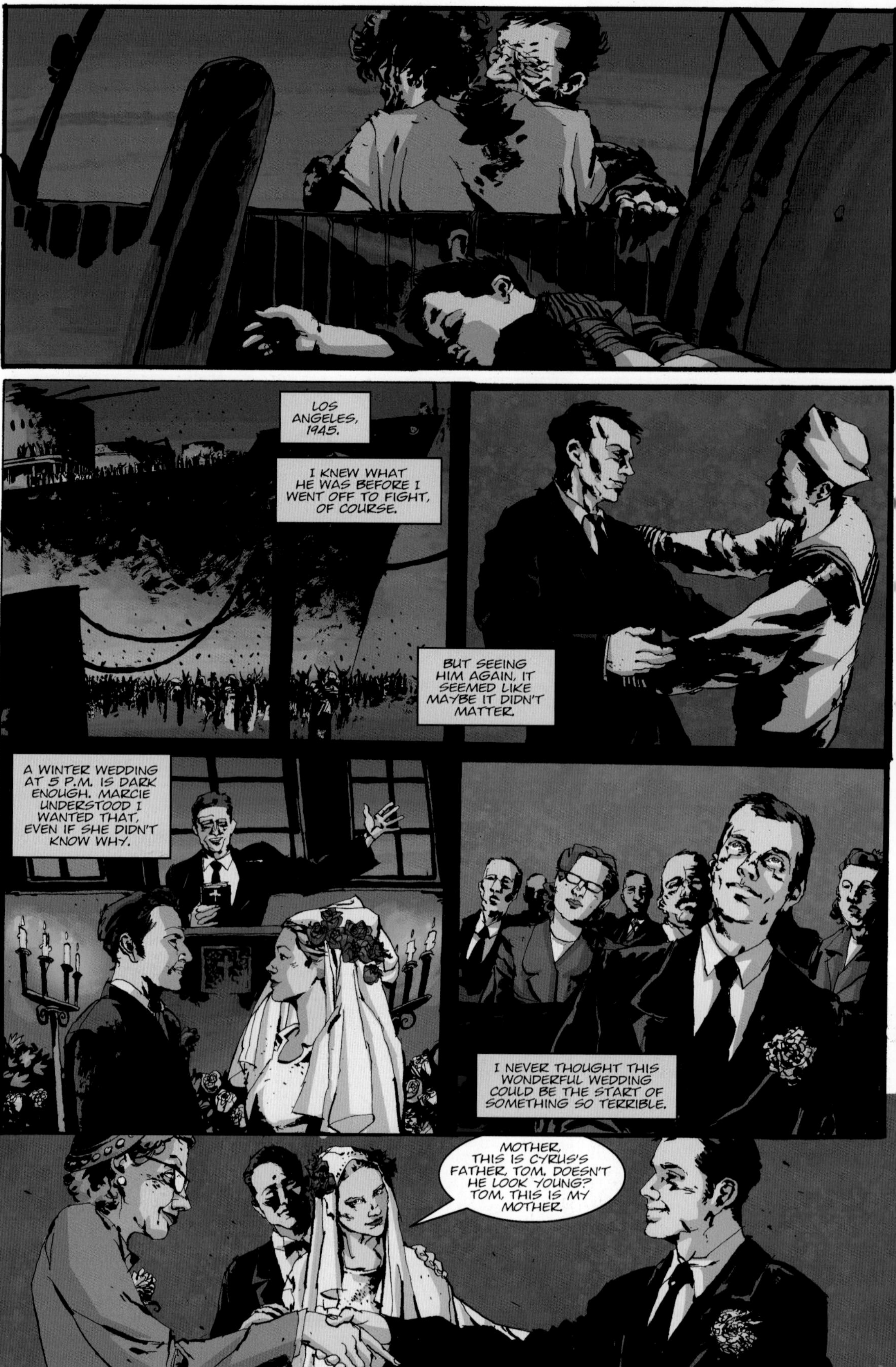
LOS ANGELES, 1945.
I KNEW WHAT HE WAS BEFORE I WENT OFF TO FIGHT, OF COURSE.
BUT SEEING HIM AGAIN, IT SEEMED LIKE MAYBE IT DIDN'T MATTER.
A WINTER WEDDING AT 5 P.M. IS DARK ENOUGH. MARCIE UNDERSTOOD I WANTED THAT, EVEN IF SHE DIDN'T KNOW WHY.
I NEVER THOUGHT THIS WONDERFUL WEDDING COULD BE THE START OF SOMETHING SO TERRIBLE.
MOTHER, THIS IS CYRUS'S FATHER, TOM. DOESN'T HE LOOK YOUNG? TOM, THIS IS MY MOTHER.

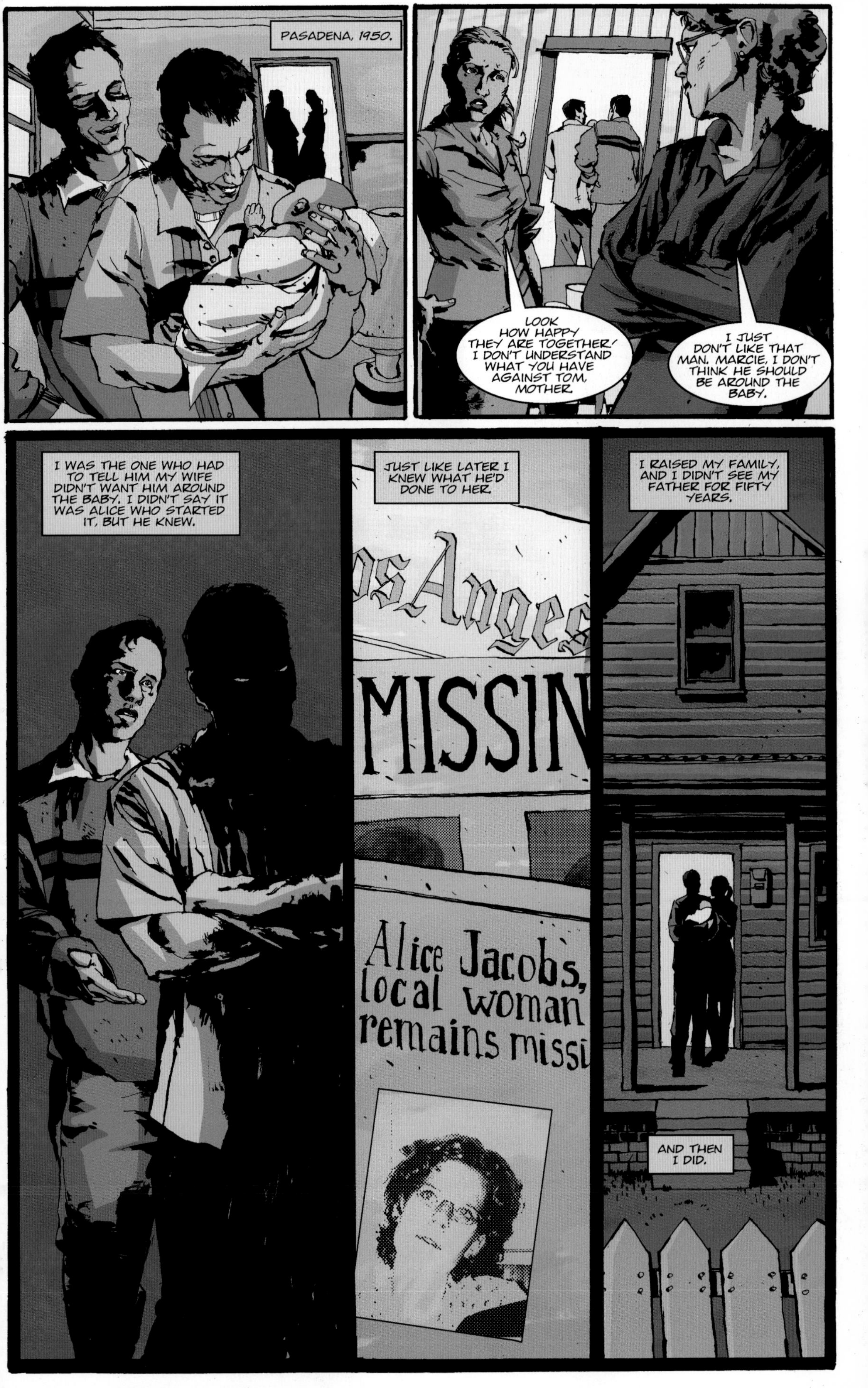
PASADENA, 1950.
LOOK HOW HAPPY THEY ARE TOGETHER! I DON'T UNDERSTAND WHAT YOU HAVE AGAINST TOM, MOTHER.
I JUST DON'T LIKE THAT MAN, MARCIE. I DON'T THINK HE SHOULD BE AROUND THE BABY.
I WAS THE ONE WHO HAD TO TELL HIM MY WIFE DIDN'T WANT HIM AROUND THE BABY. I DIDN'T SAY IT WAS ALICE WHO STARTED IT, BUT HE KNEW.
JUST LIKE LATER I KNEW WHAT HE'D DONE TO HER.
os Anges
MISSIN
Alice Jacobs, local woman remains missi
I RAISED MY FAMILY, AND I DIDN'T SEE MY FATHER FOR FIFTY YEARS.
AND THEN I DID.

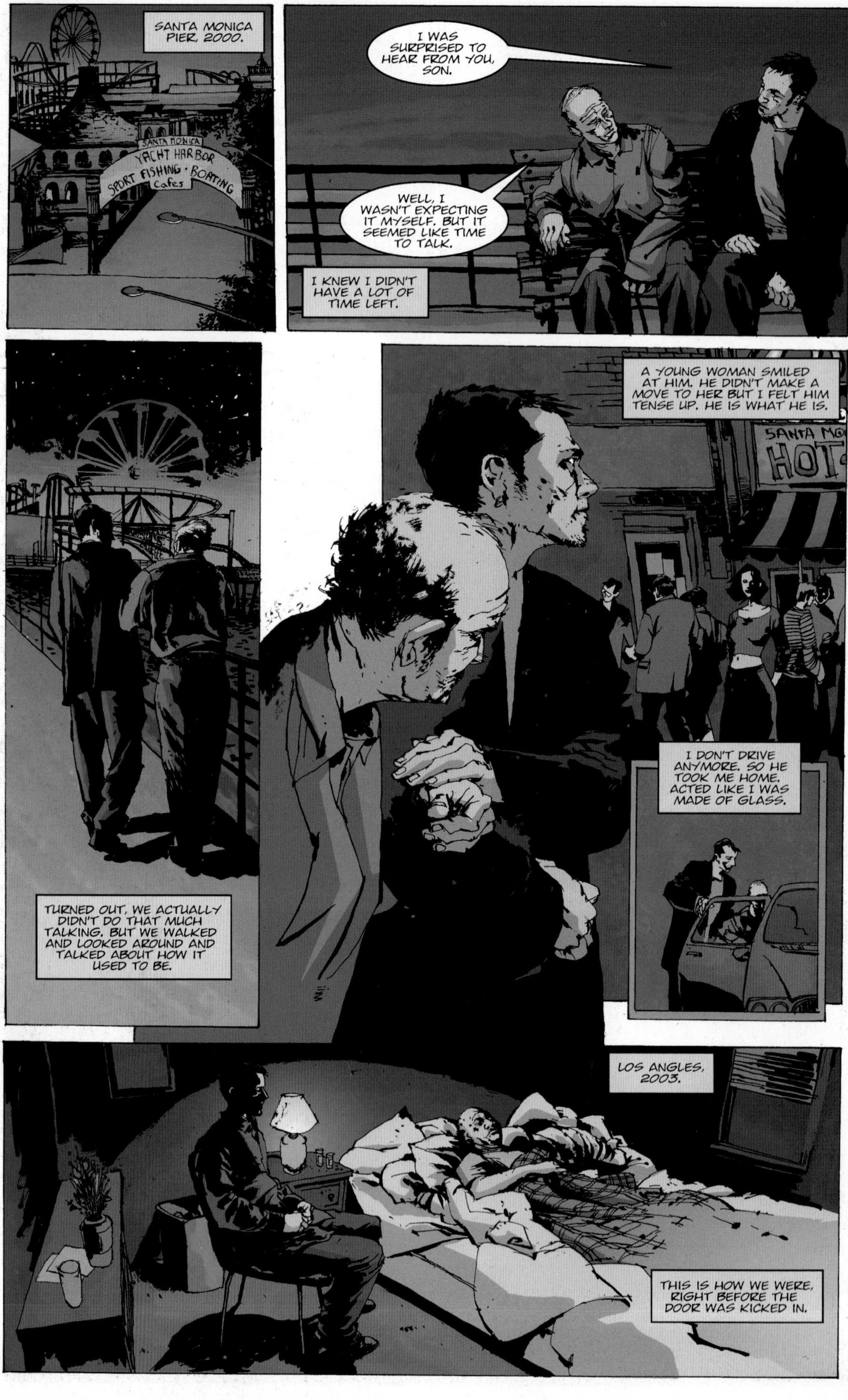
SANTA MONICA PIER, 2000.
SANTA MONICA
YACHT HARBOR
SPORT FISHING • BOATING
Cafes
I WAS SURPRISED TO HEAR FROM YOU, SON.
WELL, I WASN'T EXPECTING IT MYSELF. BUT IT SEEMED LIKE TIME TO TALK.
I KNEW I DIDN'T HAVE A LOT OF TIME LEFT.
TURNED OUT, WE ACTUALLY DIDN'T DO THAT MUCH TALKING. BUT WE WALKED AND LOOKED AROUND AND TALKED ABOUT HOW IT USED TO BE.
A YOUNG WOMAN SMILED AT HIM. HE DIDN'T MAKE A MOVE TO HER BUT I FELT HIM TENSE UP. HE IS WHAT HE IS.
I DON'T DRIVE ANYMORE. SO HE TOOK ME HOME. ACTED LIKE I WAS MADE OF GLASS.
LOS ANGLES, 2003.
THIS IS HOW WE WERE, RIGHT BEFORE THE DOOR WAS KICKED IN.

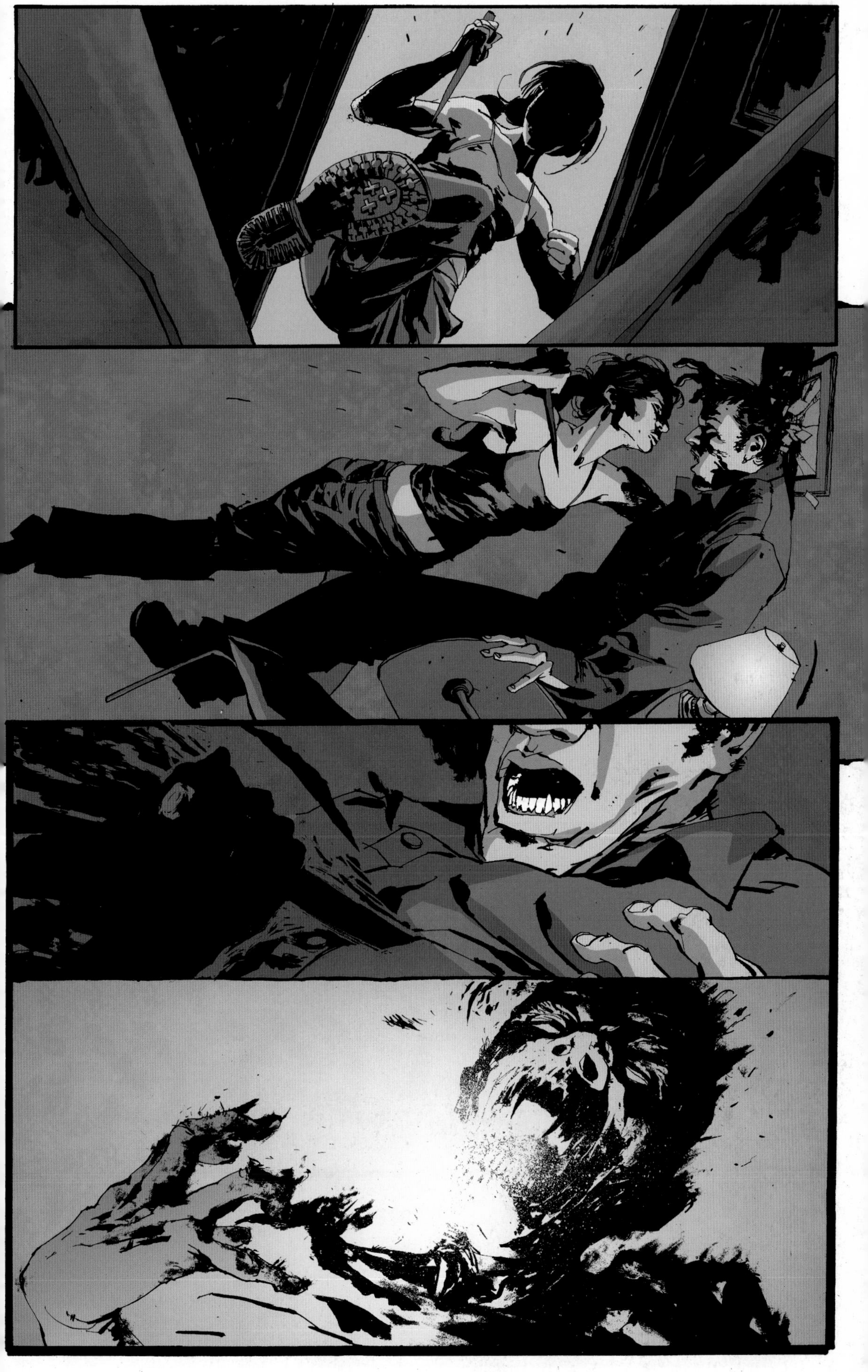

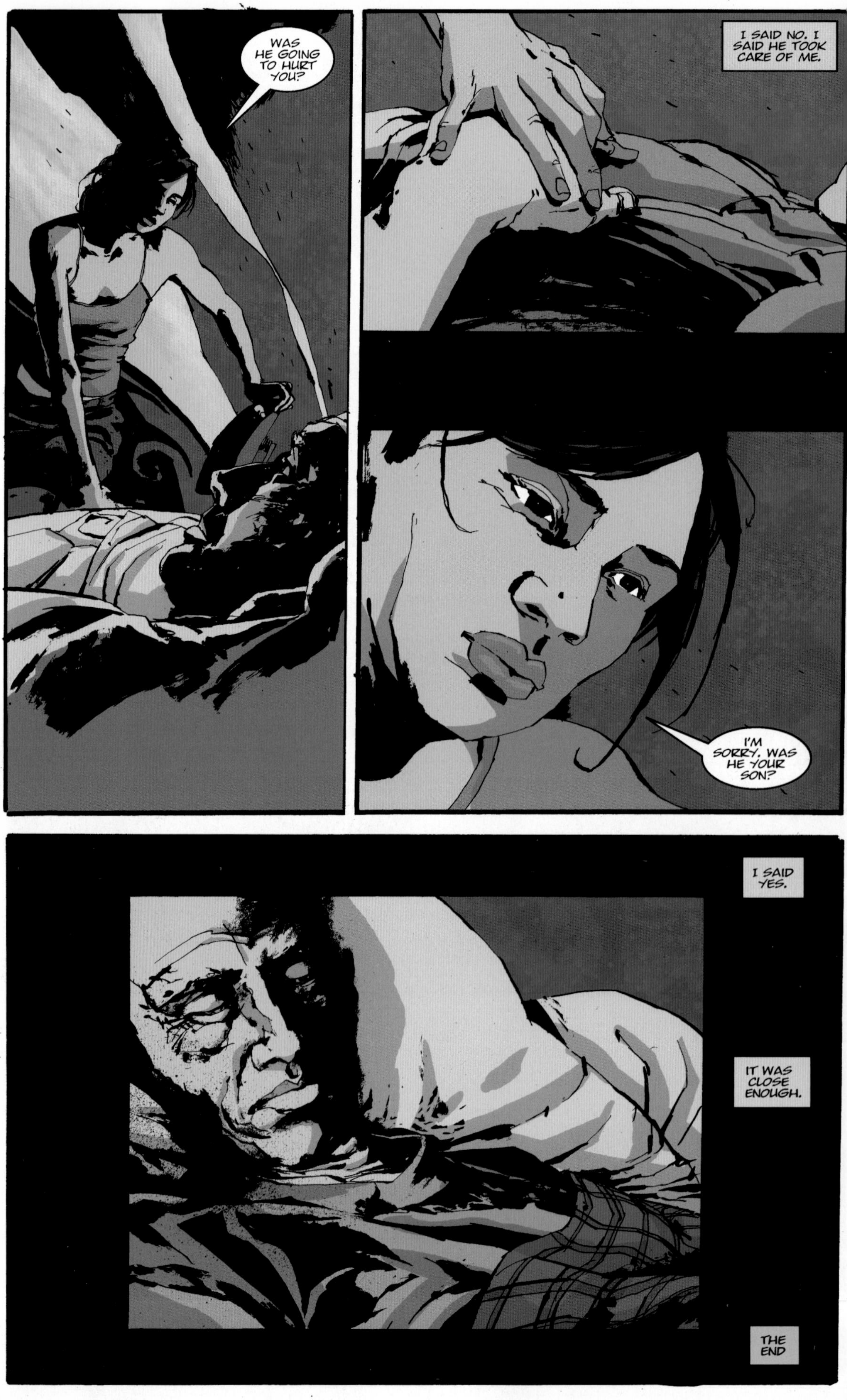
WAS HE GOING TO HURT YOU?
I SAID NO. I SAID HE TOOK CARE OF ME.
I'M SORRY. WAS HE YOUR SON?
I SAID YES.
IT WAS CLOSE ENOUGH.
THE END

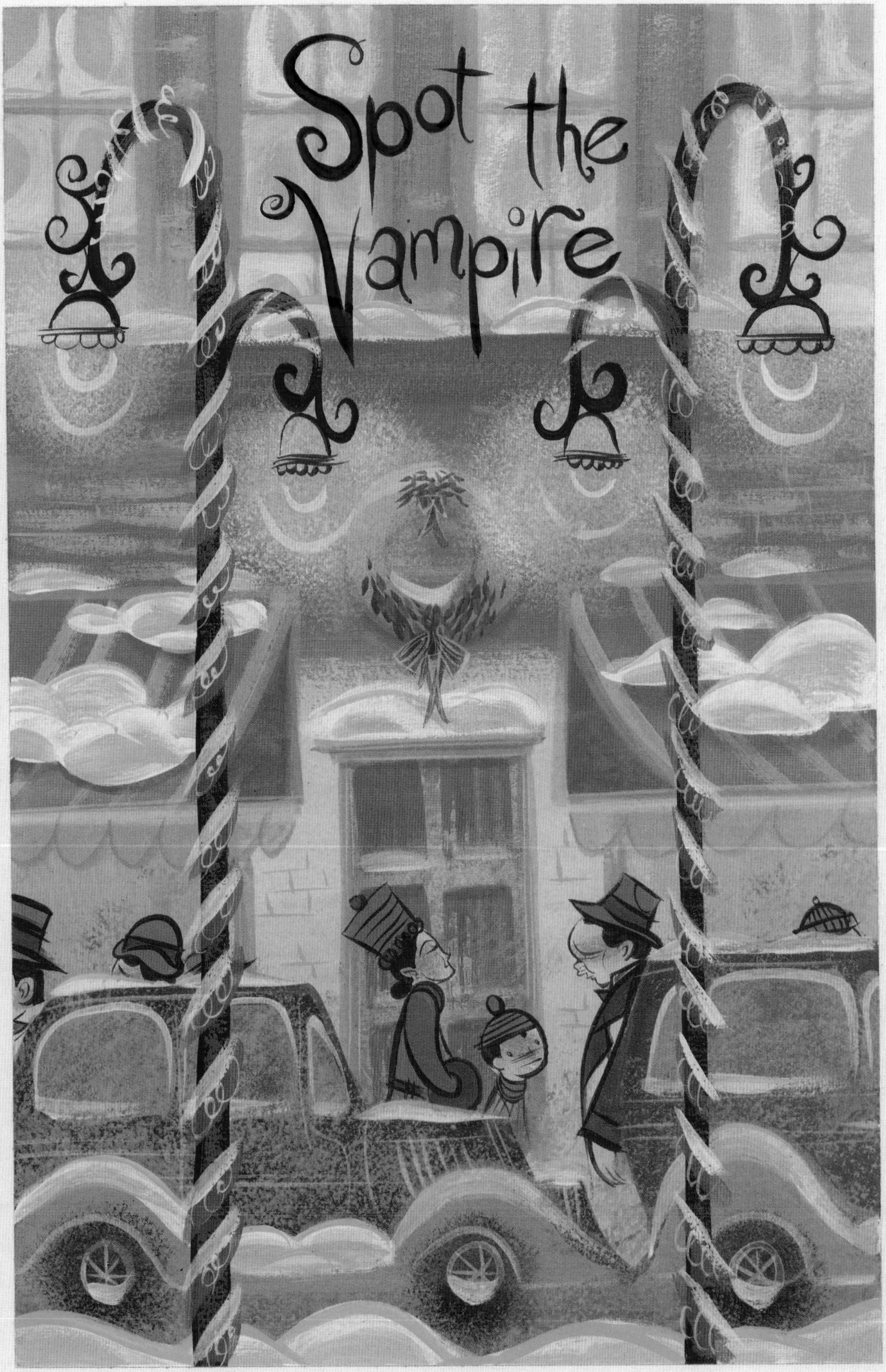
Spot the Vampire

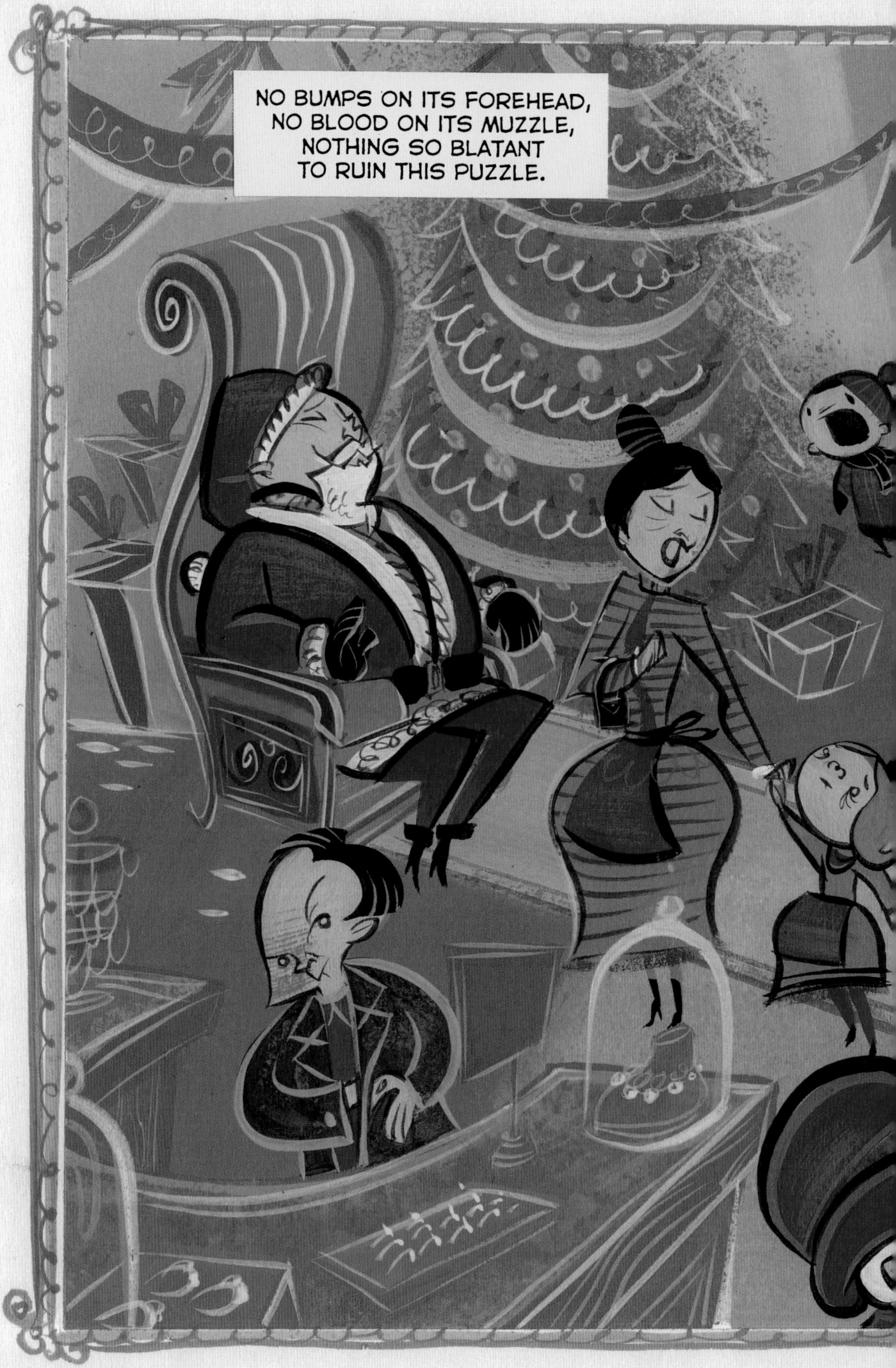
NO BUMPS ON ITS FOREHEAD,
NO BLOOD ON ITS MUZZLE,
NOTHING SO BLATANT
TO RUIN THIS PUZZLE.

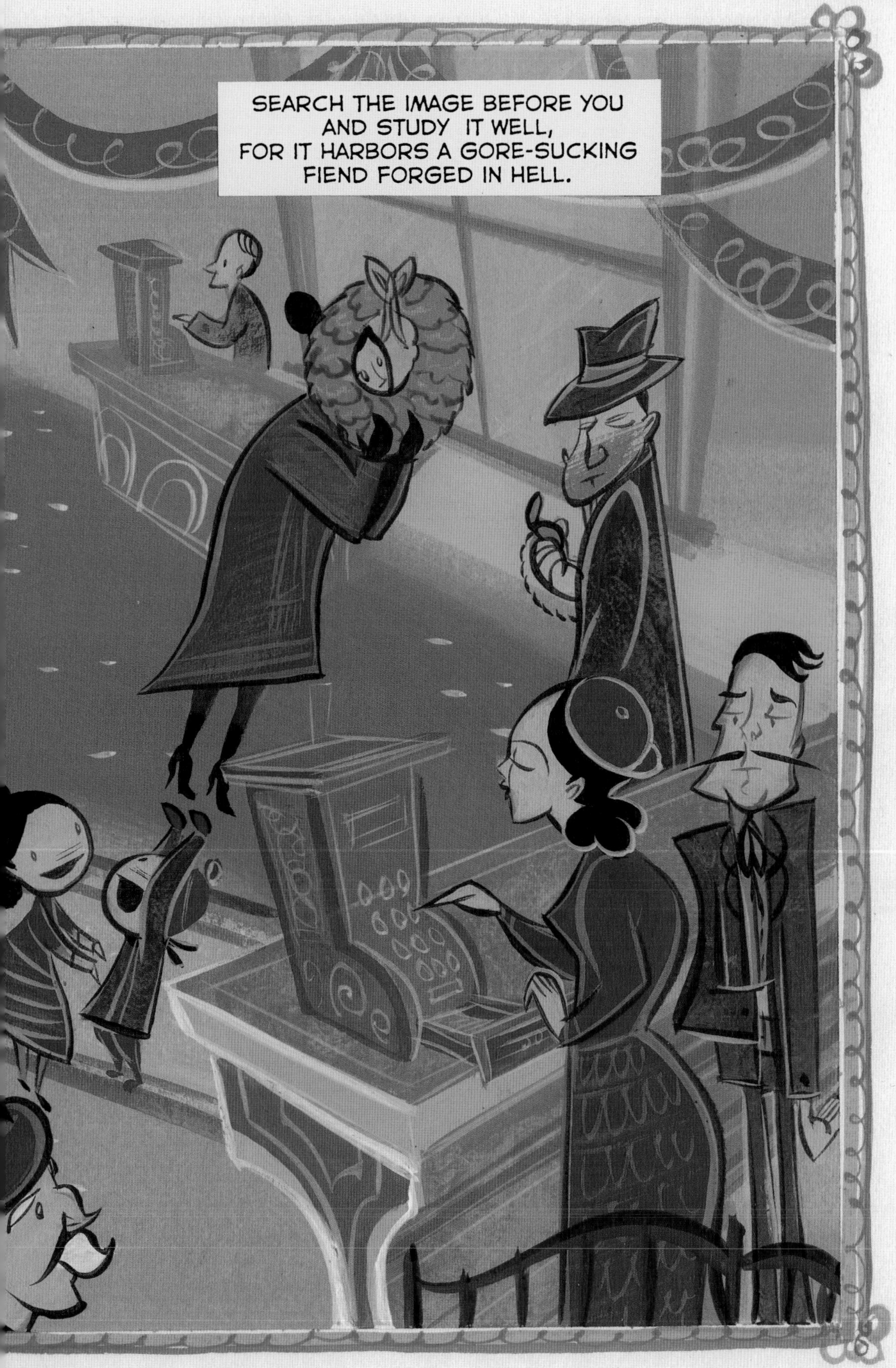
SEARCH THE IMAGE BEFORE YOU
AND STUDY IT WELL,
FOR IT HARBORS A GORE-SUCKING
FIEND FORGED IN HELL.

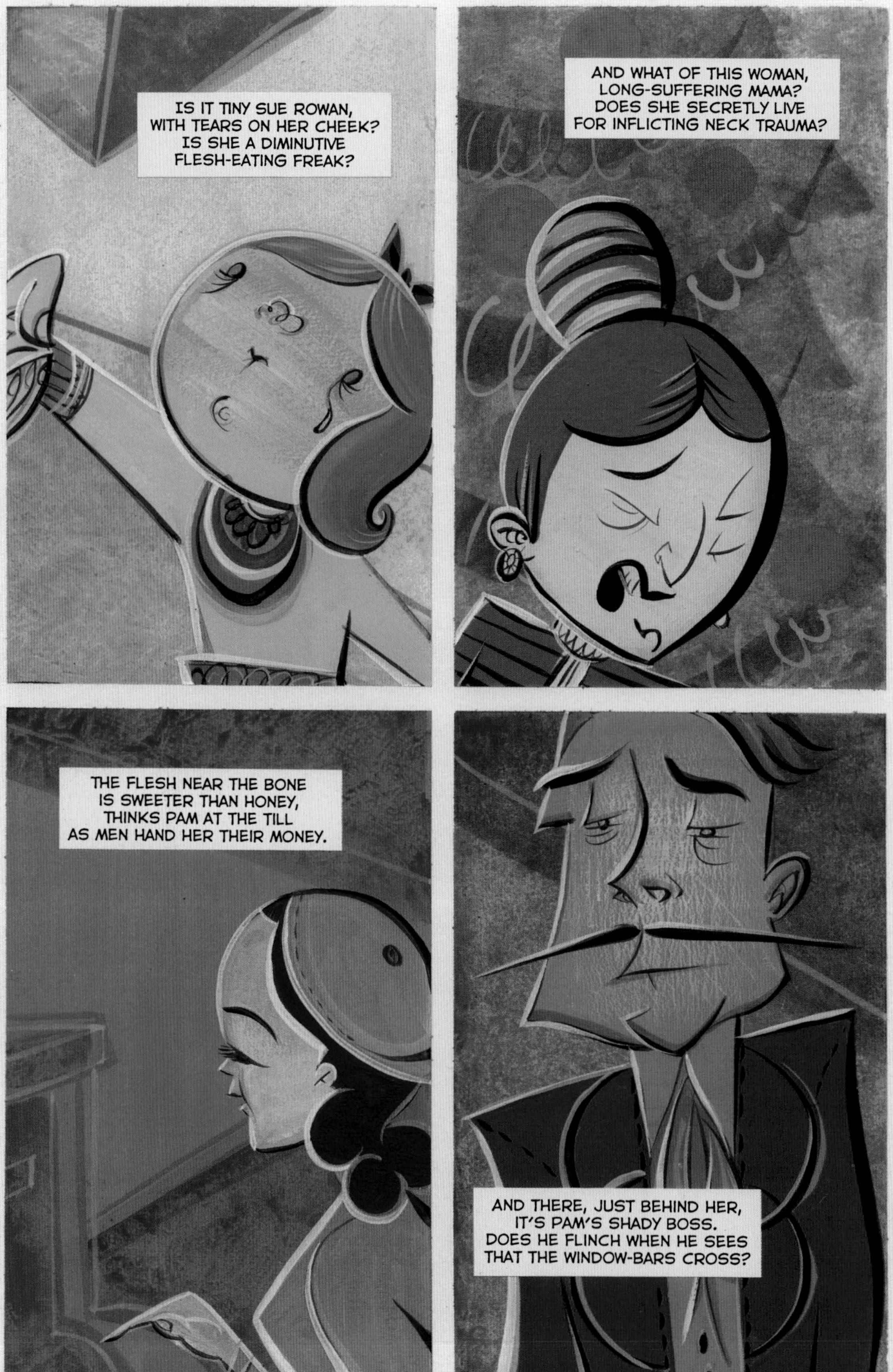
IS IT TINY SUE ROWAN, WITH TEARS ON HER CHEEK? IS SHE A DIMINUTIVE FLESH-EATING FREAK?
AND WHAT OF THIS WOMAN, LONG-SUFFERING MAMA? DOES SHE SECRETLY LIVE FOR INFLICTING NECK TRAUMA?
THE FLESH NEAR THE BONE IS SWEETER THAN HONEY, THINKS PAM AT THE TILL AS MEN HAND HER THEIR MONEY.
AND THERE, JUST BEHIND HER, IT'S PAM'S SHADY BOSS. DOES HE FLINCH WHEN HE SEES THAT THE WINDOW-BARS CROSS?

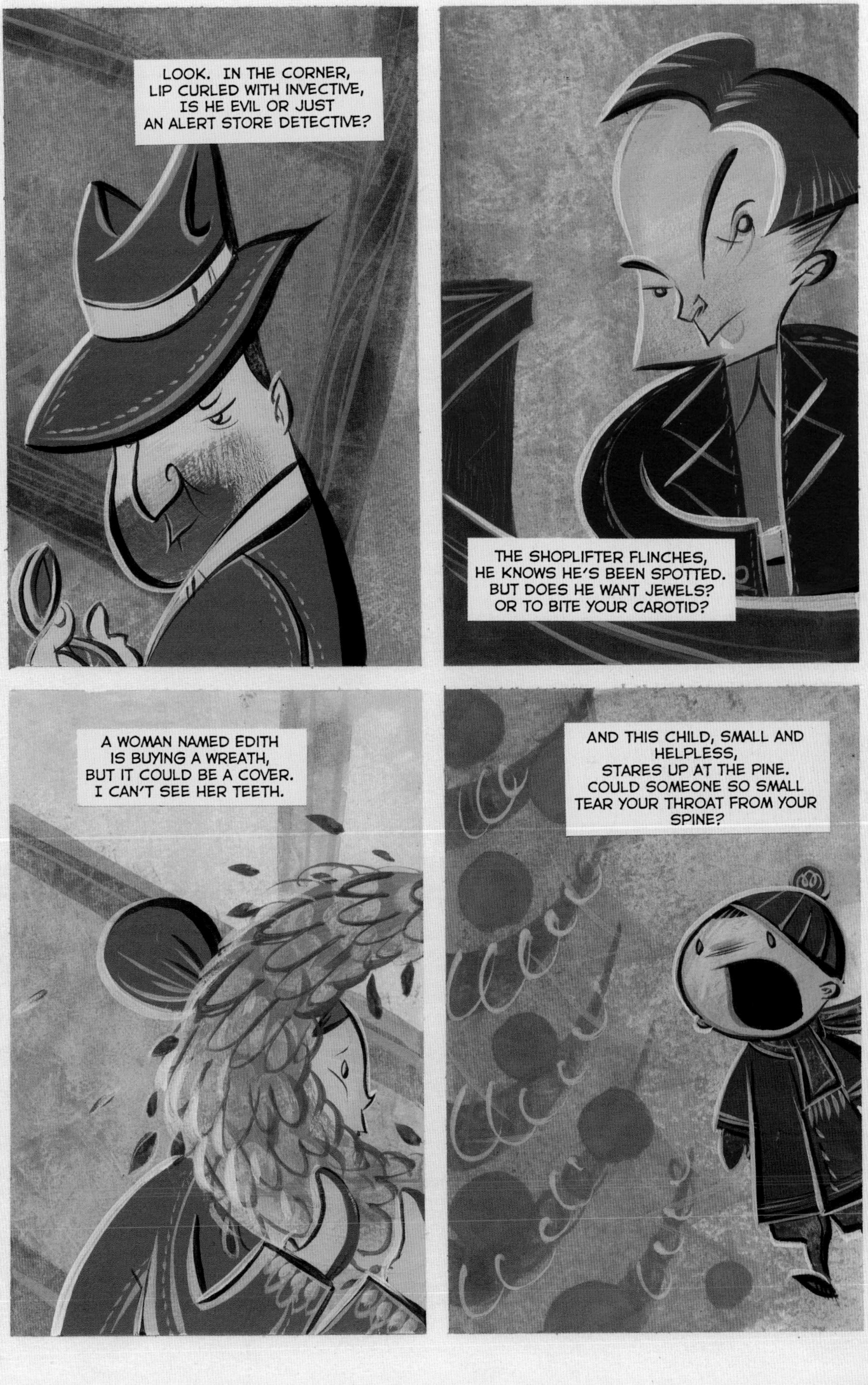
LOOK. IN THE CORNER, LIP CURLED WITH INVECTIVE, IS HE EVIL OR JUST AN ALERT STORE DETECTIVE?
THE SHOPLIFTER FLINCHES, HE KNOWS HE'S BEEN SPOTTED. BUT DOES HE WANT JEWELS? OR TO BITE YOUR CAROTID?
A WOMAN NAMED EDITH IS BUYING A WREATH, BUT IT COULD BE A COVER. I CAN'T SEE HER TEETH.
AND THIS CHILD, SMALL AND HELPLESS, STARES UP AT THE PINE. COULD SOMEONE SO SMALL TEAR YOUR THROAT FROM YOUR SPINE?

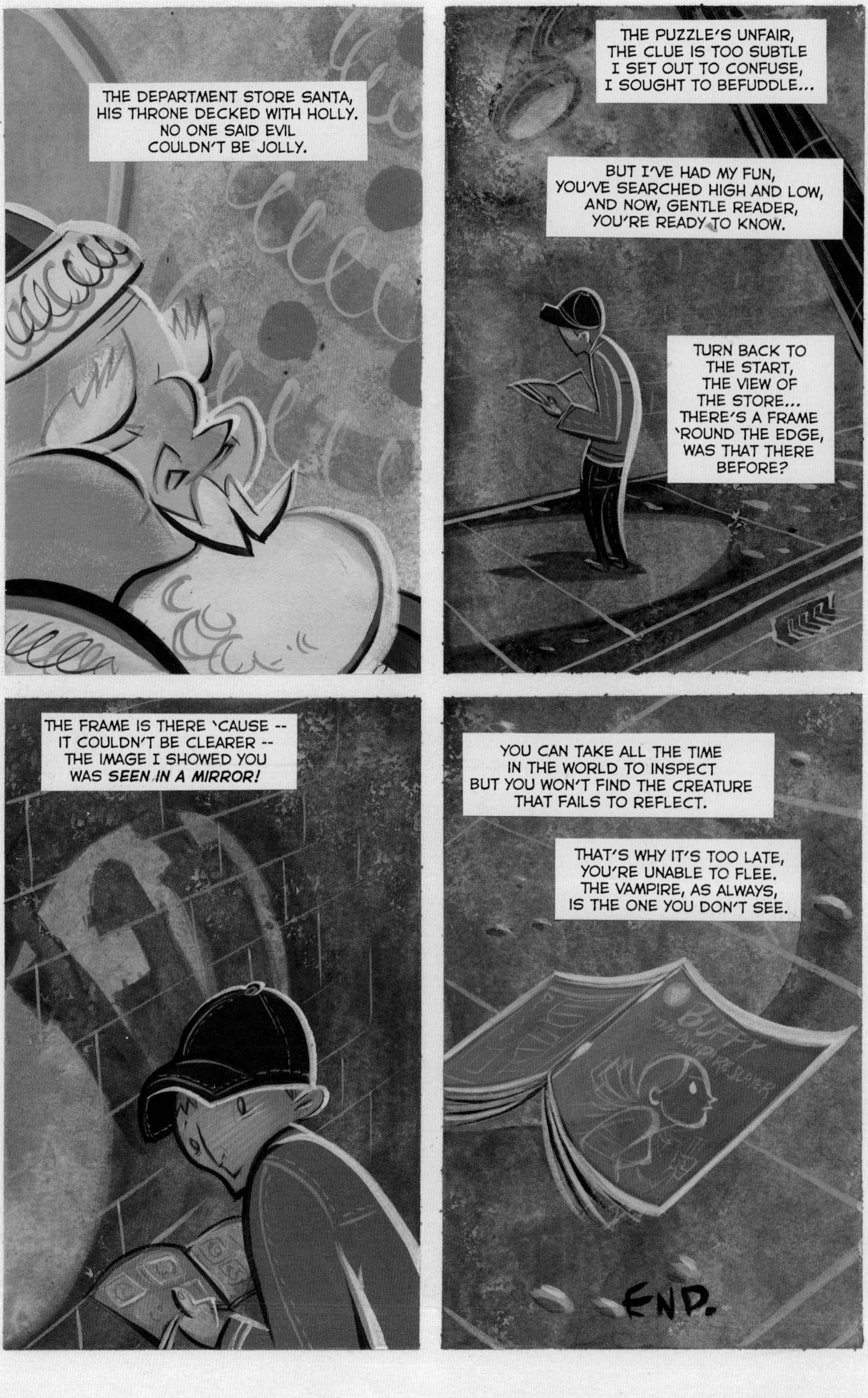
THE DEPARTMENT STORE SANTA, HIS THRONE DECKED WITH HOLLY. NO ONE SAID EVIL COULDN'T BE JOLLY.
THE PUZZLE'S UNFAIR, THE CLUE IS TOO SUBTLE I SET OUT TO CONFUSE, I SOUGHT TO BEFUDDLE...
BUT I'VE HAD MY FUN, YOU'VE SEARCHED HIGH AND LOW, AND NOW, GENTLE READER, YOU'RE READY TO KNOW.
TURN BACK TO THE START, THE VIEW OF THE STORE... THERE'S A FRAME 'ROUND THE EDGE, WAS THAT THERE BEFORE?
THE FRAME IS THERE 'CAUSE -- IT COULDN'T BE CLEARER -- THE IMAGE I SHOWED YOU WAS *SEEN IN A MIRROR!*
YOU CAN TAKE ALL THE TIME IN THE WORLD TO INSPECT BUT YOU WON'T FIND THE CREATURE THAT FAILS TO REFLECT.
THAT'S WHY IT'S TOO LATE, YOU'RE UNABLE TO FLEE. THE VAMPIRE, AS ALWAYS, IS THE ONE YOU DON'T SEE.
BUFFY
END.

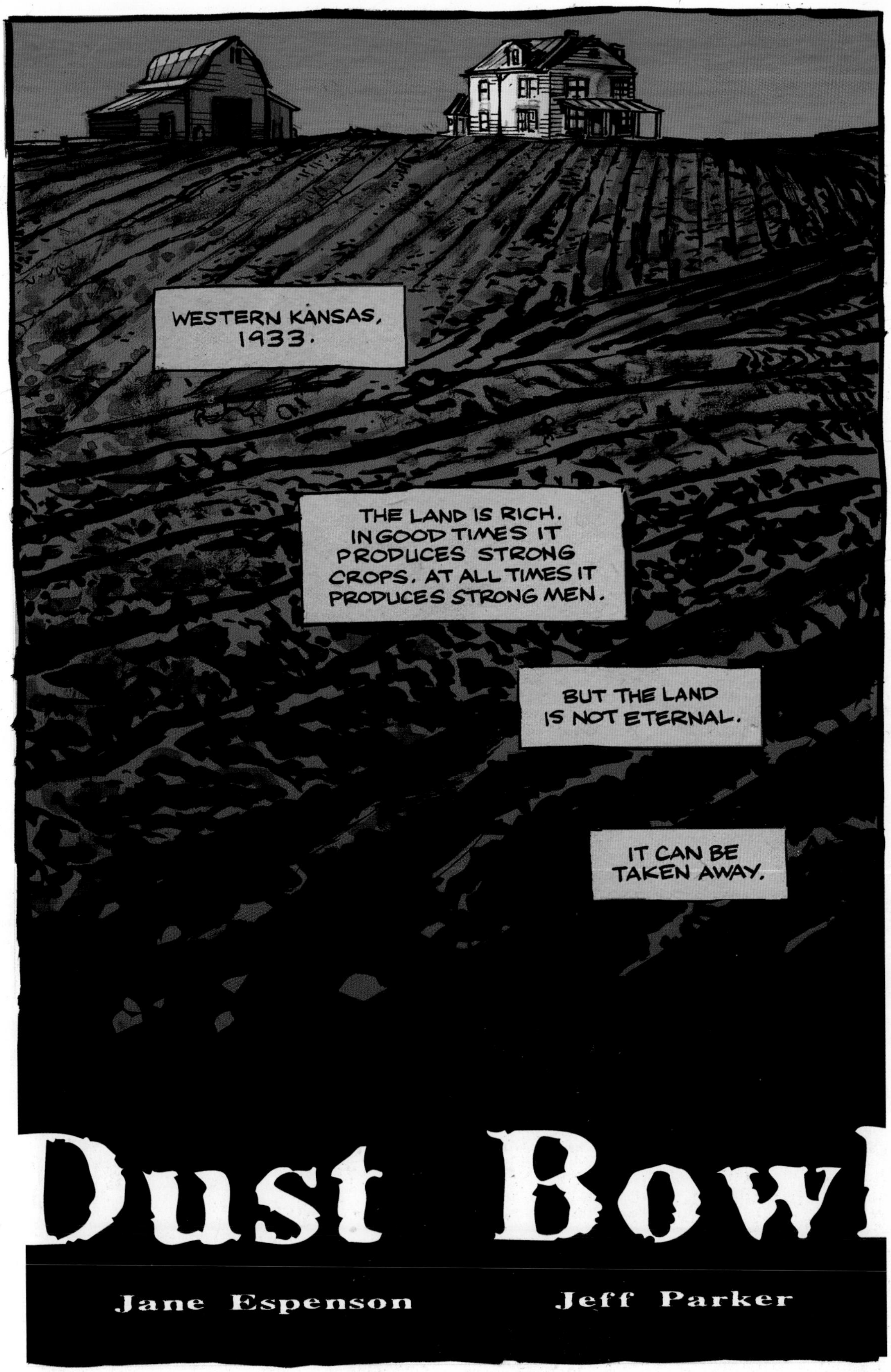
WESTERN KANSAS, 1933.
THE LAND IS RICH. IN GOOD TIMES IT PRODUCES STRONG CROPS. AT ALL TIMES IT PRODUCES STRONG MEN.
BUT THE LAND IS NOT ETERNAL.
IT CAN BE TAKEN AWAY.

Dust Bowl

Jane Espenson   Jeff Parker

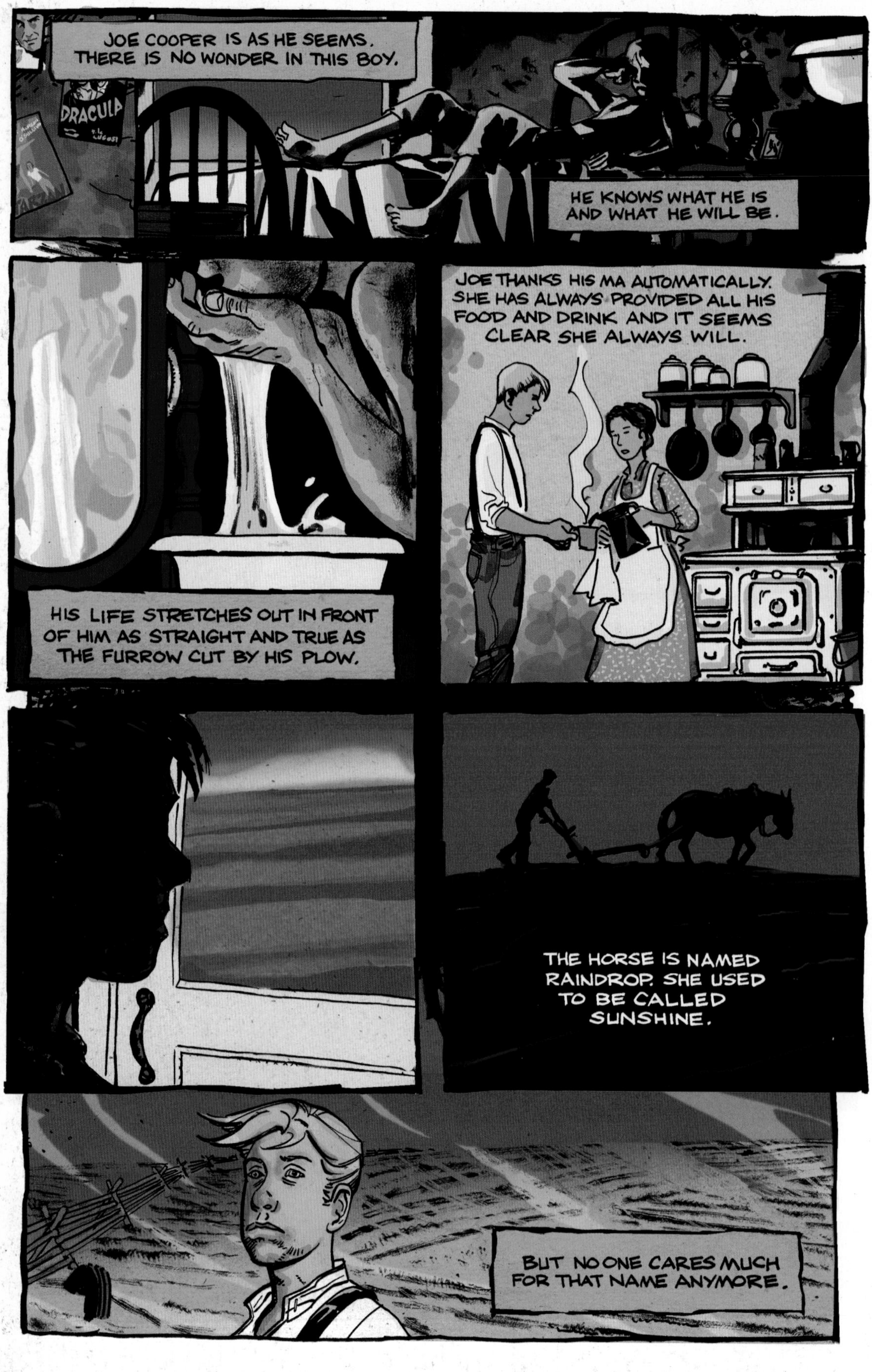
JOE COOPER IS AS HE SEEMS. THERE IS NO WONDER IN THIS BOY.
DRACULA
HE KNOWS WHAT HE IS AND WHAT HE WILL BE.
HIS LIFE STRETCHES OUT IN FRONT OF HIM AS STRAIGHT AND TRUE AS THE FURROW CUT BY HIS PLOW.
JOE THANKS HIS MA AUTOMATICALLY. SHE HAS ALWAYS PROVIDED ALL HIS FOOD AND DRINK AND IT SEEMS CLEAR SHE ALWAYS WILL.
THE HORSE IS NAMED RAINDROP. SHE USED TO BE CALLED SUNSHINE.
BUT NO ONE CARES MUCH FOR THAT NAME ANYMORE.

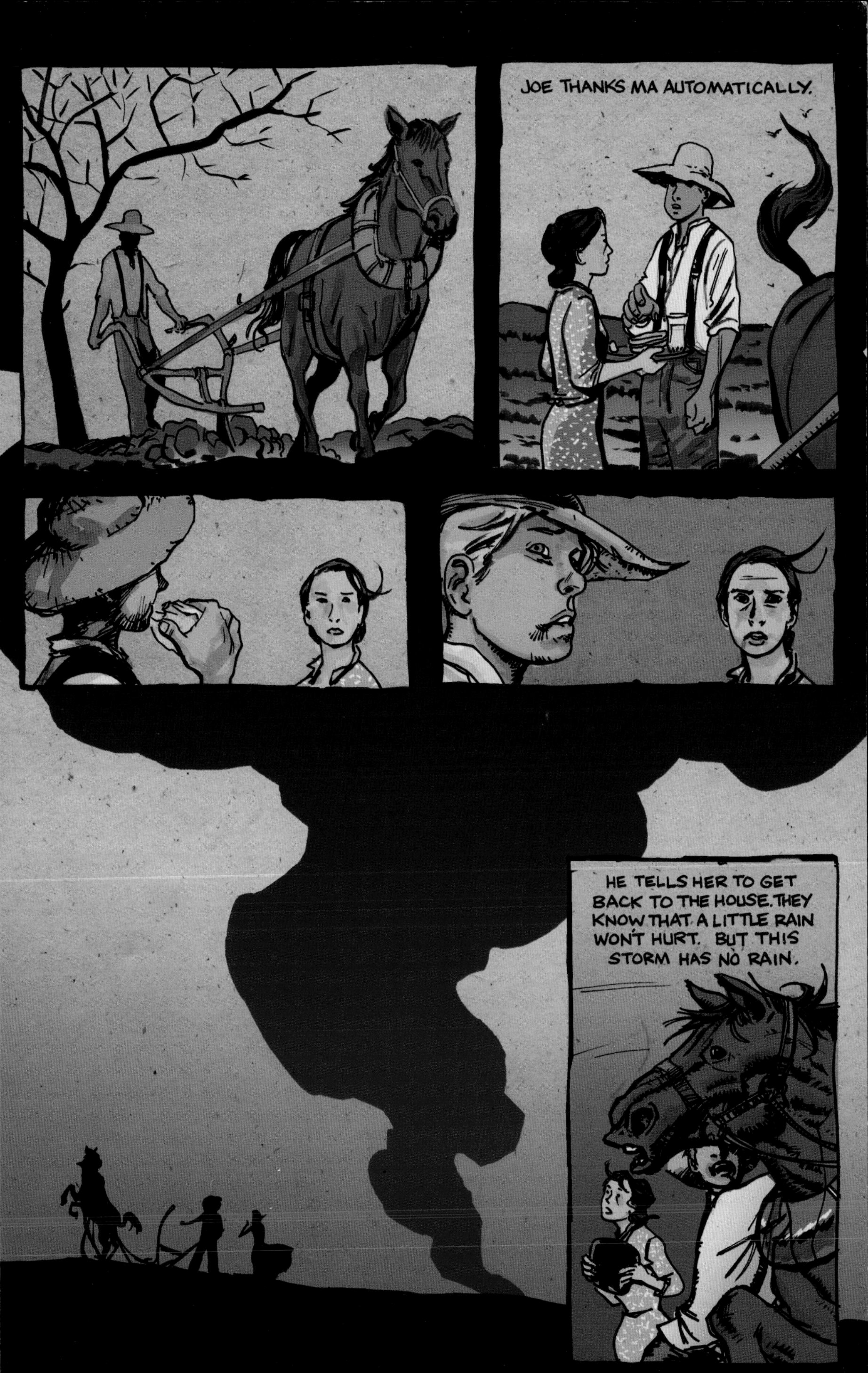
JOE THANKS MA AUTOMATICALLY.
HE TELLS HER TO GET BACK TO THE HOUSE. THEY KNOW THAT A LITTLE RAIN WON'T HURT. BUT THIS STORM HAS NO RAIN.

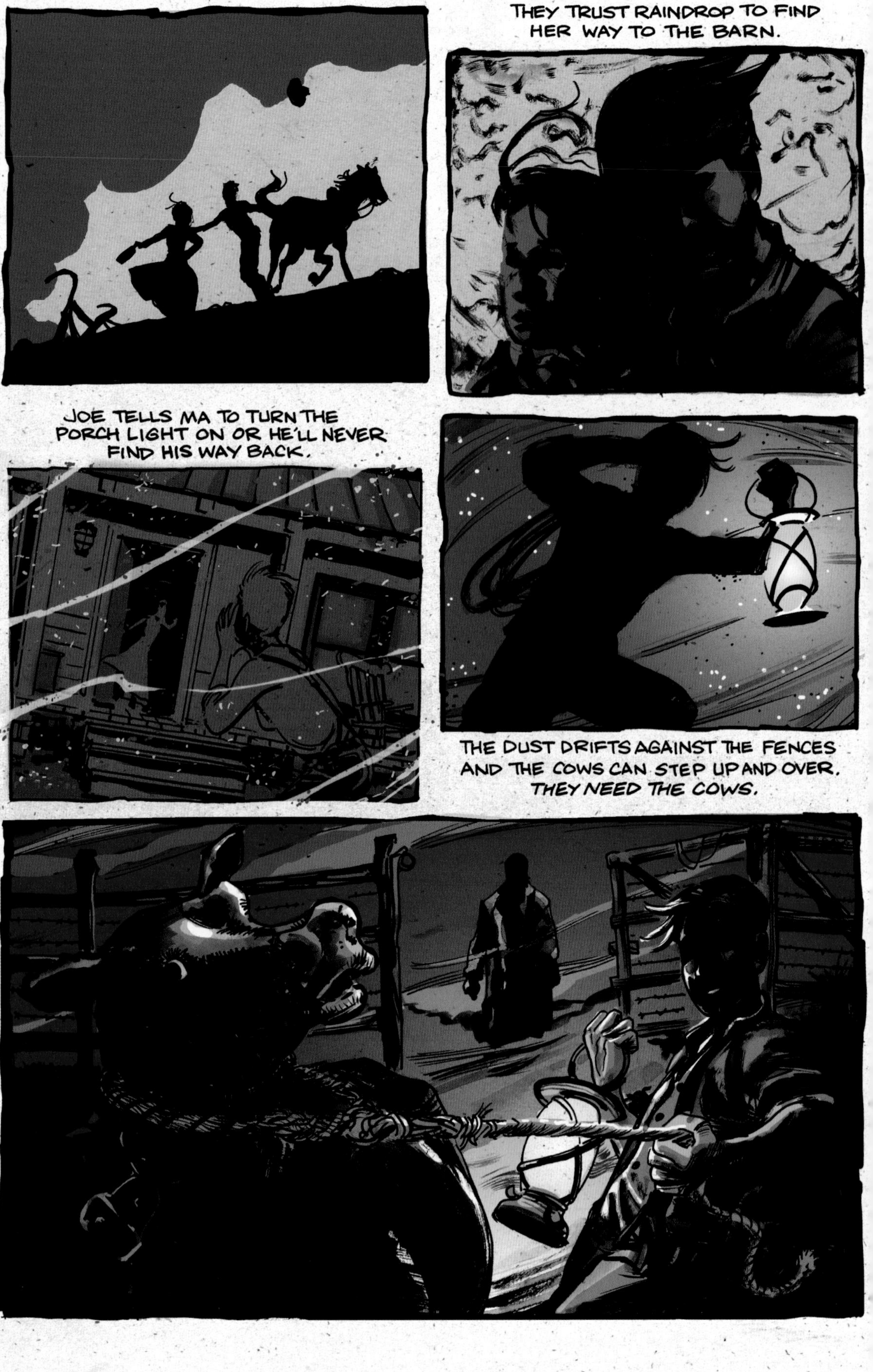
THEY TRUST RAINDROP TO FIND HER WAY TO THE BARN.
JOE TELLS MA TO TURN THE PORCH LIGHT ON OR HE'LL NEVER FIND HIS WAY BACK.
THE DUST DRIFTS AGAINST THE FENCES AND THE COWS CAN STEP UP AND OVER. THEY NEED THE COWS.

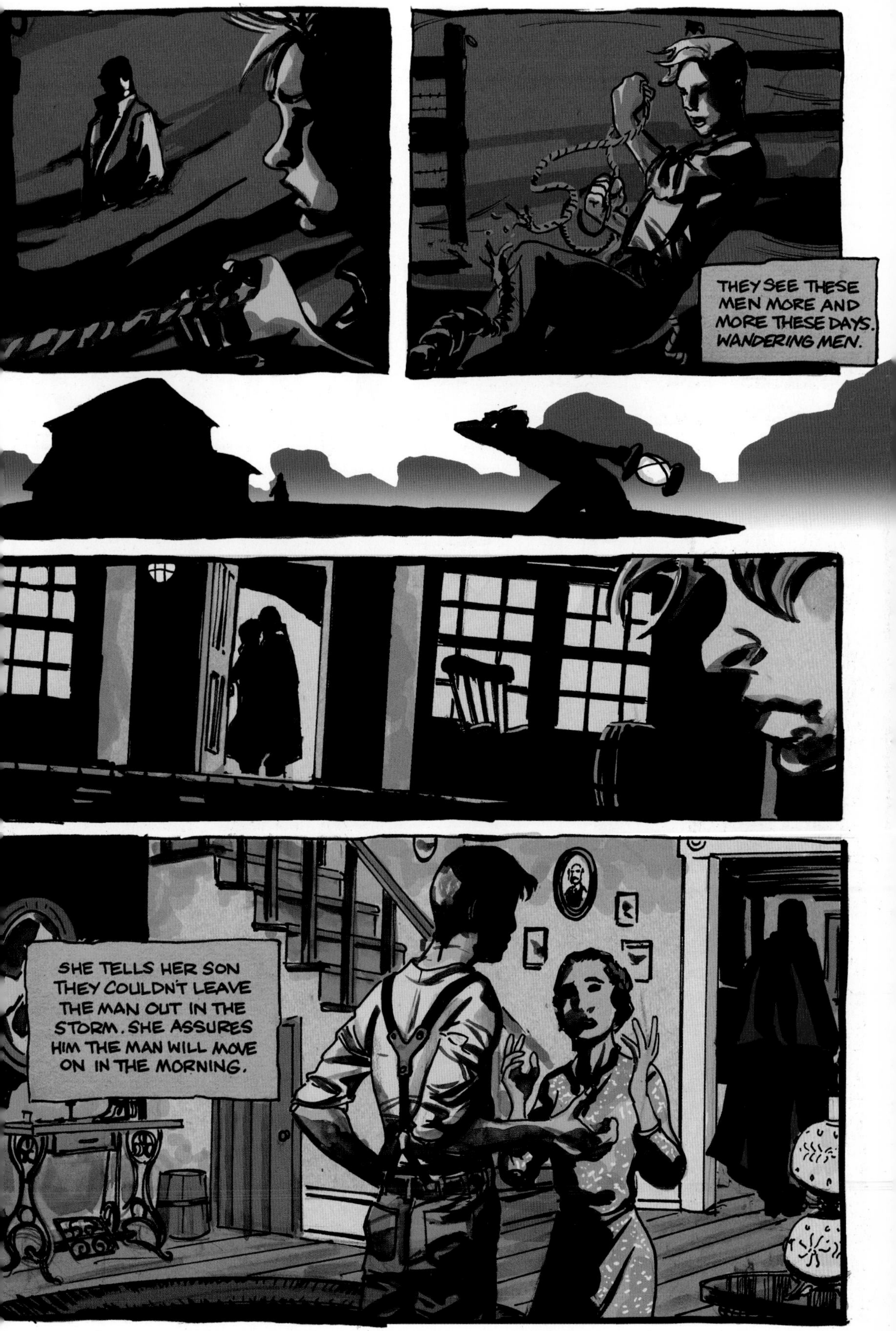
THEY SEE THESE MEN MORE AND MORE THESE DAYS. WANDERING MEN.
SHE TELLS HER SON THEY COULDN'T LEAVE THE MAN OUT IN THE STORM. SHE ASSURES HIM THE MAN WILL MOVE ON IN THE MORNING.

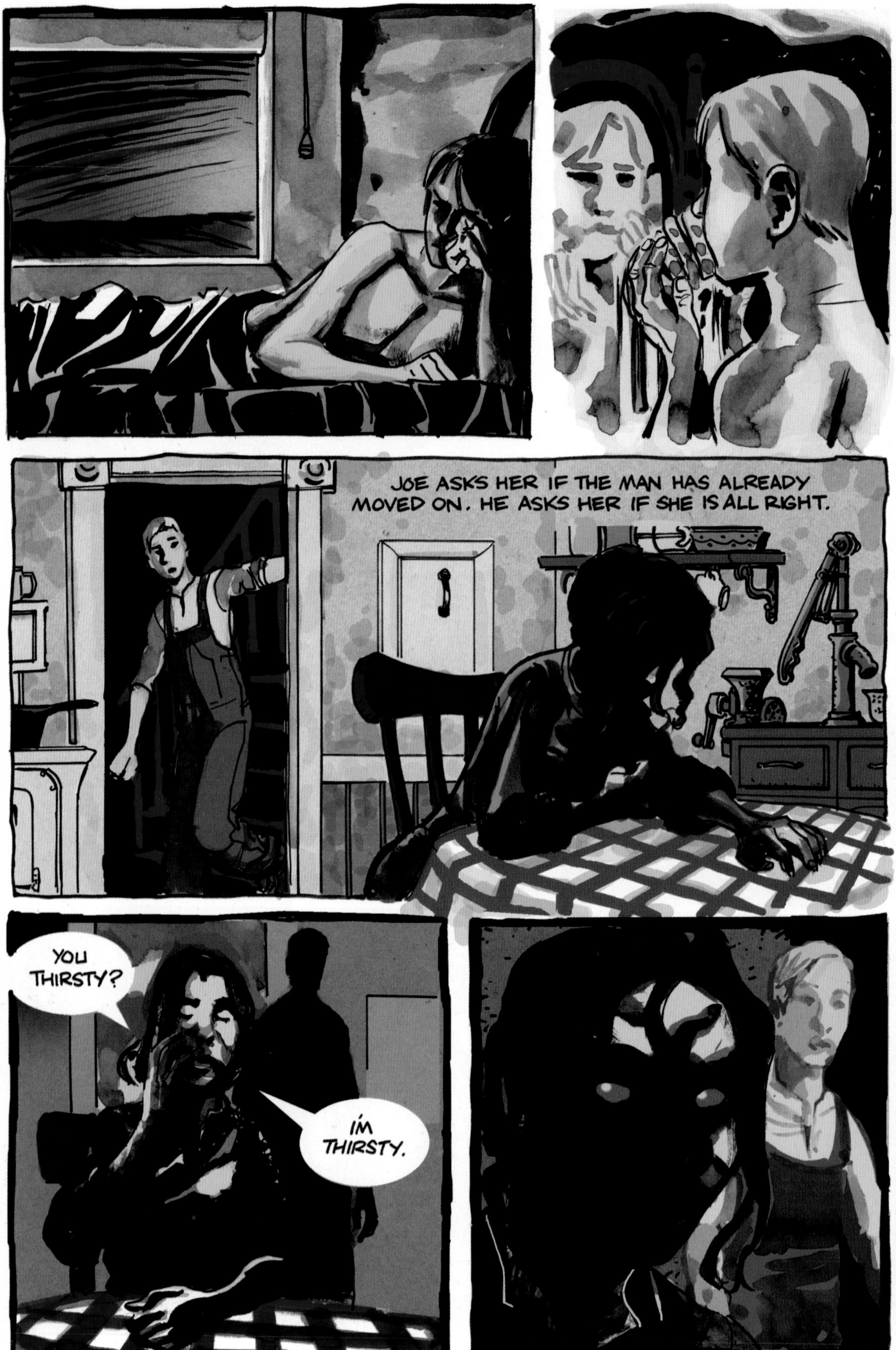
JOE ASKS HER IF THE MAN HAS ALREADY MOVED ON. HE ASKS HER IF SHE IS ALL RIGHT.
YOU THIRSTY?
I'M THIRSTY.

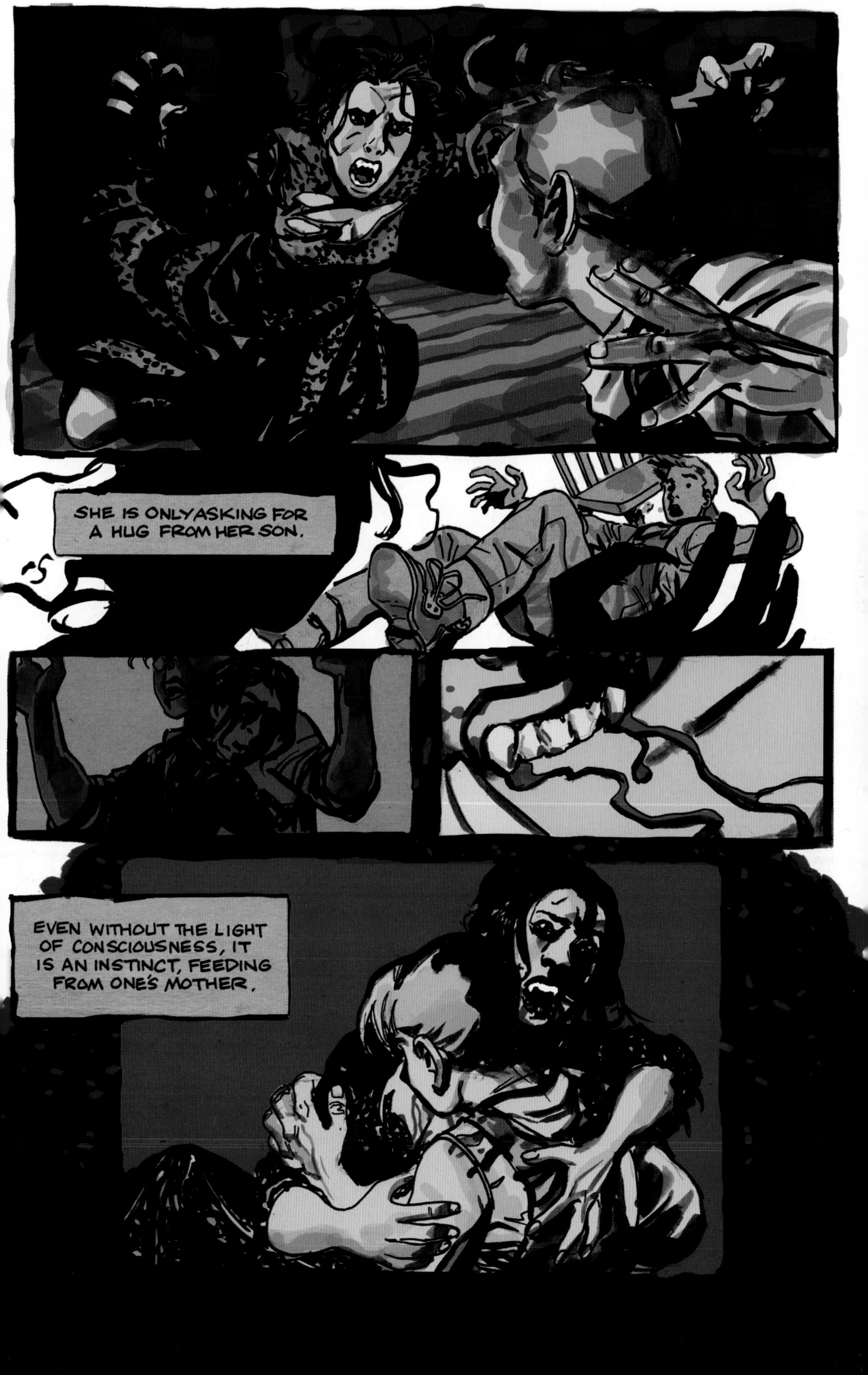
SHE IS ONLYASKING FOR A HUG FROM HER SON.
EVEN WITHOUT THE LIGHT OF CONSCIOUSNESS, IT IS AN INSTINCT, FEEDING FROM ONE'S MOTHER.

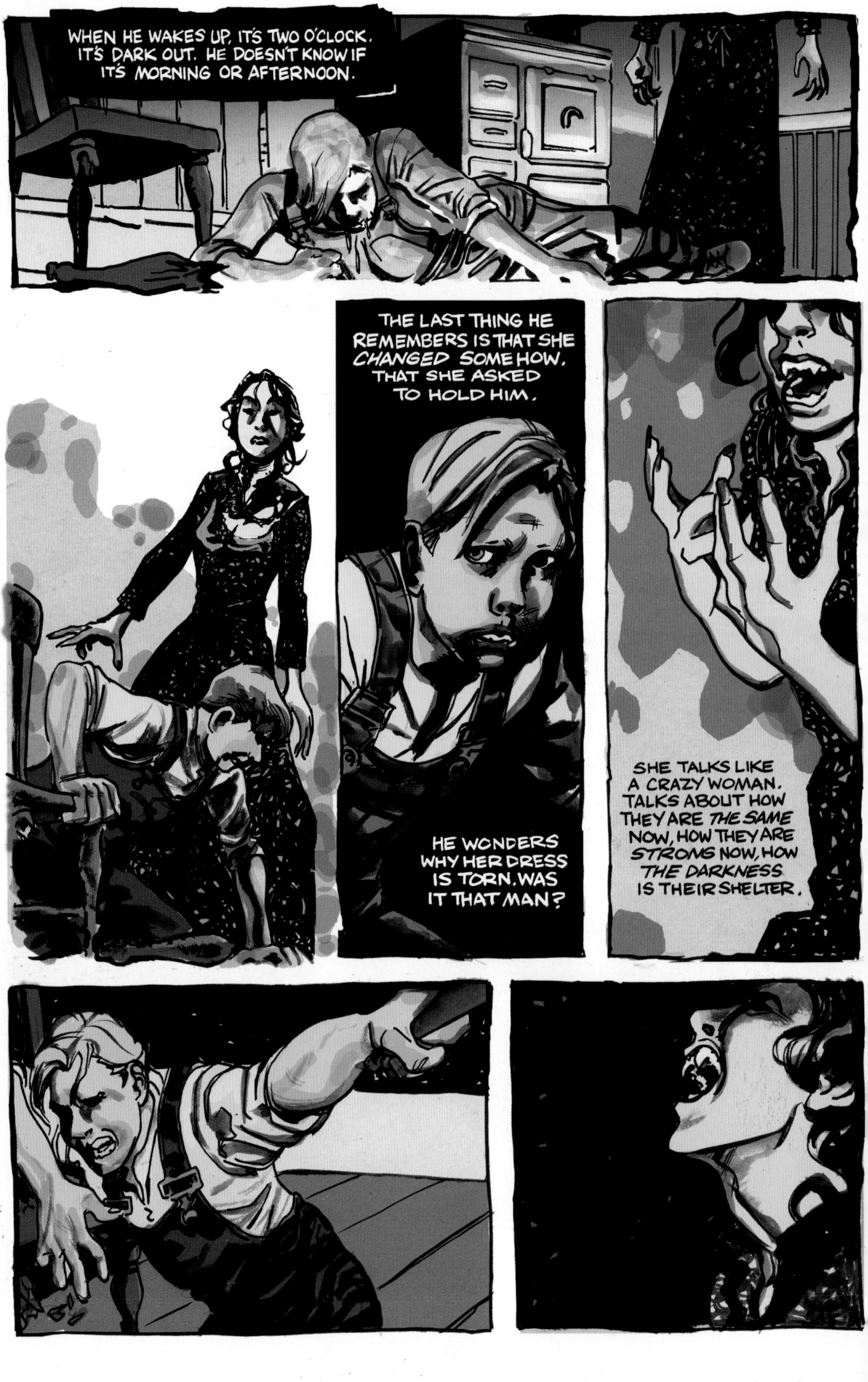
WHEN HE WAKES UP, IT'S TWO O'CLOCK. IT'S DARK OUT. HE DOESN'T KNOW IF IT'S MORNING OR AFTERNOON.
THE LAST THING HE REMEMBERS IS THAT SHE CHANGED SOMEHOW, THAT SHE ASKED TO HOLD HIM.
HE WONDERS WHY HER DRESS IS TORN. WAS IT THAT MAN?
SHE TALKS LIKE A CRAZY WOMAN. TALKS ABOUT HOW THEY ARE THE SAME NOW, HOW THEY ARE STRONG NOW, HOW THE DARKNESS IS THEIR SHELTER.

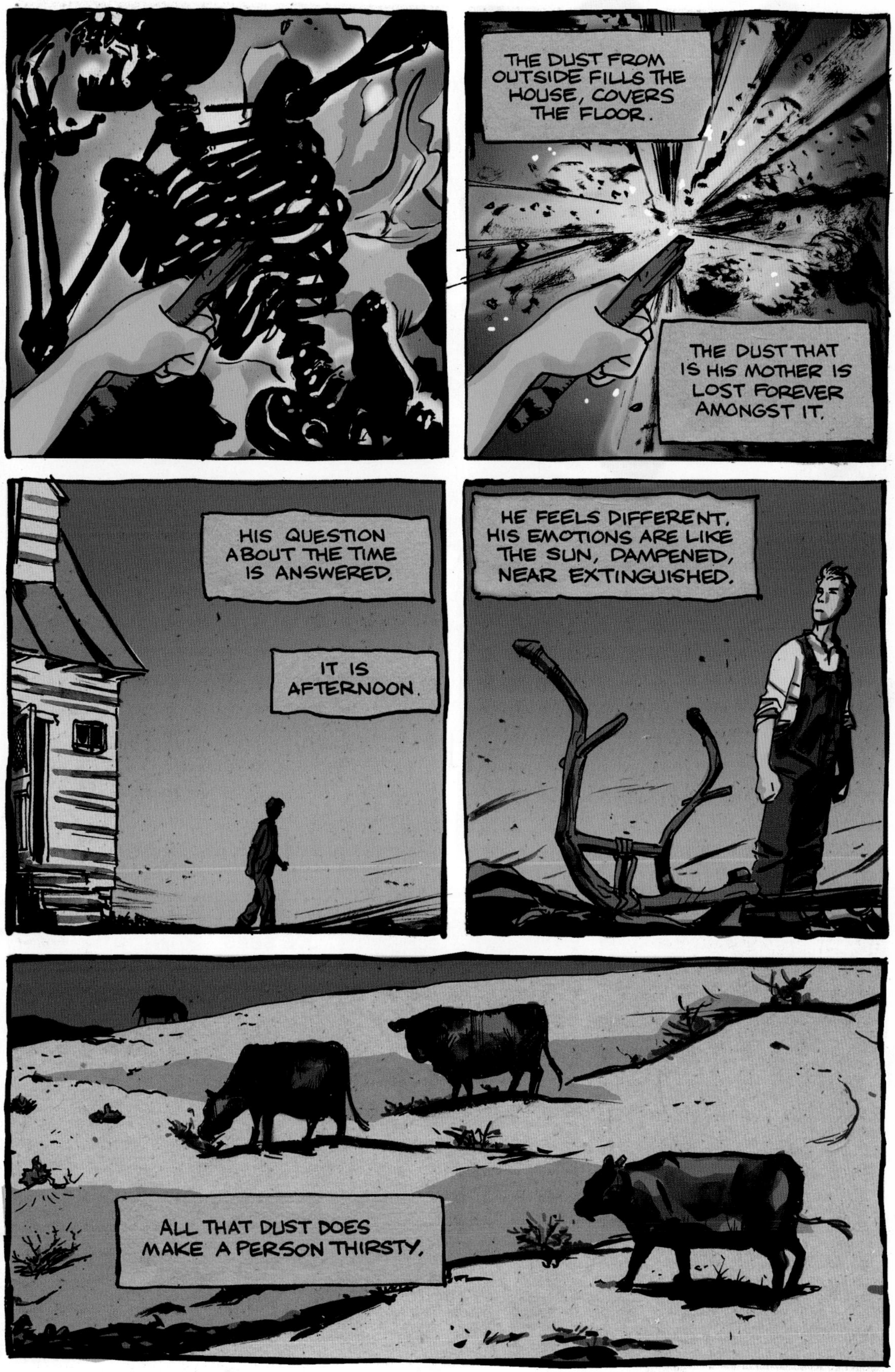
THE DUST FROM OUTSIDE FILLS THE HOUSE, COVERS THE FLOOR.
THE DUST THAT IS HIS MOTHER IS LOST FOREVER AMONGST IT.
HIS QUESTION ABOUT THE TIME IS ANSWERED.
IT IS AFTERNOON.
HE FEELS DIFFERENT. HIS EMOTIONS ARE LIKE THE SUN, DAMPENED, NEAR EXTINGUISHED.
ALL THAT DUST DOES MAKE A PERSON THIRSTY.

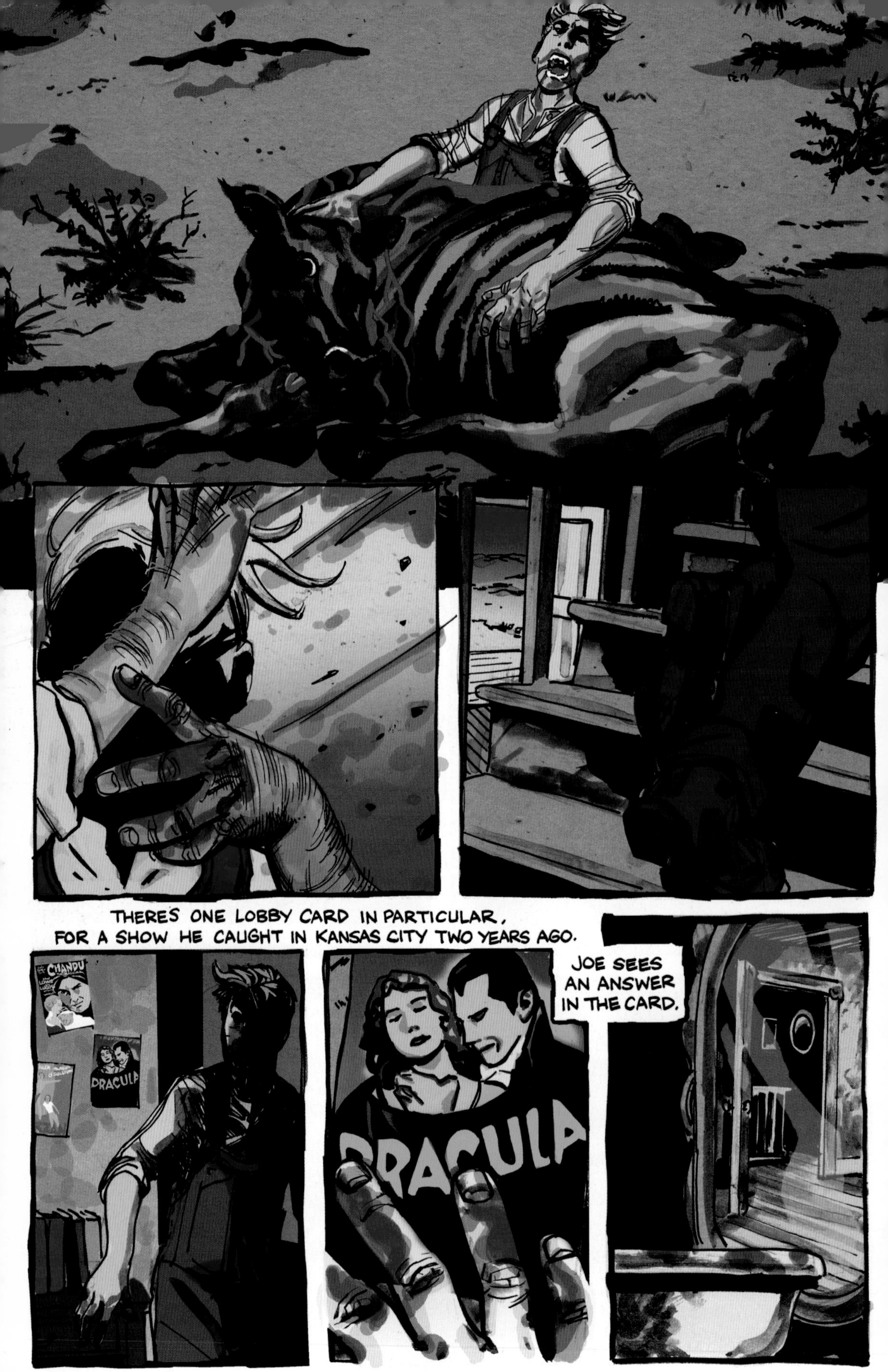
THERES ONE LOBBY CARD IN PARTICULAR, FOR A SHOW HE CAUGHT IN KANSAS CITY TWO YEARS AGO.
CHANDU
DRACULA
JOE SEES AN ANSWER IN THE CARD.
DRACULA

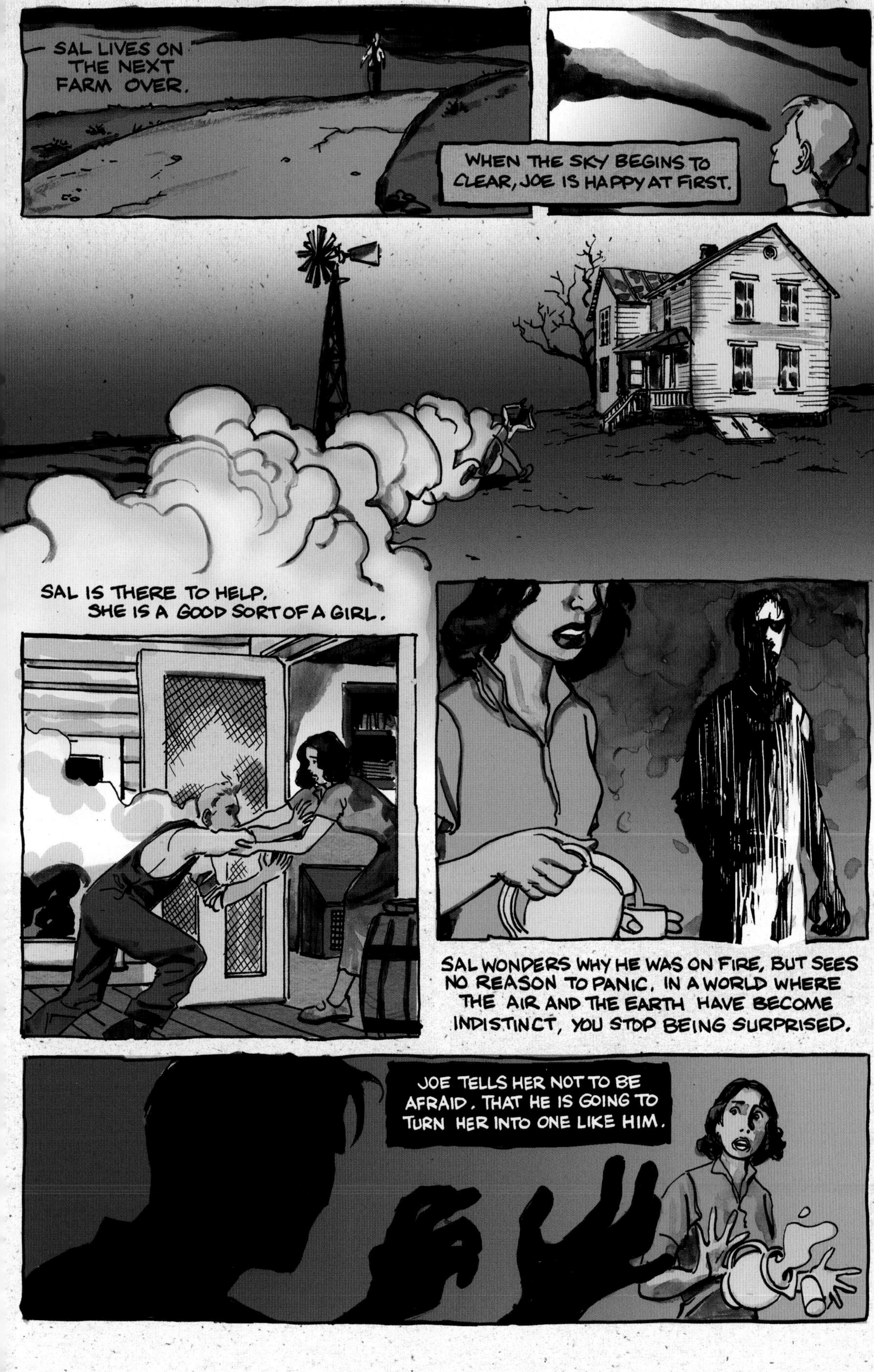
SAL LIVES ON THE NEXT FARM OVER.
WHEN THE SKY BEGINS TO CLEAR, JOE IS HAPPY AT FIRST.
SAL IS THERE TO HELP. SHE IS A GOOD SORT OF A GIRL.
SAL WONDERS WHY HE WAS ON FIRE, BUT SEES NO REASON TO PANIC. IN A WORLD WHERE THE AIR AND THE EARTH HAVE BECOME INDISTINCT, YOU STOP BEING SURPRISED.
JOE TELLS HER NOT TO BE AFRAID. THAT HE IS GOING TO TURN HER INTO ONE LIKE HIM.

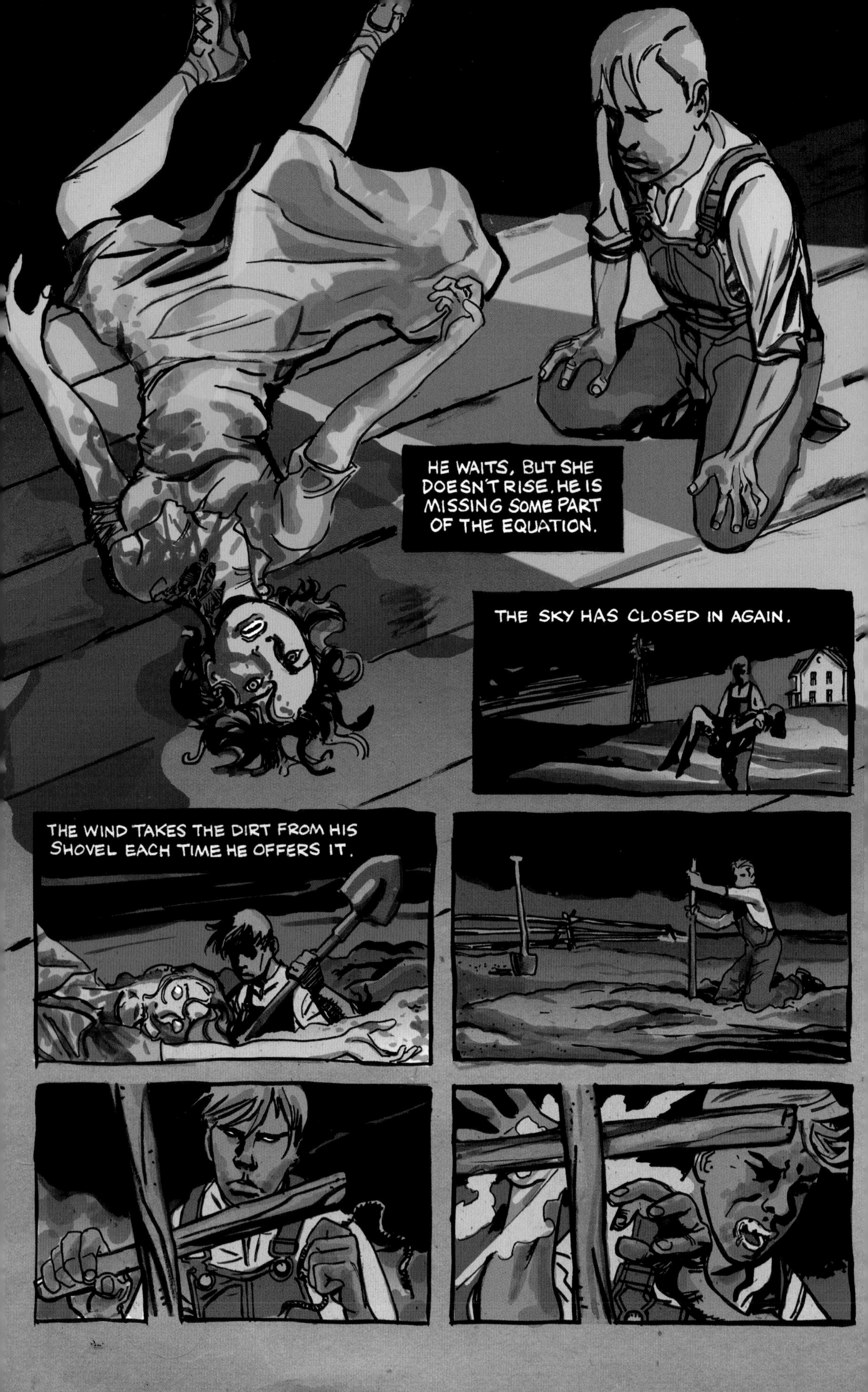
HE WAITS, BUT SHE DOESN'T RISE. HE IS MISSING SOME PART OF THE EQUATION.
THE SKY HAS CLOSED IN AGAIN.
THE WIND TAKES THE DIRT FROM HIS SHOVEL EACH TIME HE OFFERS IT.

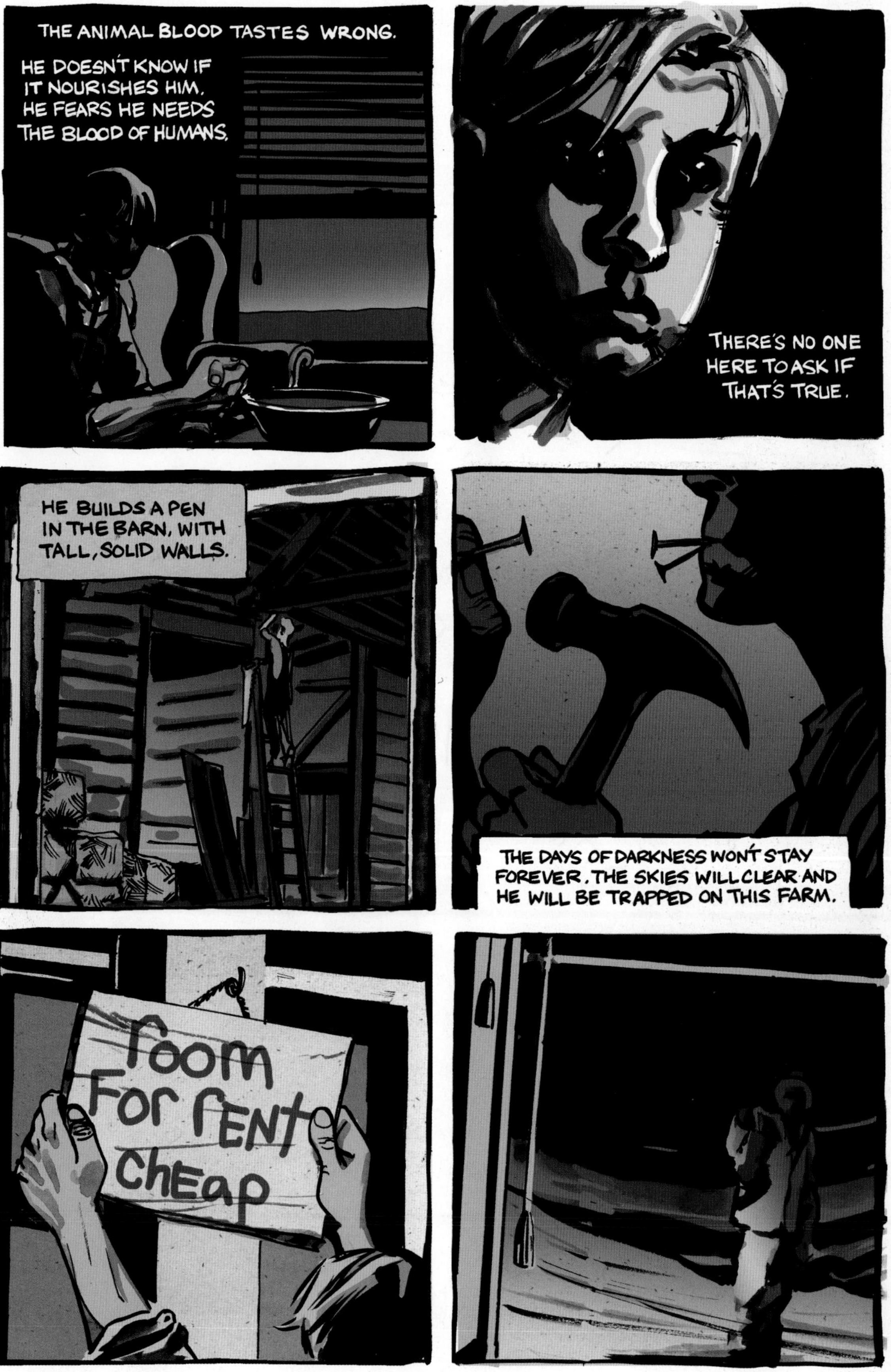
THE ANIMAL BLOOD TASTES WRONG.
HE DOESN'T KNOW IF IT NOURISHES HIM. HE FEARS HE NEEDS THE BLOOD OF HUMANS.
THERE'S NO ONE HERE TO ASK IF THAT'S TRUE.
HE BUILDS A PEN IN THE BARN, WITH TALL, SOLID WALLS.
THE DAYS OF DARKNESS WON'T STAY FOREVER. THE SKIES WILL CLEAR AND HE WILL BE TRAPPED ON THIS FARM.
room For rent cheap

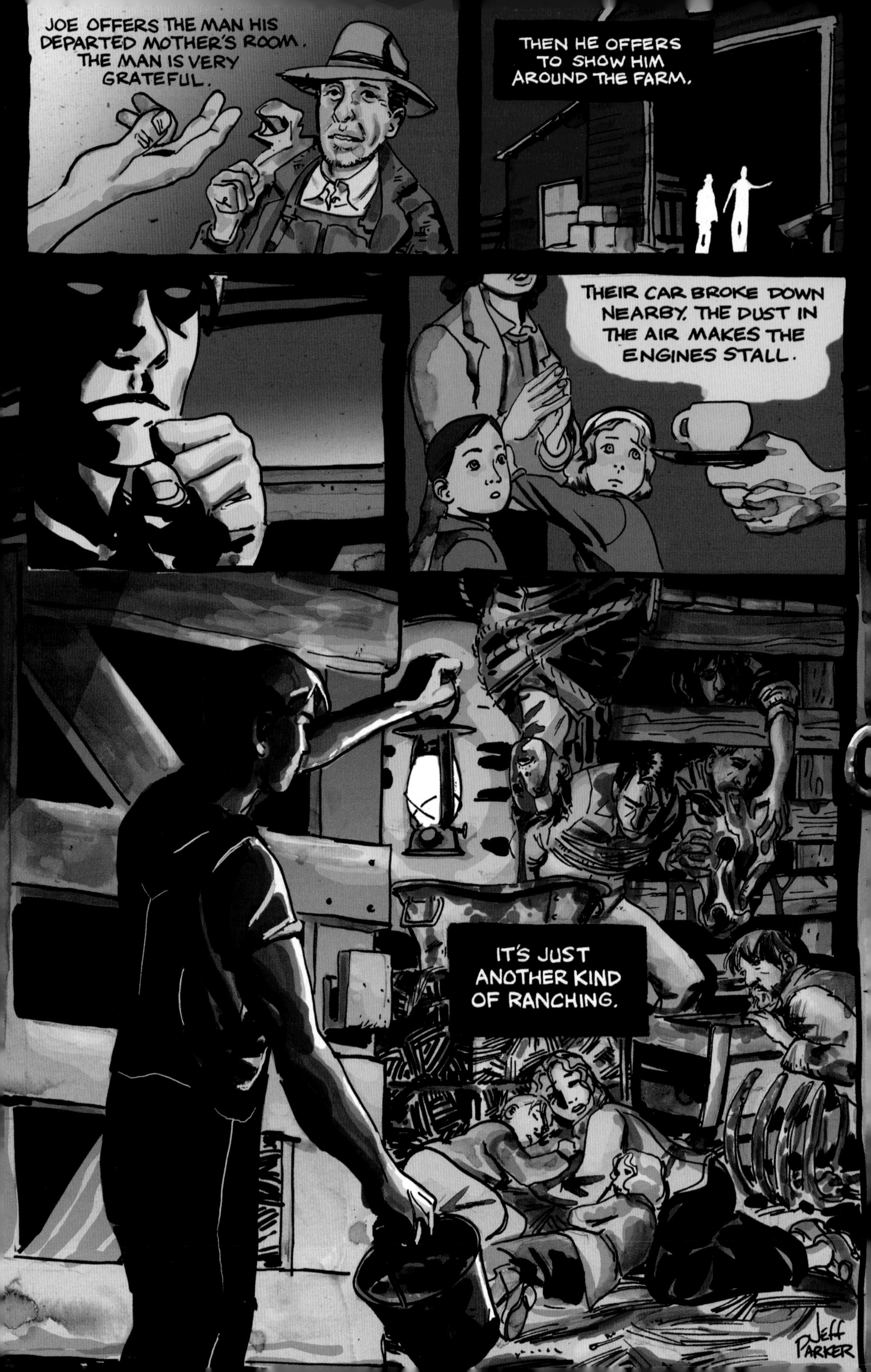
JOE OFFERS THE MAN HIS DEPARTED MOTHER'S ROOM. THE MAN IS VERY GRATEFUL.
THEN HE OFFERS TO SHOW HIM AROUND THE FARM.
THEIR CAR BROKE DOWN NEARBY. THE DUST IN THE AIR MAKES THE ENGINES STALL.
IT'S JUST ANOTHER KIND OF RANCHING.
JEFF PARKER

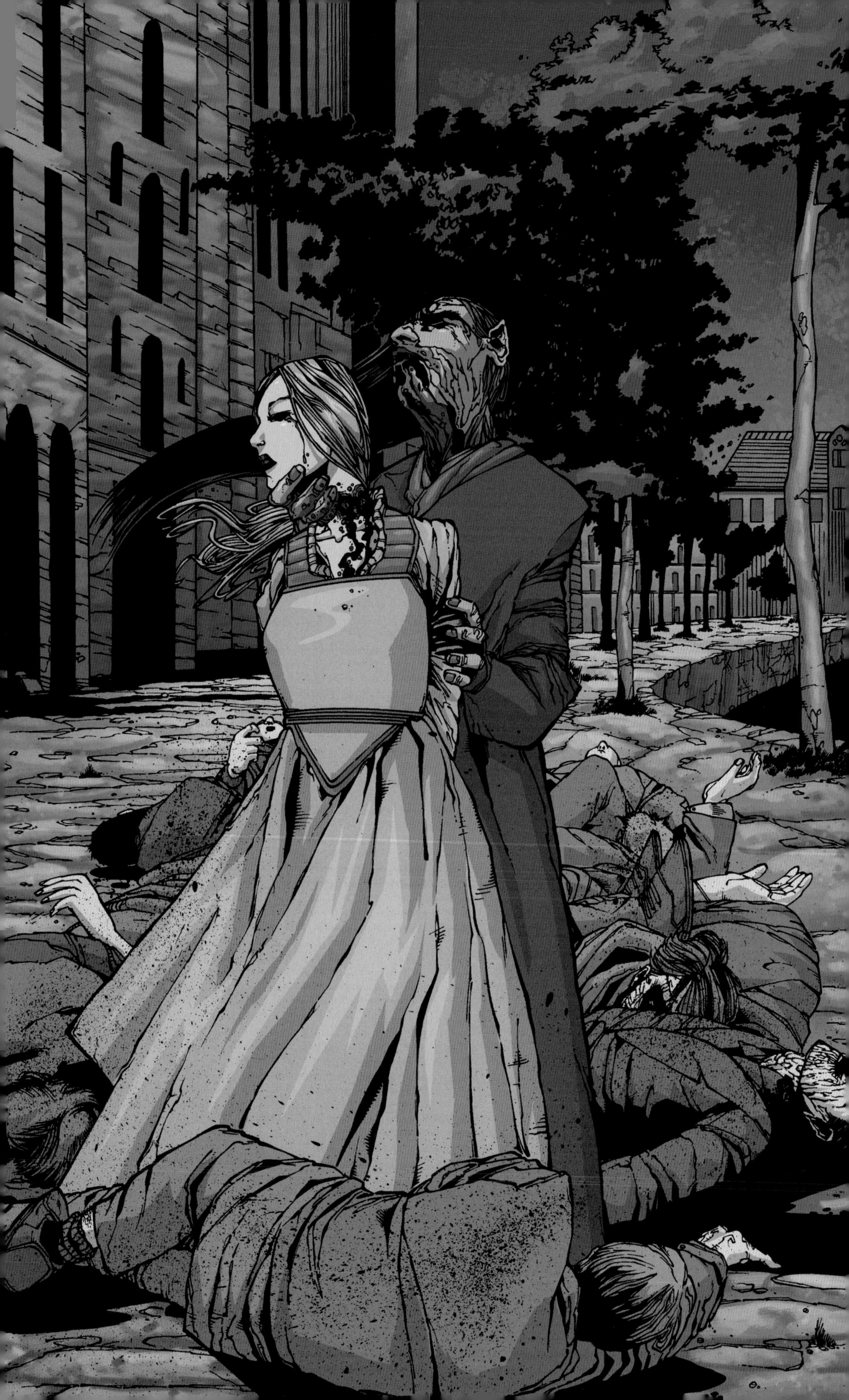

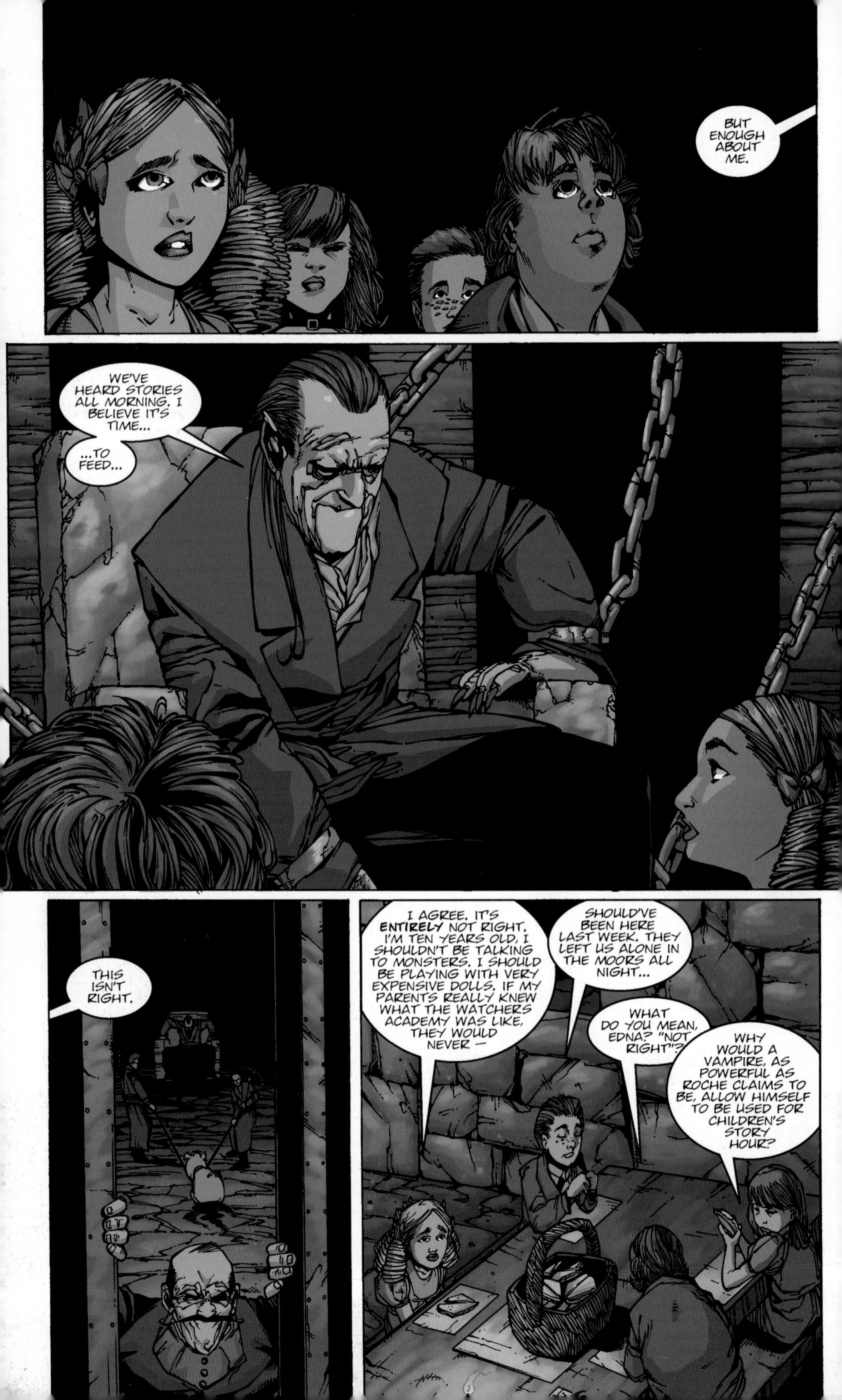
BUT ENOUGH ABOUT ME.
WE'VE HEARD STORIES ALL MORNING. I BELIEVE IT'S TIME...
...TO FEED...
THIS ISN'T RIGHT.
I AGREE. IT'S **ENTIRELY** NOT RIGHT. I'M TEN YEARS OLD, I SHOULDN'T BE TALKING TO MONSTERS. I SHOULD BE PLAYING WITH VERY EXPENSIVE DOLLS. IF MY PARENTS REALLY KNEW WHAT THE WATCHERS ACADEMY WAS LIKE, THEY WOULD NEVER —
SHOULD'VE BEEN HERE LAST WEEK. THEY LEFT US ALONE IN THE MOORS ALL NIGHT...
WHAT DO YOU MEAN, EDNA? "NOT RIGHT"?
WHY WOULD A VAMPIRE, AS POWERFUL AS ROCHE CLAIMS TO BE, ALLOW HIMSELF TO BE USED FOR CHILDREN'S STORY HOUR?

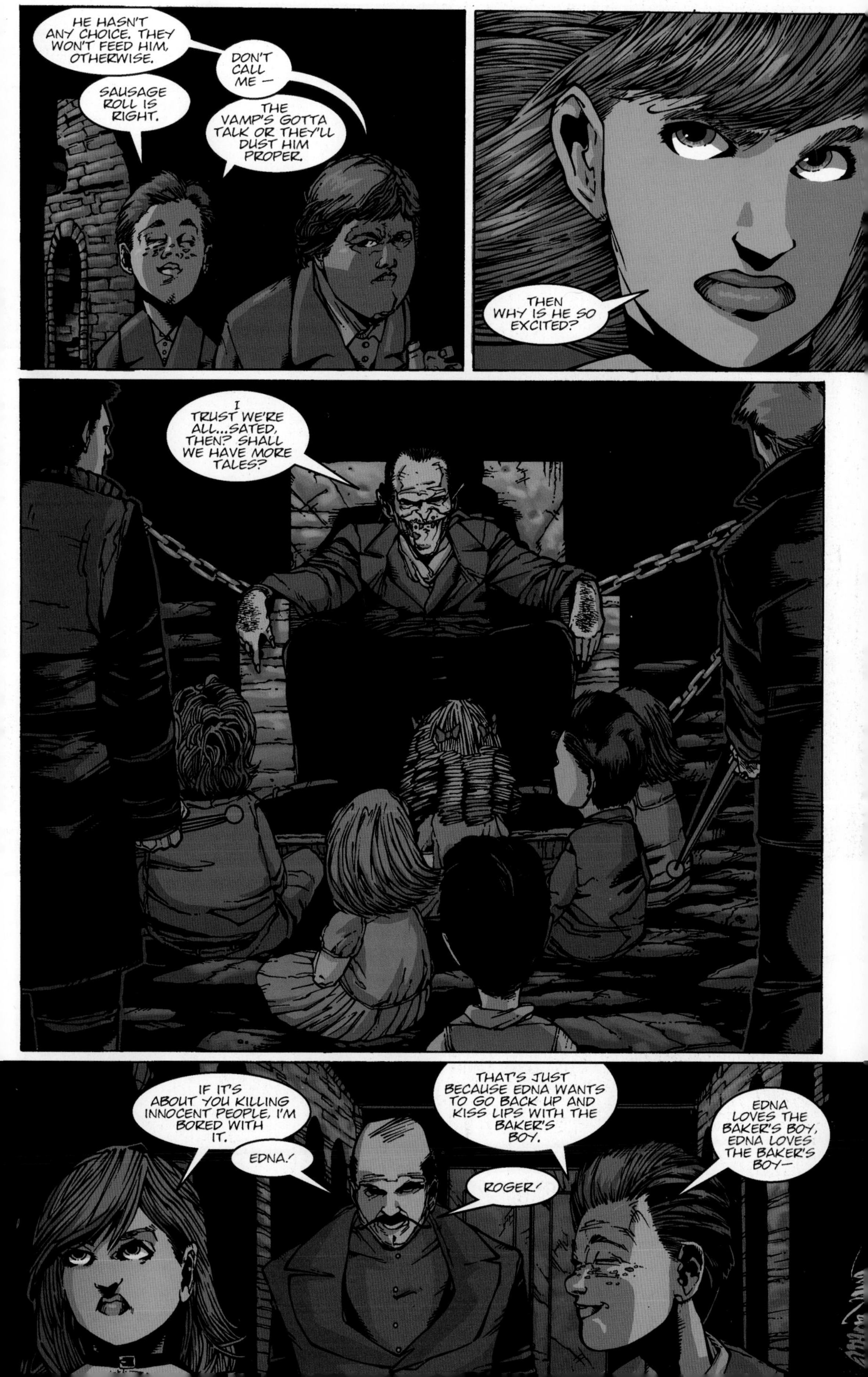

HE HASN'T ANY CHOICE. THEY WON'T FEED HIM, OTHERWISE.
DON'T CALL ME —
SAUSAGE ROLL IS RIGHT.
THE VAMP'S GOTTA TALK OR THEY'LL DUST HIM PROPER.
THEN WHY IS HE SO EXCITED?
I TRUST WE'RE ALL...SATED, THEN? SHALL WE HAVE MORE TALES?
IF IT'S ABOUT YOU KILLING INNOCENT PEOPLE, I'M BORED WITH IT.
EDNA!
THAT'S JUST BECAUSE EDNA WANTS TO GO BACK UP AND KISS LIPS WITH THE BAKER'S BOY.
ROGER!
EDNA LOVES THE BAKER'S BOY, EDNA LOVES THE BAKER'S BOY—

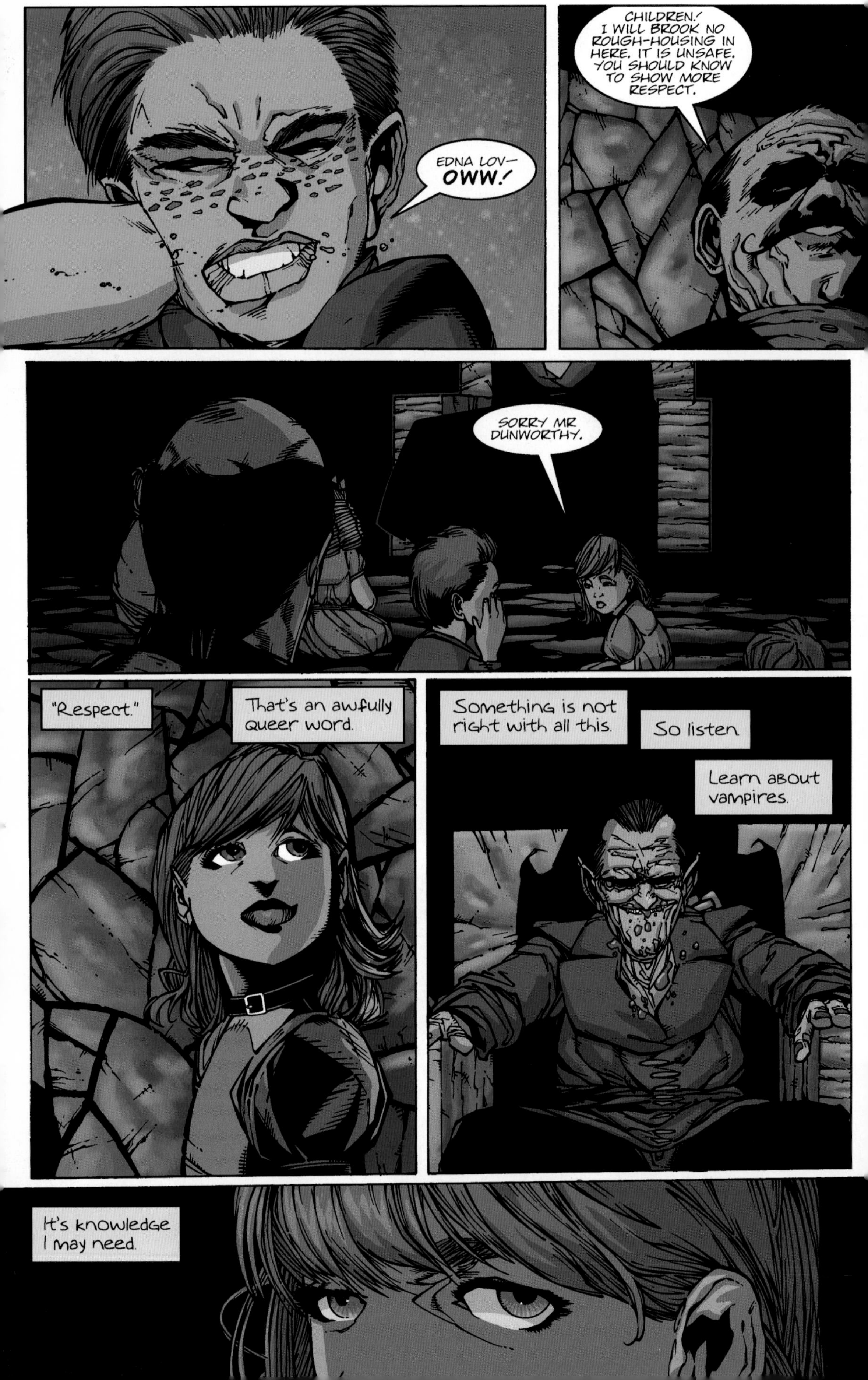
EDNA LOV—
OWW!
CHILDREN! I WILL BROOK NO ROUGH-HOUSING IN HERE. IT IS UNSAFE. YOU SHOULD KNOW TO SHOW MORE RESPECT.
SORRY MR DUNWORTHY.
"Respect."
That's an awfully queer word.
Something is not right with all this.
So listen.
Learn about vampires.
It's knowledge I may need.

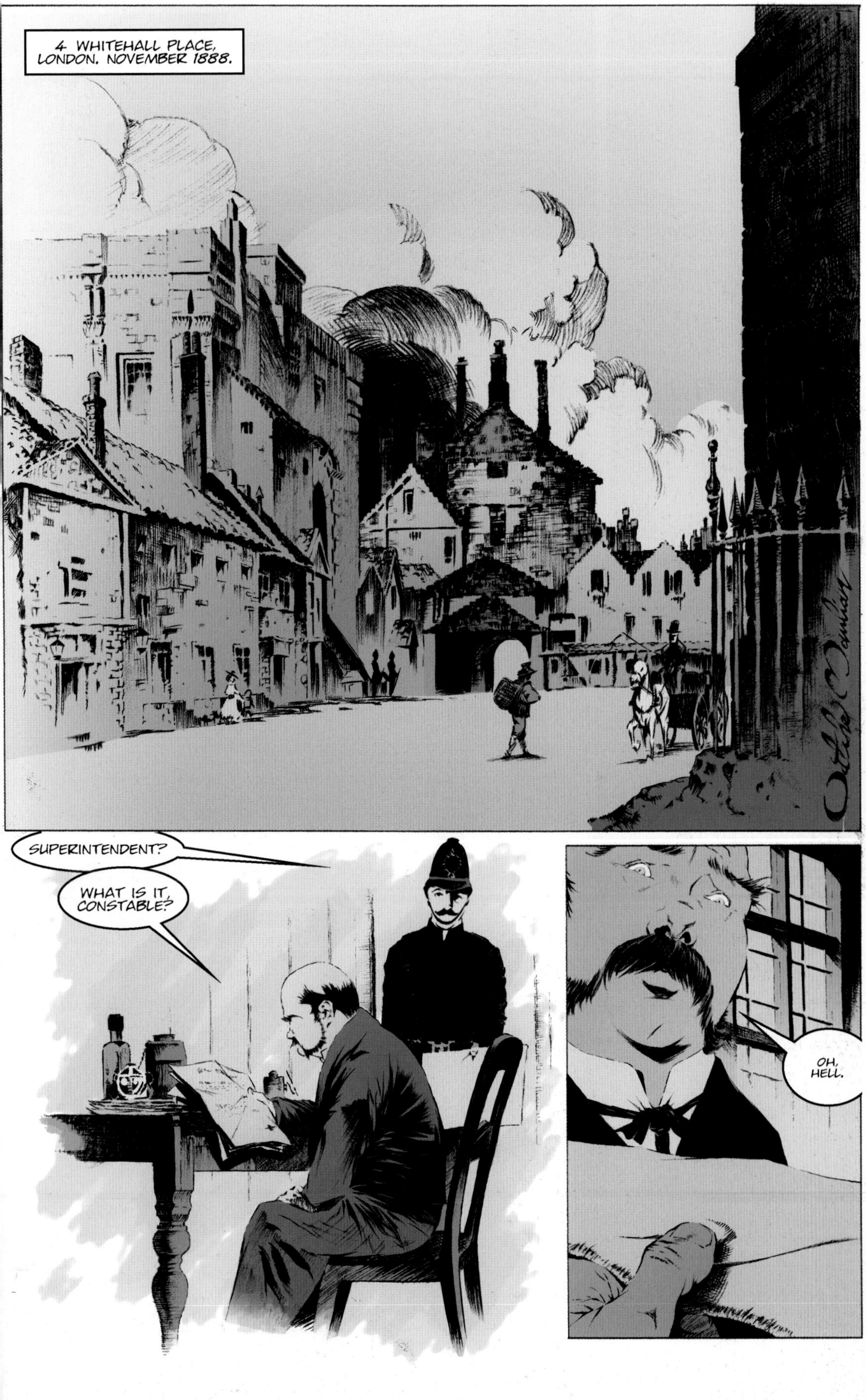
4 WHITEHALL PLACE, LONDON. NOVEMBER 1888.
SUPERINTENDENT?
WHAT IS IT, CONSTABLE?
OH, HELL.

INSPECTOR?

JAMES, ARE YOU —

OH.

WHAT CAN I DO FOR YOU, SUPERINTENDENT?

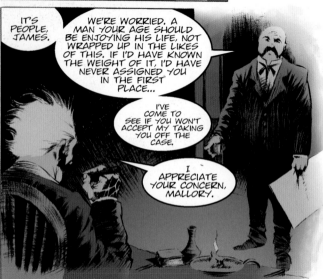

IT'S PEOPLE, JAMES.

WE'RE WORRIED. A MAN YOUR AGE SHOULD BE ENJOYING HIS LIFE, NOT WRAPPED UP IN THE LIKES OF THIS. IF I'D HAVE KNOWN THE WEIGHT OF IT, I'D HAVE NEVER ASSIGNED YOU IN THE FIRST PLACE...

I'VE COME TO SEE IF YOU WON'T ACCEPT MY TAKING YOU OFF THE CASE.

I APPRECIATE YOUR CONCERN, MALLORY.

AS ALWAYS.

BUT MY ANSWER IS SIMILARLY CONSTANT. NOW, WILL THAT BE ALL?

UNFORTUNATELY IT'S NOT, JAMES...

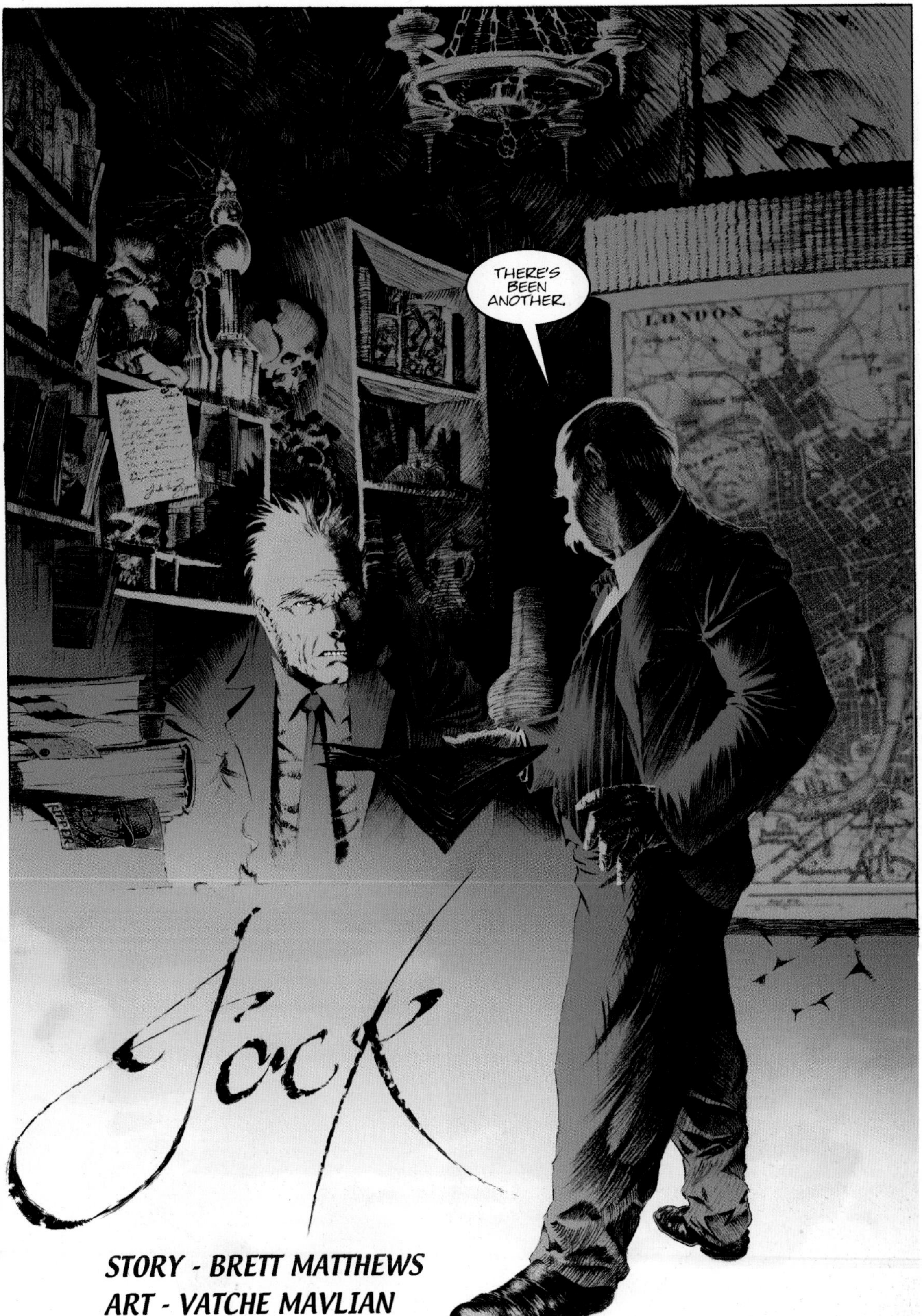
THERE'S BEEN ANOTHER.
LONDON
Jack
STORY - BRETT MATTHEWS
ART - VATCHE MAVLIAN

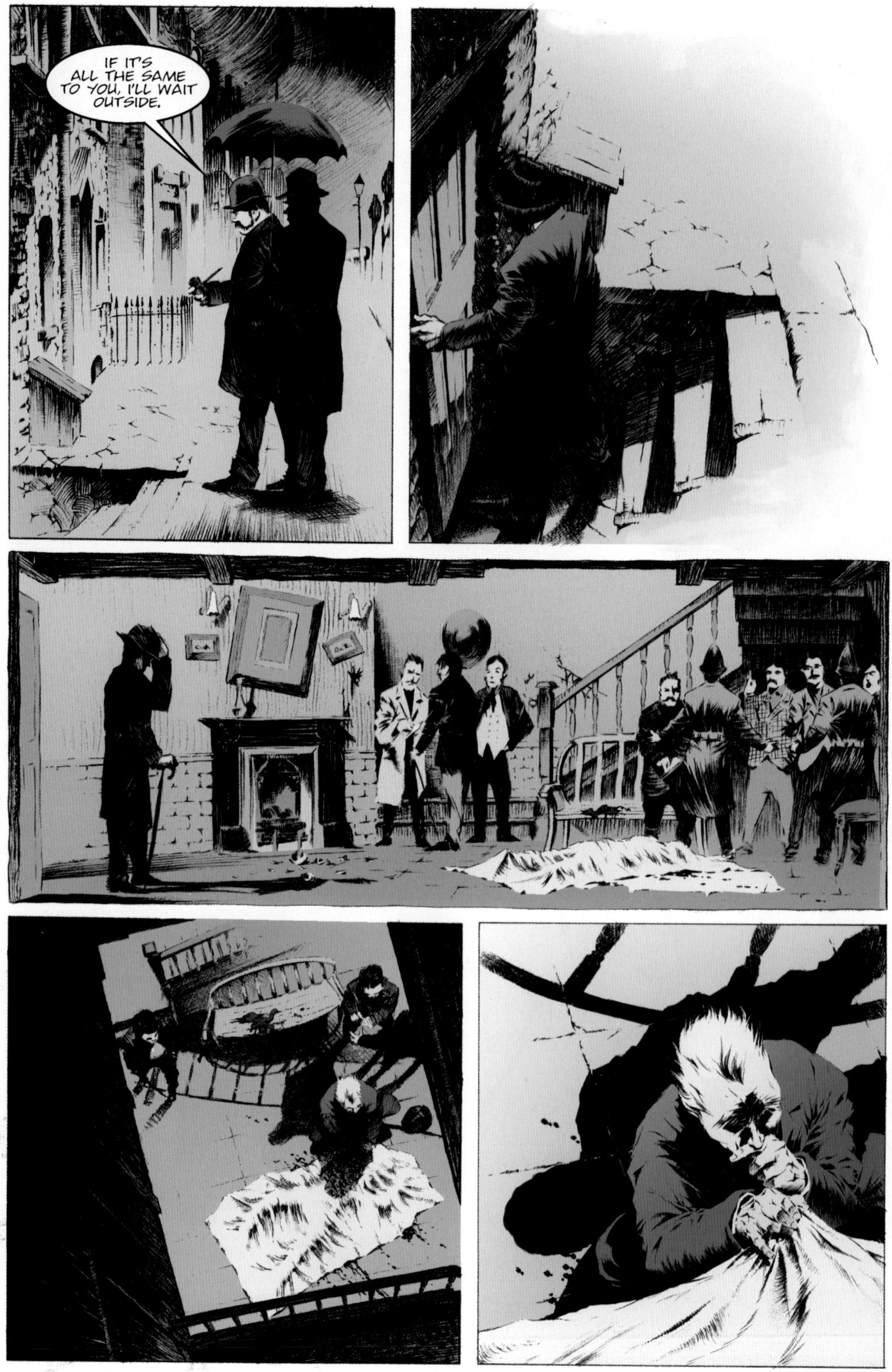
IF IT'S ALL THE SAME TO YOU, I'LL WAIT OUTSIDE.

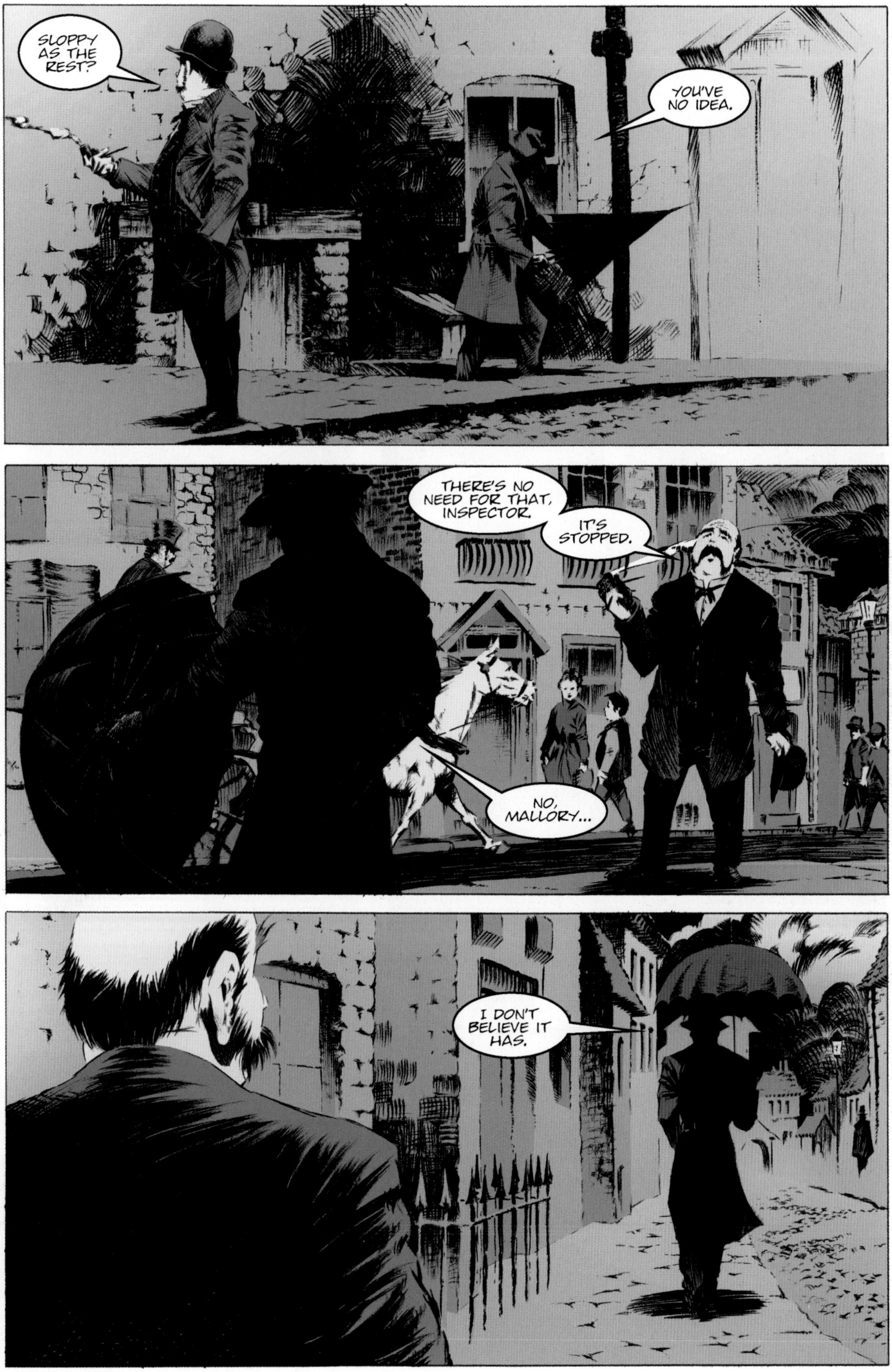
SLOPPY AS THE REST?
YOU'VE NO IDEA.
THERE'S NO NEED FOR THAT, INSPECTOR.
IT'S STOPPED.
NO, MALLORY...
I DON'T BELIEVE IT HAS.

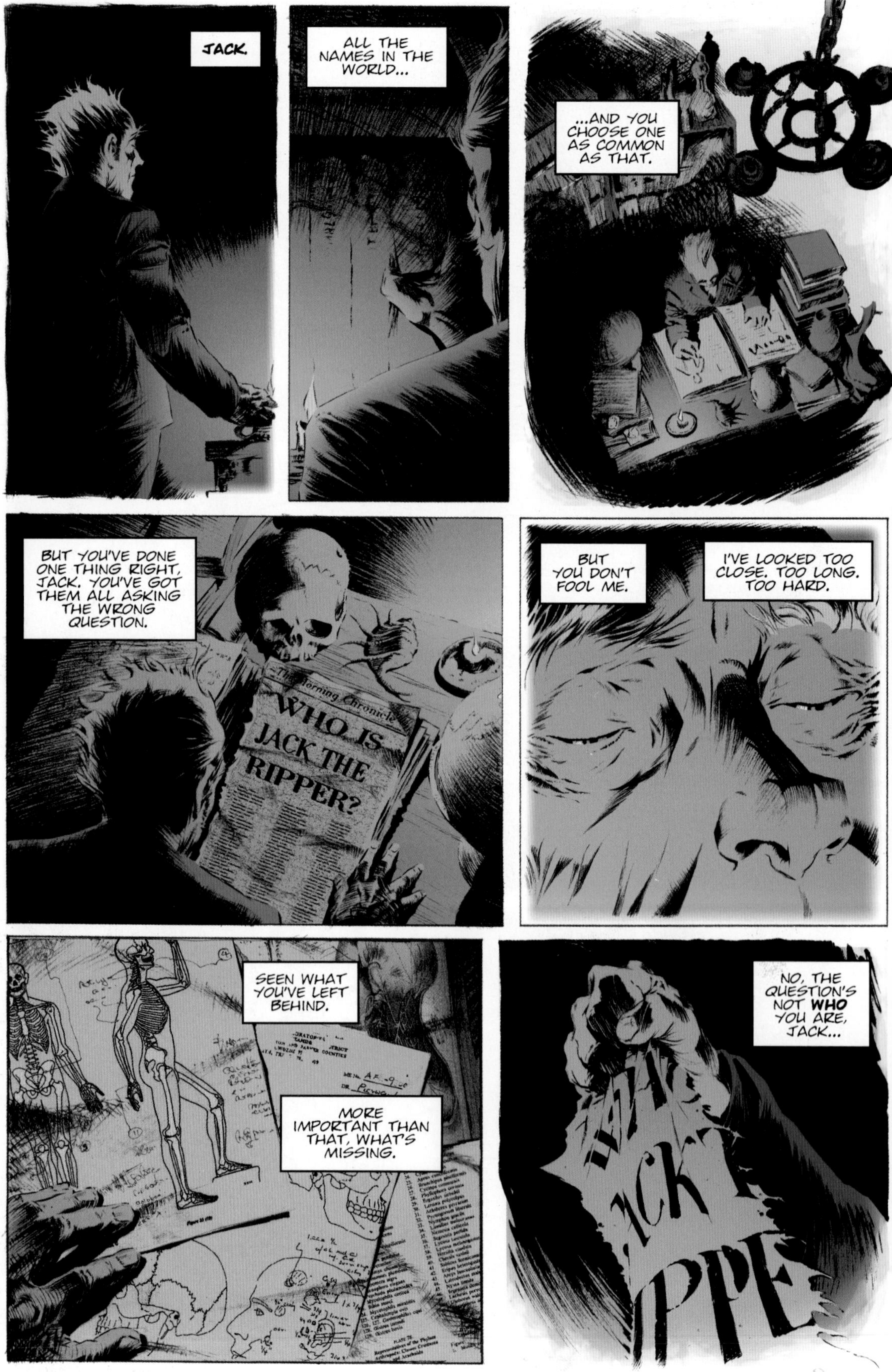
JACK.
ALL THE NAMES IN THE WORLD...
...AND YOU CHOOSE ONE AS COMMON AS THAT.
BUT YOU'VE DONE ONE THING RIGHT, JACK. YOU'VE GOT THEM ALL ASKING THE WRONG QUESTION.
WHO IS JACK THE RIPPER?
BUT YOU DON'T FOOL ME.
I'VE LOOKED TOO CLOSE. TOO LONG. TOO HARD.
SEEN WHAT YOU'VE LEFT BEHIND.
MORE IMPORTANT THAN THAT, WHAT'S MISSING.
NO, THE QUESTION'S NOT **WHO** YOU ARE, JACK...

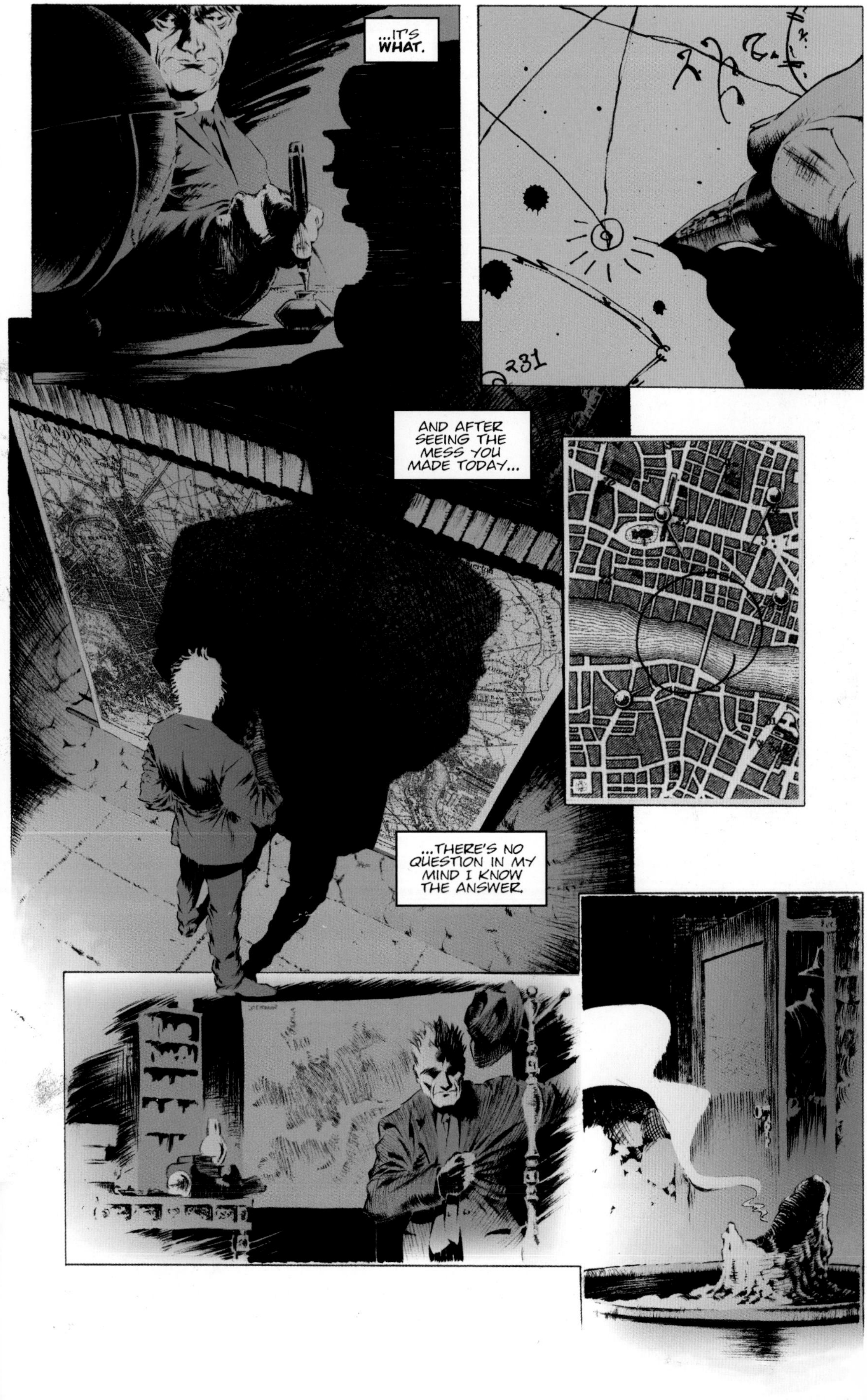
...IT'S WHAT.
LONDON
231
AND AFTER SEEING THE MESS YOU MADE TODAY...
...THERE'S NO QUESTION IN MY MIND I KNOW THE ANSWER.

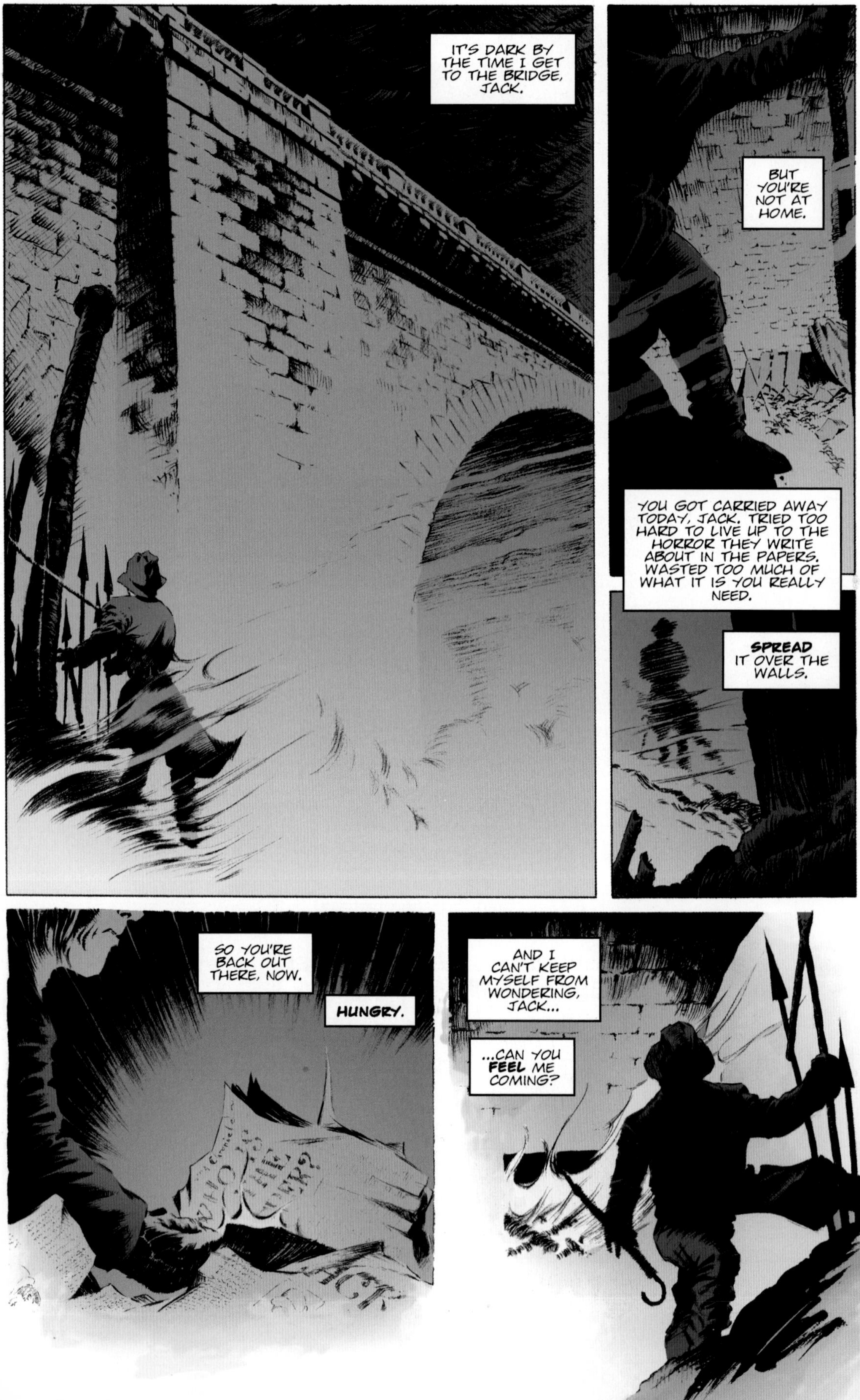
IT'S DARK BY THE TIME I GET TO THE BRIDGE, JACK.
BUT YOU'RE NOT AT HOME.
YOU GOT CARRIED AWAY TODAY, JACK. TRIED TOO HARD TO LIVE UP TO THE HORROR THEY WRITE ABOUT IN THE PAPERS. WASTED TOO MUCH OF WHAT IT IS YOU REALLY NEED.
SPREAD IT OVER THE WALLS.
SO YOU'RE BACK OUT THERE, NOW.
HUNGRY.
AND I CAN'T KEEP MYSELF FROM WONDERING, JACK...
...CAN YOU **FEEL** ME COMING?

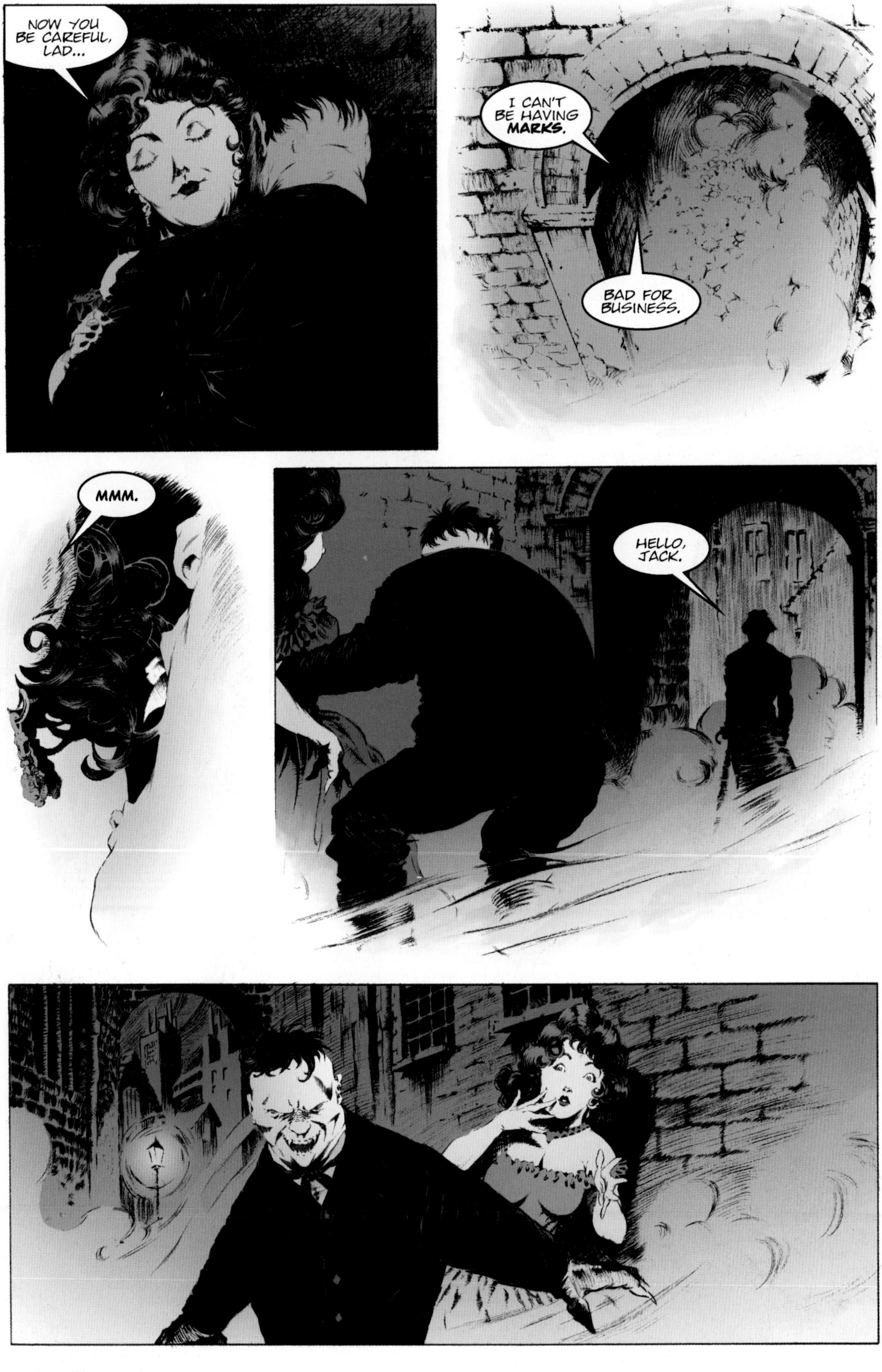
NOW YOU BE CAREFUL, LAD...
I CAN'T BE HAVING **MARKS.**
BAD FOR BUSINESS.
MMM.
HELLO, JACK.

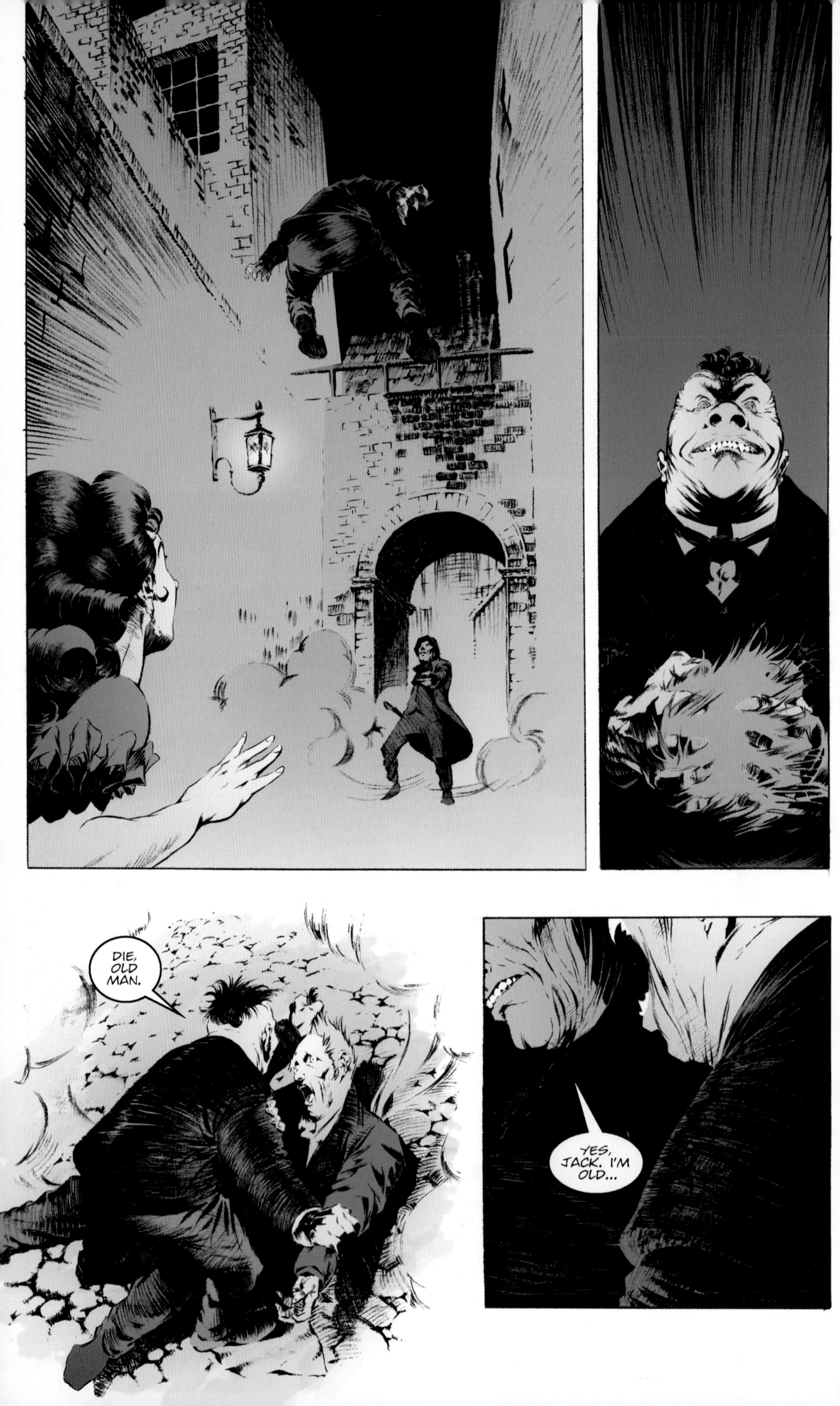
DIE, OLD MAN.
YES, JACK. I'M OLD...

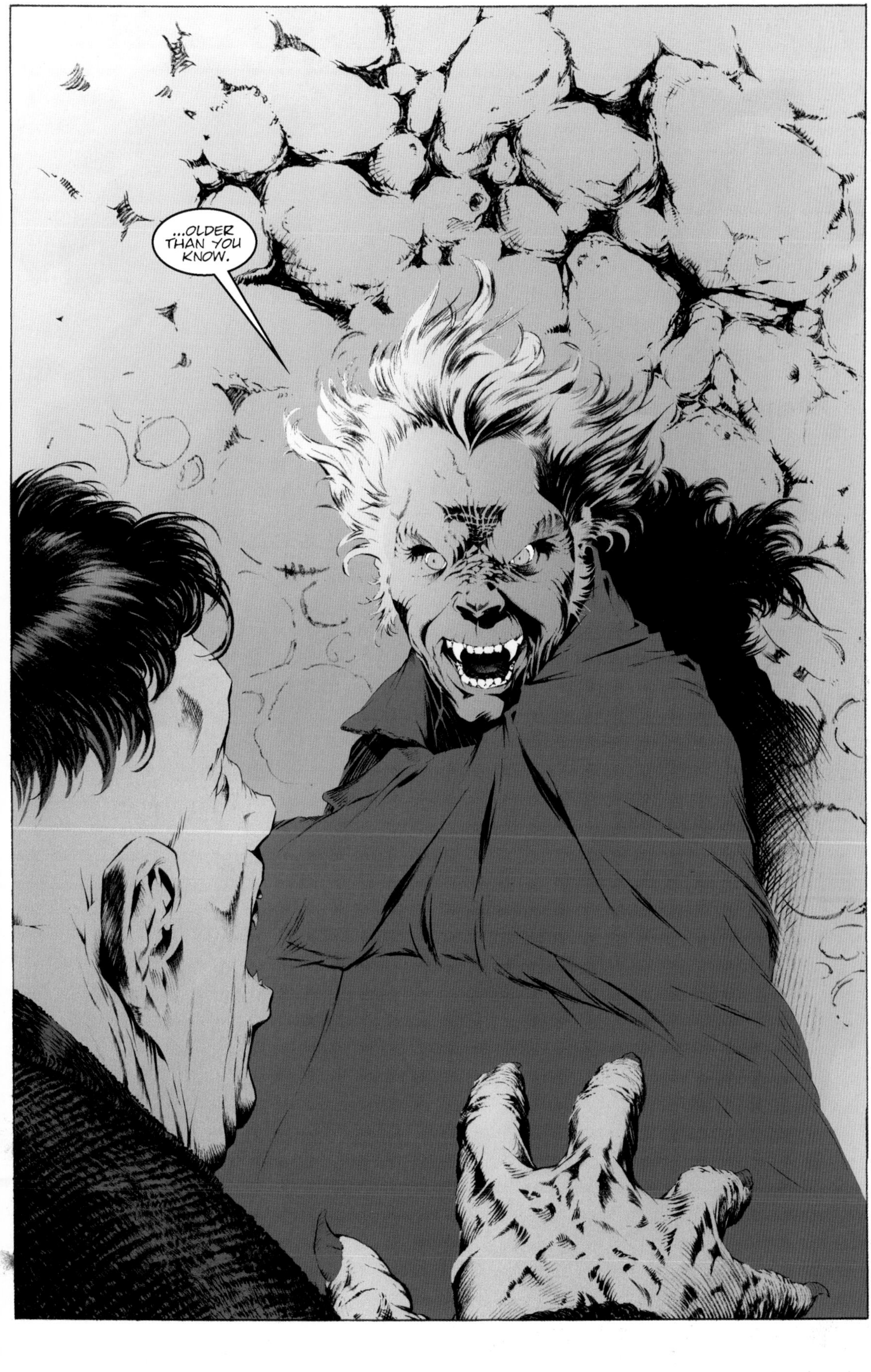
...OLDER THAN YOU KNOW.

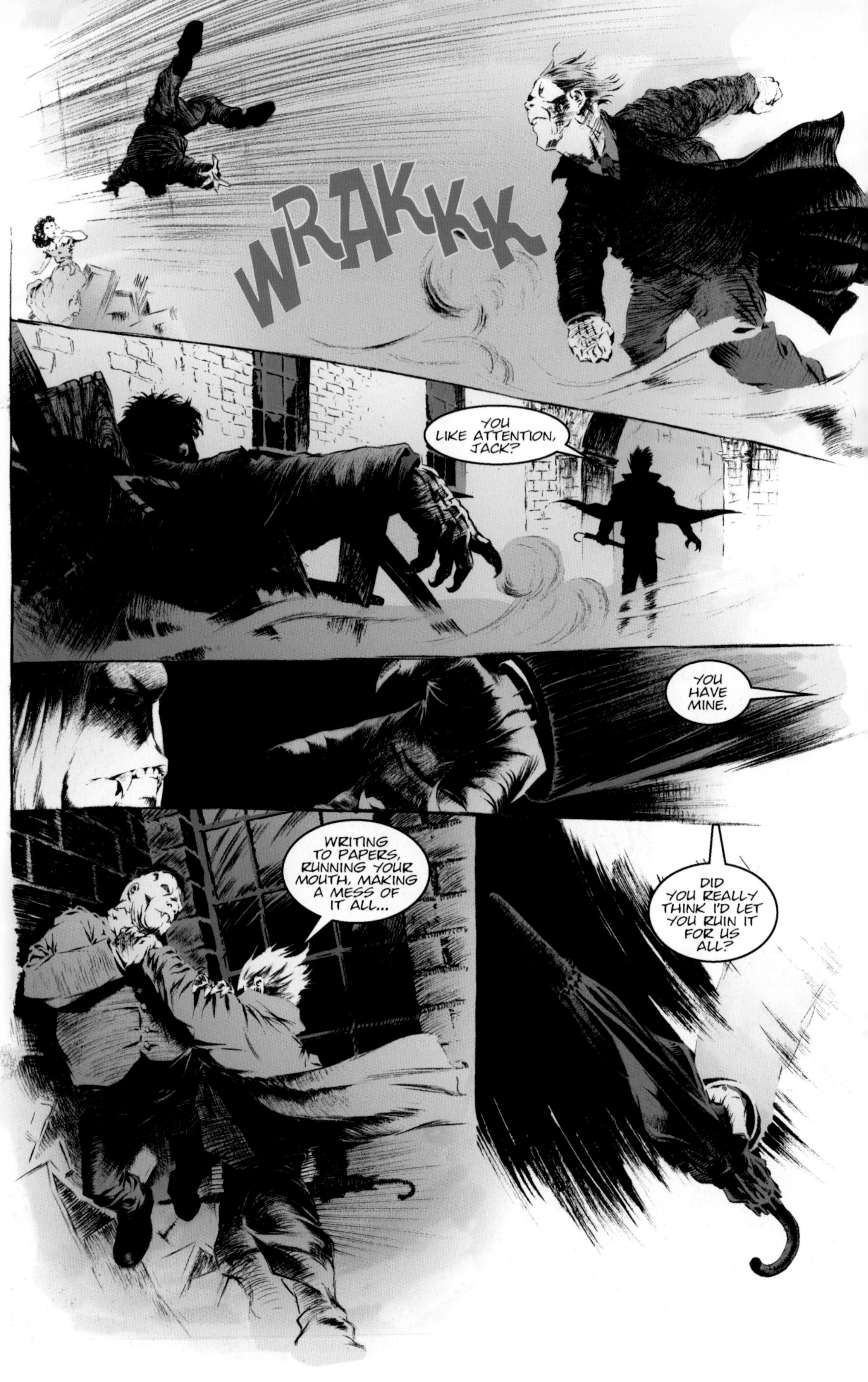
WRAKKK
YOU LIKE ATTENTION, JACK?
YOU HAVE MINE.
WRITING TO PAPERS, RUNNING YOUR MOUTH, MAKING A MESS OF IT ALL...
DID YOU REALLY THINK I'D LET YOU RUIN IT FOR US ALL?

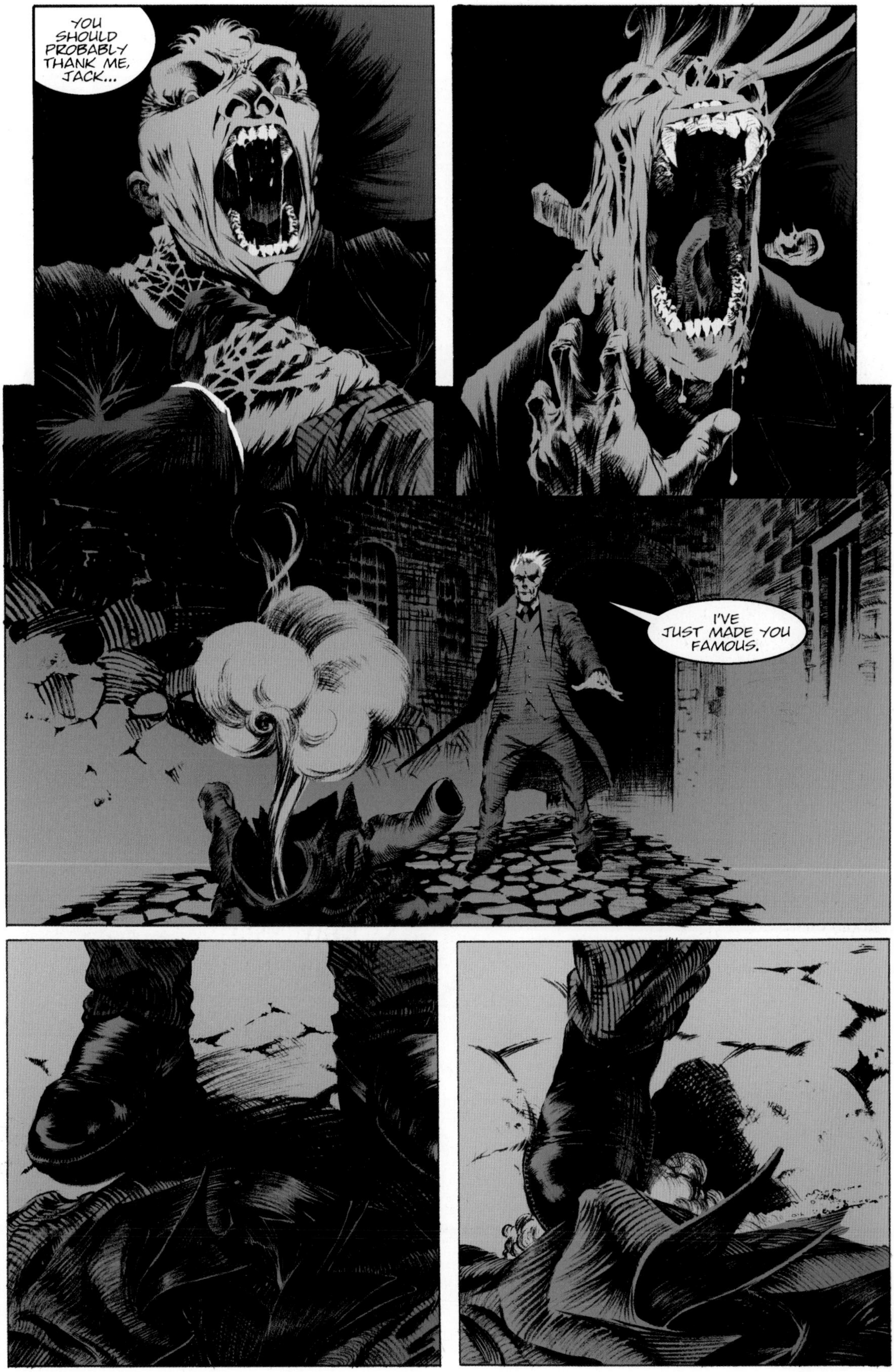
YOU SHOULD PROBABLY THANK ME, JACK...
I'VE JUST MADE YOU FAMOUS.

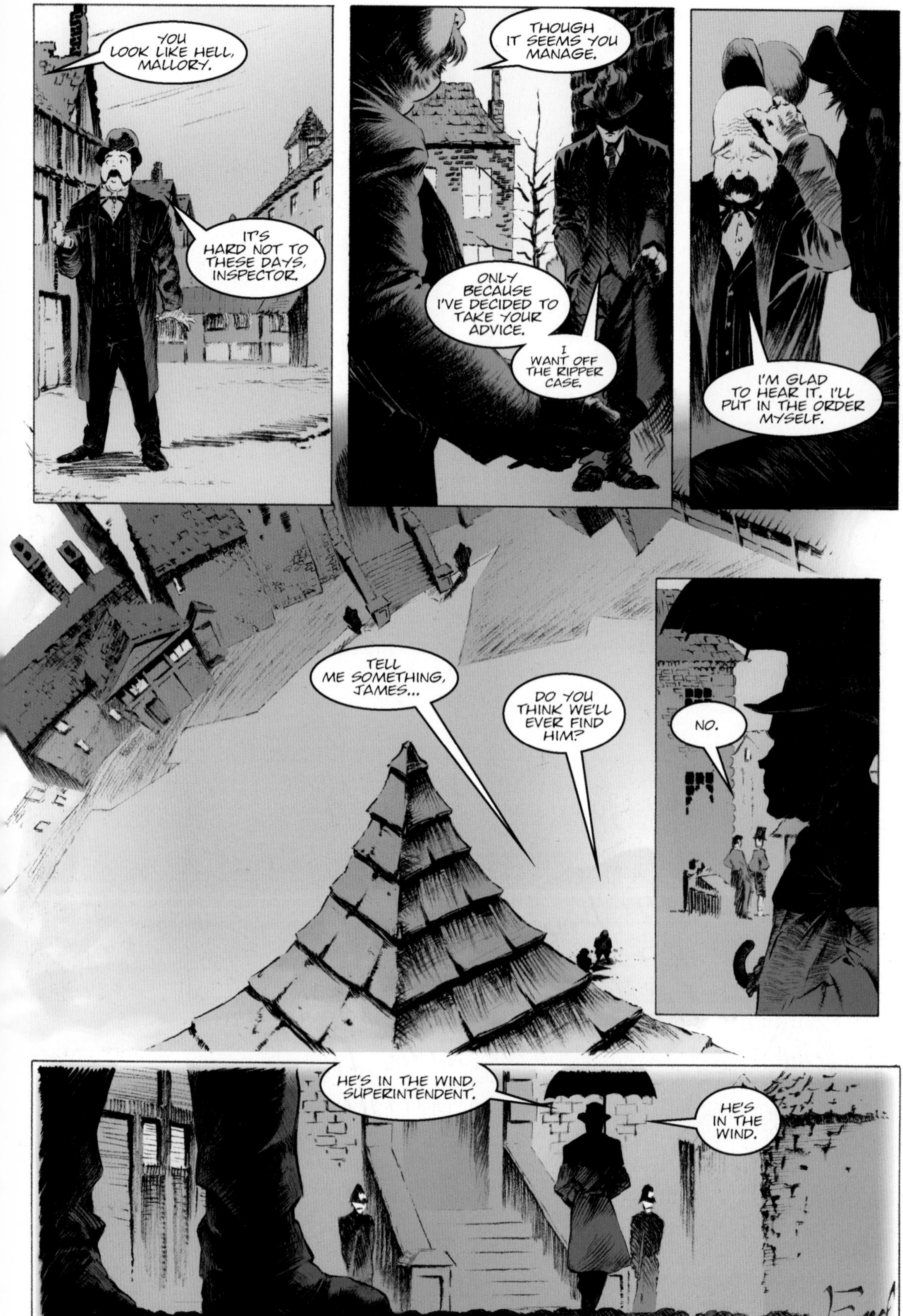
YOU LOOK LIKE HELL, MALLORY.
IT'S HARD NOT TO THESE DAYS, INSPECTOR.
THOUGH IT SEEMS YOU MANAGE.
ONLY BECAUSE I'VE DECIDED TO TAKE YOUR ADVICE.
I WANT OFF THE RIPPER CASE.
I'M GLAD TO HEAR IT. I'LL PUT IN THE ORDER MYSELF.
TELL ME SOMETHING, JAMES...
DO YOU THINK WE'LL EVER FIND HIM?
NO.
HE'S IN THE WIND, SUPERINTENDENT.
HE'S IN THE WIND.
End

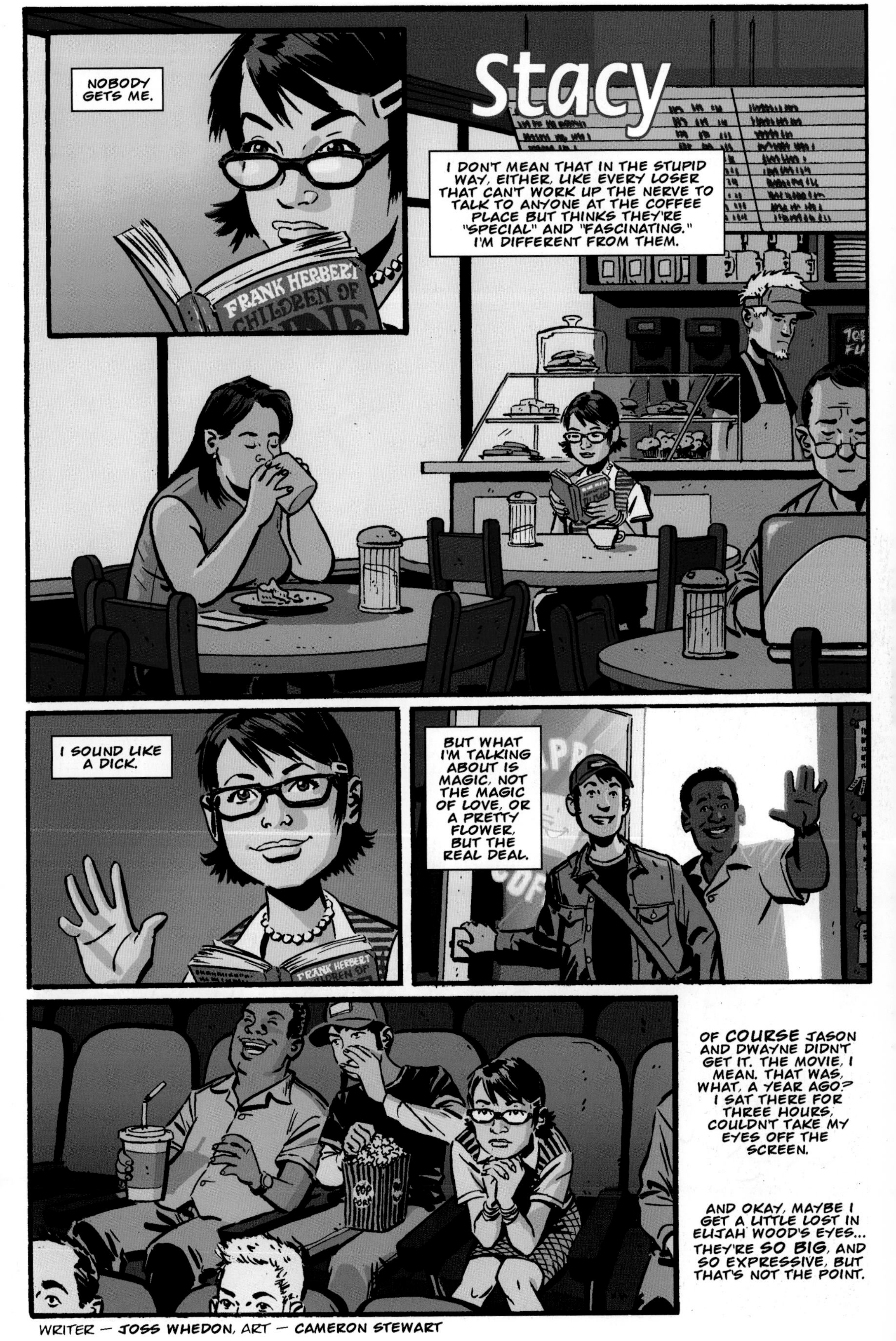
Stacy
NOBODY GETS ME.
I DON'T MEAN THAT IN THE STUPID WAY, EITHER, LIKE EVERY LOSER THAT CAN'T WORK UP THE NERVE TO TALK TO ANYONE AT THE COFFEE PLACE BUT THINKS THEY'RE "SPECIAL" AND "FASCINATING." I'M DIFFERENT FROM THEM.
FRANK HERBERT CHILDREN OF
I SOUND LIKE A DICK.
FRANK HERBERT
BUT WHAT I'M TALKING ABOUT IS MAGIC, NOT THE MAGIC OF LOVE, OR A PRETTY FLOWER, BUT THE REAL DEAL.
OF COURSE JASON AND DWAYNE DIDN'T GET IT. THE MOVIE, I MEAN. THAT WAS, WHAT, A YEAR AGO? I SAT THERE FOR THREE HOURS, COULDN'T TAKE MY EYES OFF THE SCREEN.
AND OKAY, MAYBE I GET A LITTLE LOST IN ELIJAH WOOD'S EYES... THEY'RE SO BIG, AND SO EXPRESSIVE, BUT THAT'S NOT THE POINT.

WRITER — JOSS WHEDON, ART — CAMERON STEWART

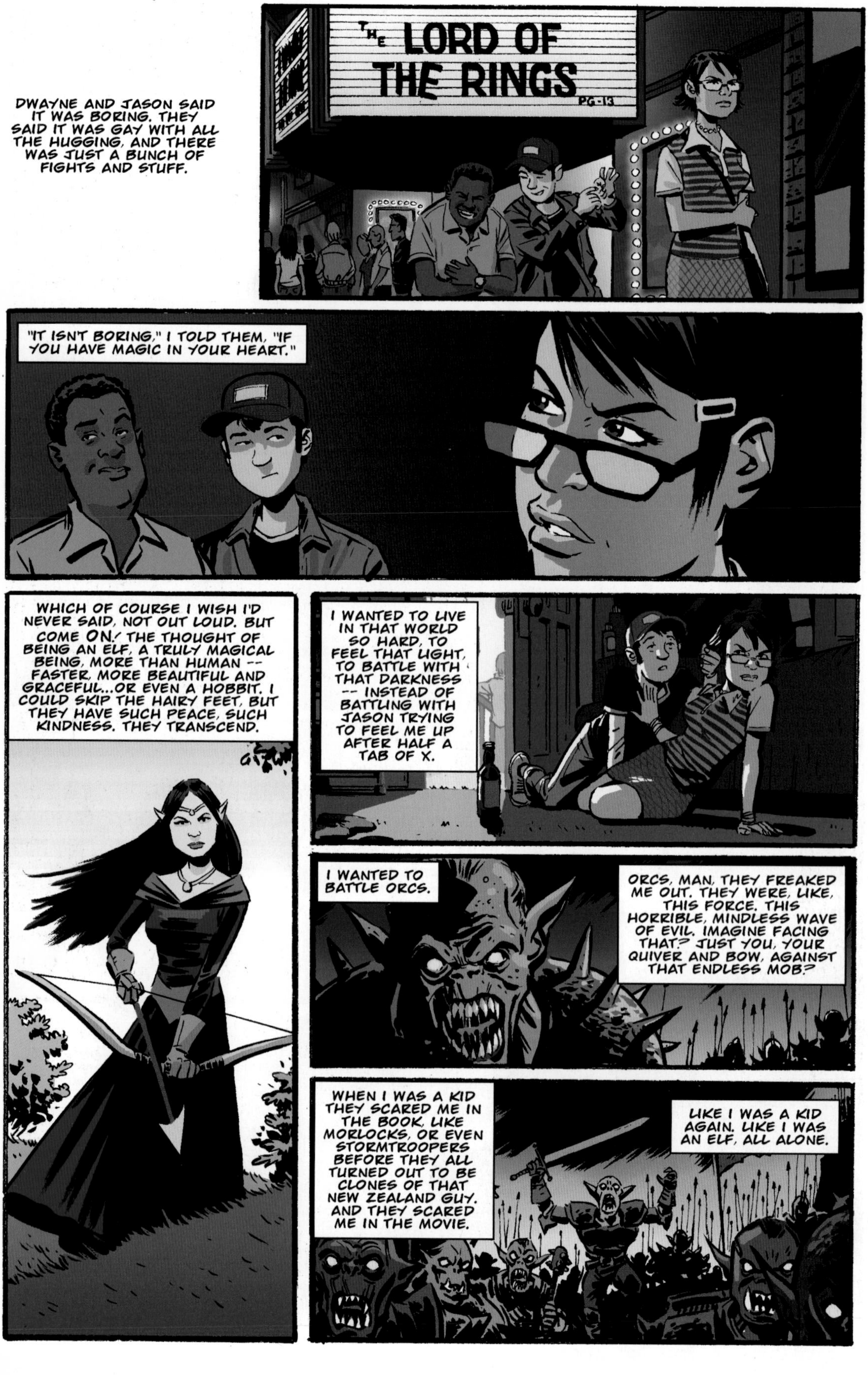
DWAYNE AND JASON SAID IT WAS BORING. THEY SAID IT WAS GAY WITH ALL THE HUGGING, AND THERE WAS JUST A BUNCH OF FIGHTS AND STUFF.
THE LORD OF THE RINGS
PG-13
"IT ISN'T BORING," I TOLD THEM, "IF YOU HAVE MAGIC IN YOUR HEART."
WHICH OF COURSE I WISH I'D NEVER SAID, NOT OUT LOUD. BUT COME ON! THE THOUGHT OF BEING AN ELF, A TRULY MAGICAL BEING, MORE THAN HUMAN -- FASTER, MORE BEAUTIFUL AND GRACEFUL...OR EVEN A HOBBIT. I COULD SKIP THE HAIRY FEET, BUT THEY HAVE SUCH PEACE, SUCH KINDNESS. THEY TRANSCEND.
I WANTED TO LIVE IN THAT WORLD SO HARD, TO FEEL THAT LIGHT, TO BATTLE WITH THAT DARKNESS -- INSTEAD OF BATTLING WITH JASON TRYING TO FEEL ME UP AFTER HALF A TAB OF X.
I WANTED TO BATTLE ORCS.
ORCS, MAN, THEY FREAKED ME OUT. THEY WERE, LIKE, THIS FORCE. THIS HORRIBLE, MINDLESS WAVE OF EVIL. IMAGINE FACING THAT? JUST YOU, YOUR QUIVER AND BOW, AGAINST THAT ENDLESS MOB?
WHEN I WAS A KID THEY SCARED ME IN THE BOOK, LIKE MORLOCKS, OR EVEN STORMTROOPERS BEFORE THEY ALL TURNED OUT TO BE CLONES OF THAT NEW ZEALAND GUY. AND THEY SCARED ME IN THE MOVIE.
LIKE I WAS A KID AGAIN. LIKE I WAS AN ELF, ALL ALONE.

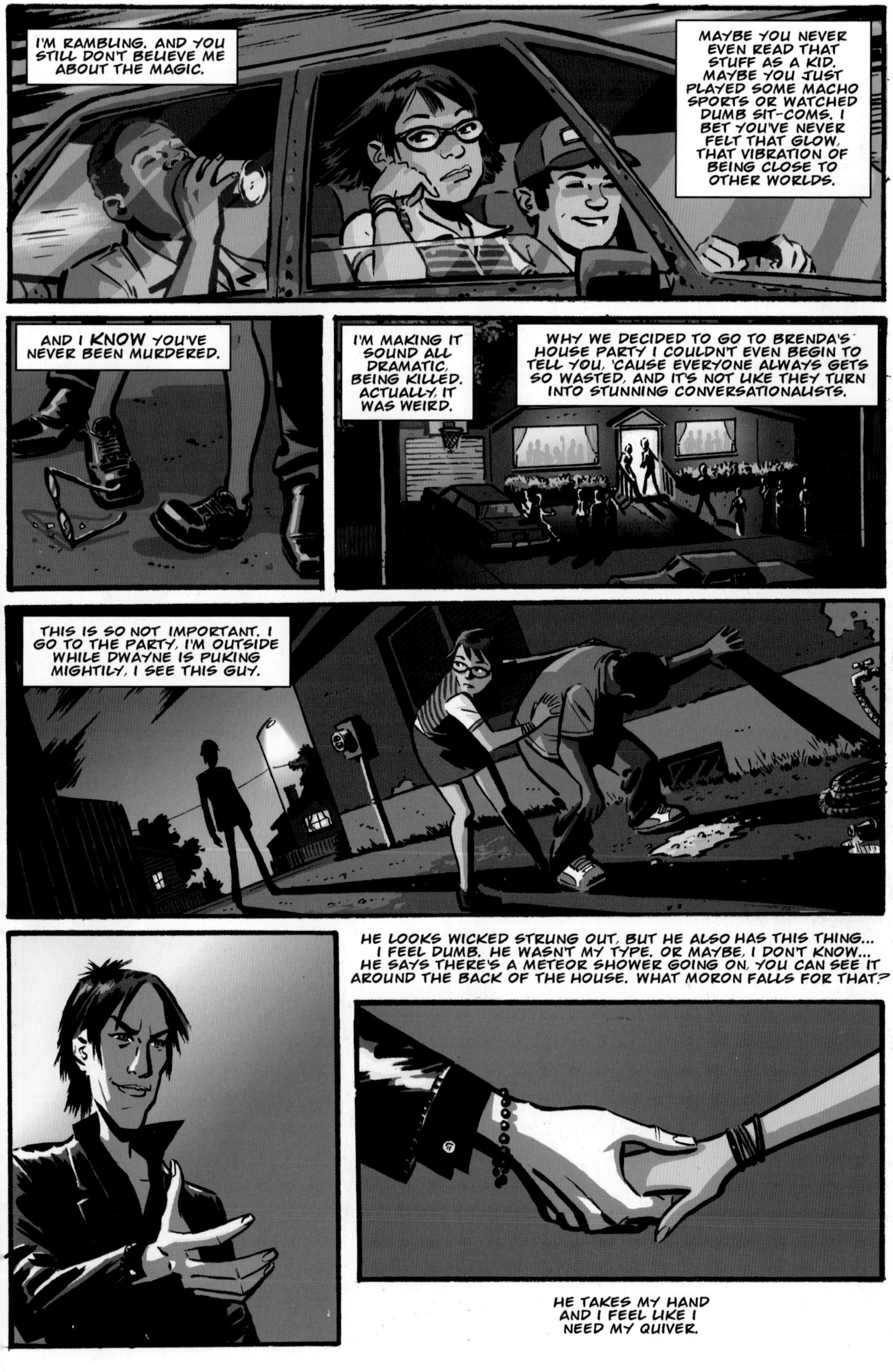
I'M RAMBLING. AND YOU STILL DON'T BELIEVE ME ABOUT THE MAGIC.
MAYBE YOU NEVER EVEN READ THAT STUFF AS A KID. MAYBE YOU JUST PLAYED SOME MACHO SPORTS OR WATCHED DUMB SIT-COMS. I BET YOU'VE NEVER FELT THAT GLOW, THAT VIBRATION OF BEING CLOSE TO OTHER WORLDS.
AND I KNOW YOU'VE NEVER BEEN MURDERED.
I'M MAKING IT SOUND ALL DRAMATIC, BEING KILLED. ACTUALLY, IT WAS WEIRD.
WHY WE DECIDED TO GO TO BRENDA'S HOUSE PARTY I COULDN'T EVEN BEGIN TO TELL YOU, 'CAUSE EVERYONE ALWAYS GETS SO WASTED, AND IT'S NOT LIKE THEY TURN INTO STUNNING CONVERSATIONALISTS.
THIS IS SO NOT IMPORTANT. I GO TO THE PARTY, I'M OUTSIDE WHILE DWAYNE IS PUKING MIGHTILY, I SEE THIS GUY.
HE LOOKS WICKED STRUNG OUT, BUT HE ALSO HAS THIS THING... I FEEL DUMB. HE WASN'T MY TYPE. OR MAYBE, I DON'T KNOW... HE SAYS THERE'S A METEOR SHOWER GOING ON, YOU CAN SEE IT AROUND THE BACK OF THE HOUSE. WHAT MORON FALLS FOR THAT?
HE TAKES MY HAND AND I FEEL LIKE I NEED MY QUIVER.

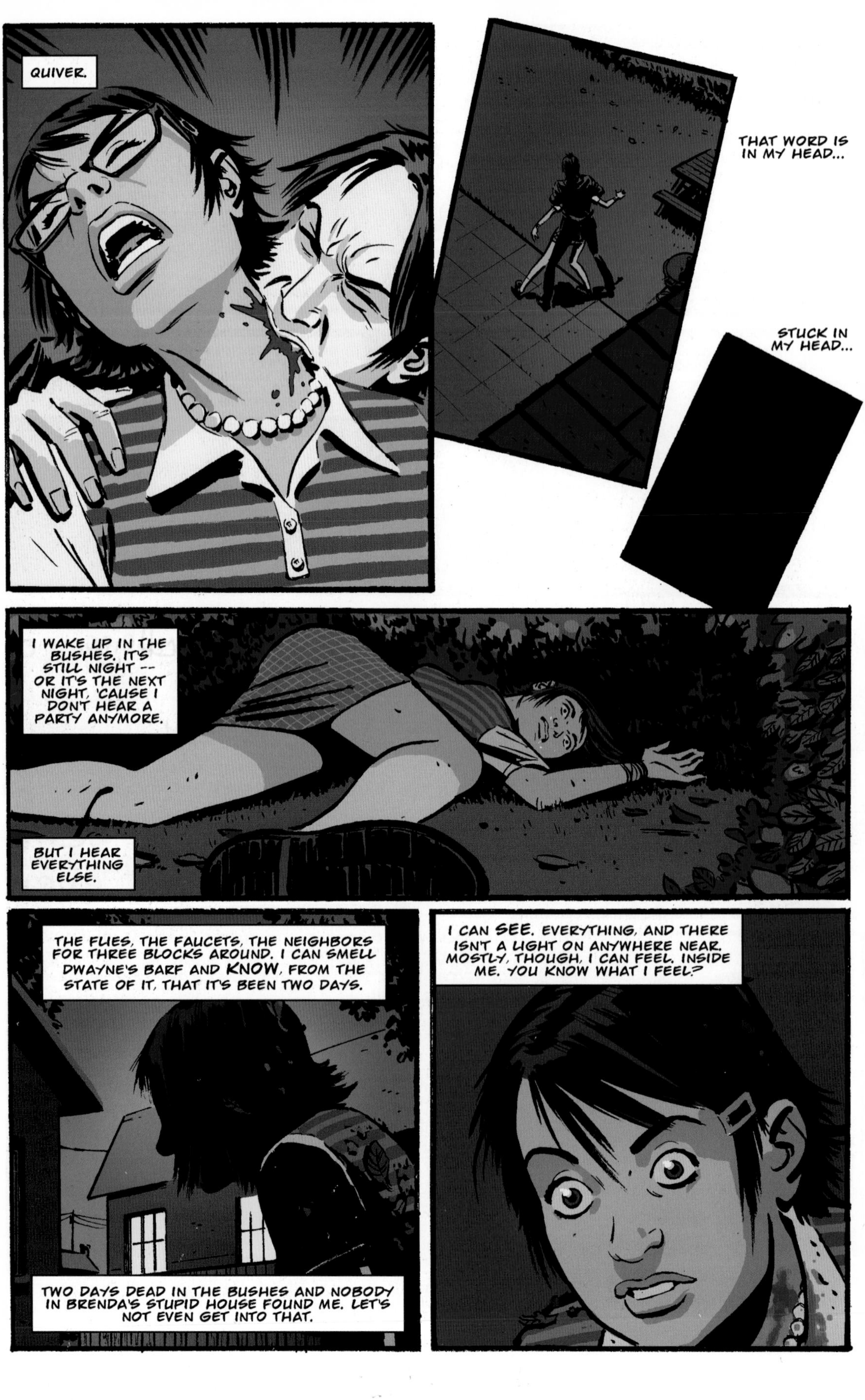
QUIVER.
THAT WORD IS IN MY HEAD...
STUCK IN MY HEAD...
I WAKE UP IN THE BUSHES. IT'S STILL NIGHT -- OR IT'S THE NEXT NIGHT, 'CAUSE I DON'T HEAR A PARTY ANYMORE.
BUT I HEAR EVERYTHING ELSE.
THE FLIES, THE FAUCETS, THE NEIGHBORS FOR THREE BLOCKS AROUND. I CAN SMELL DWAYNE'S BARF AND KNOW, FROM THE STATE OF IT, THAT IT'S BEEN TWO DAYS.
TWO DAYS DEAD IN THE BUSHES AND NOBODY IN BRENDA'S STUPID HOUSE FOUND ME. LET'S NOT EVEN GET INTO THAT.
I CAN SEE. EVERYTHING, AND THERE ISN'T A LIGHT ON ANYWHERE NEAR. MOSTLY, THOUGH, I CAN FEEL. INSIDE ME. YOU KNOW WHAT I FEEL?

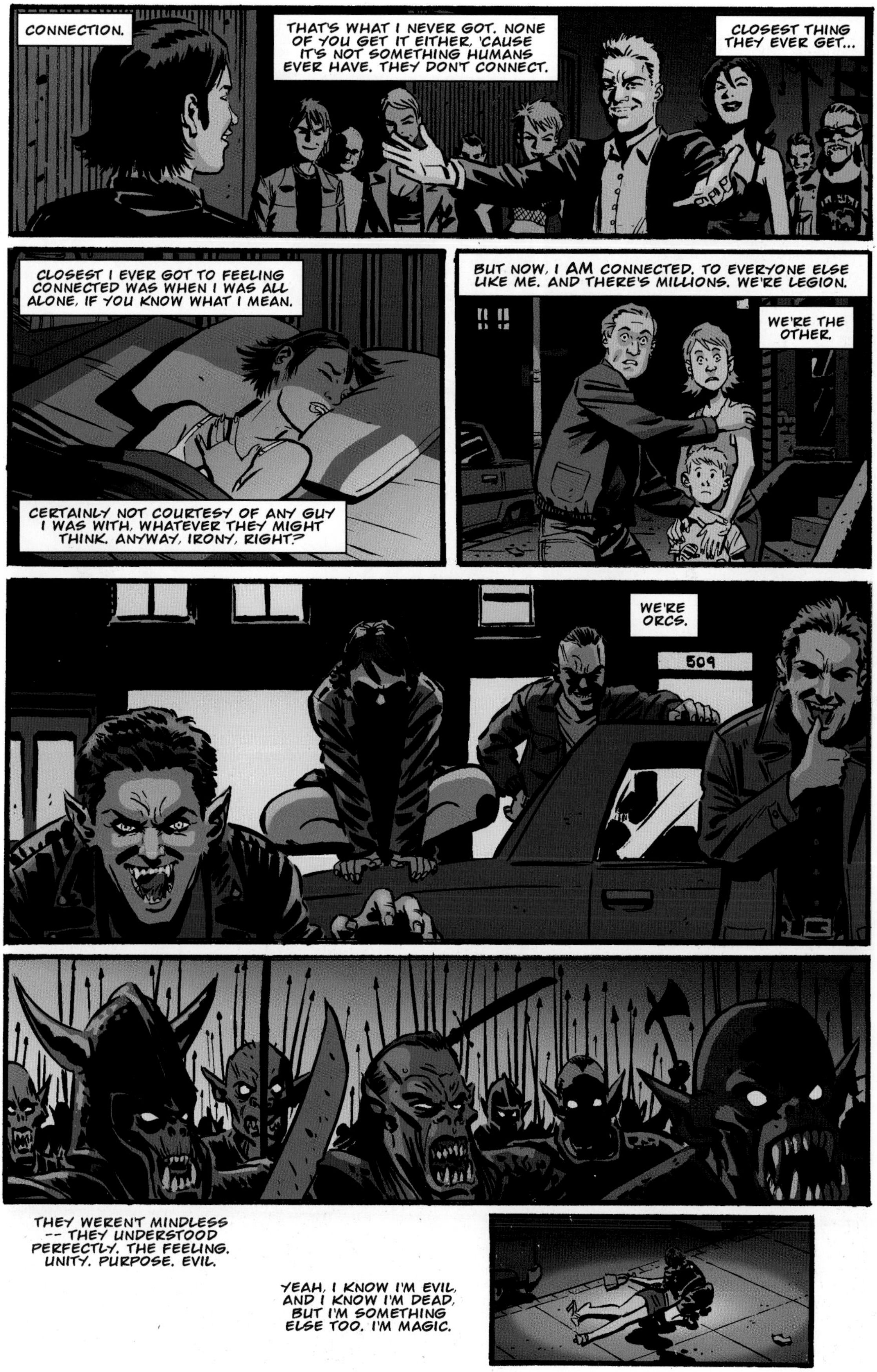
CONNECTION.
THAT'S WHAT I NEVER GOT. NONE OF YOU GET IT EITHER, 'CAUSE IT'S NOT SOMETHING HUMANS EVER HAVE. THEY DON'T CONNECT.
CLOSEST THING THEY EVER GET...
CLOSEST I EVER GOT TO FEELING CONNECTED WAS WHEN I WAS ALL ALONE, IF YOU KNOW WHAT I MEAN.
CERTAINLY NOT COURTESY OF ANY GUY I WAS WITH, WHATEVER THEY MIGHT THINK. ANYWAY, IRONY, RIGHT?
BUT NOW, I AM CONNECTED. TO EVERYONE ELSE LIKE ME. AND THERE'S MILLIONS. WE'RE LEGION.
WE'RE THE OTHER.
WE'RE ORCS.
509
THEY WEREN'T MINDLESS -- THEY UNDERSTOOD PERFECTLY. THE FEELING. UNITY. PURPOSE. EVIL.
YEAH, I KNOW I'M EVIL, AND I KNOW I'M DEAD, BUT I'M SOMETHING ELSE TOO. I'M MAGIC.

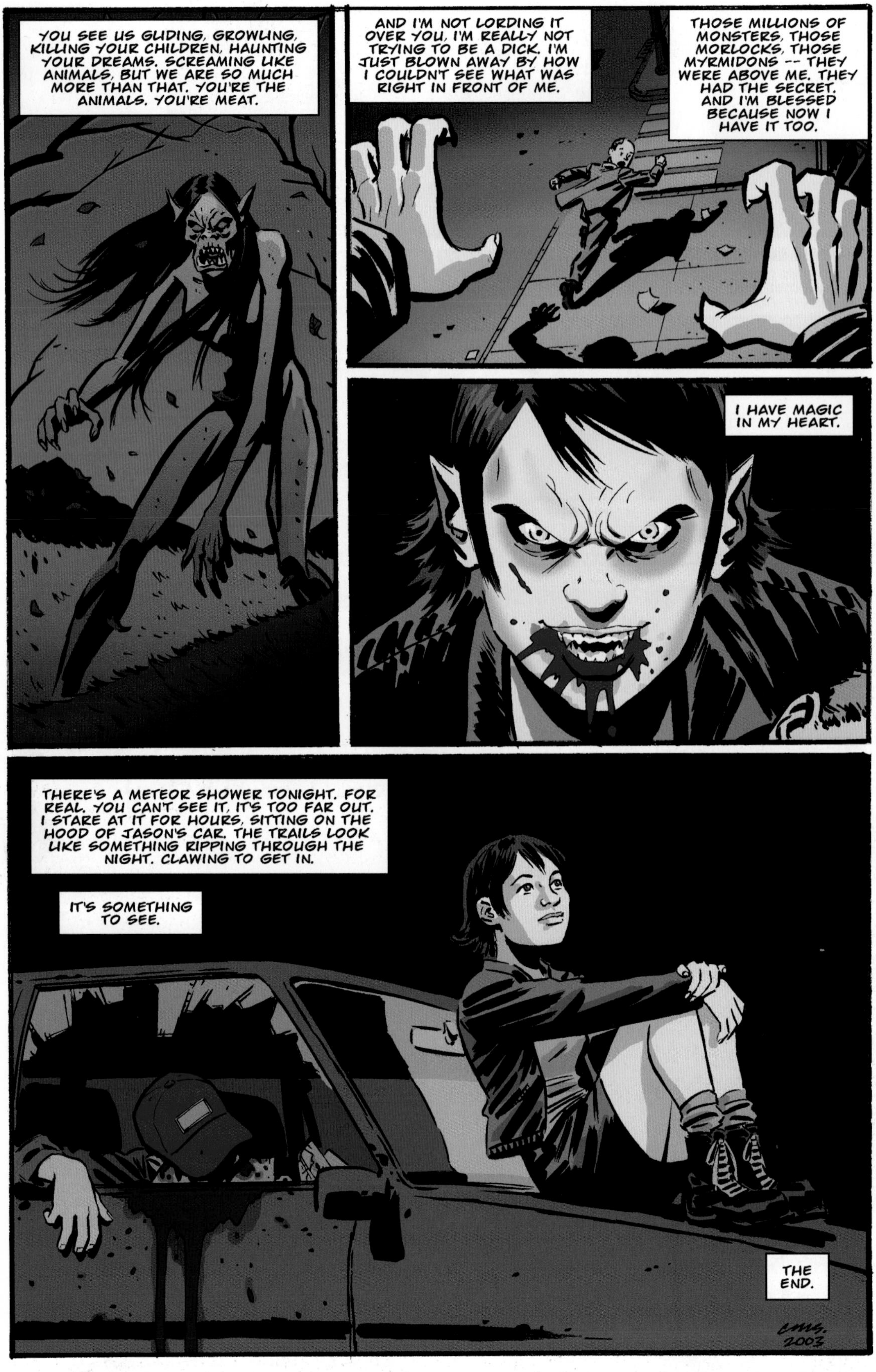
YOU SEE US GLIDING, GROWLING, KILLING YOUR CHILDREN, HAUNTING YOUR DREAMS, SCREAMING LIKE ANIMALS, BUT WE ARE SO MUCH MORE THAN THAT. YOU'RE THE ANIMALS. YOU'RE MEAT.
AND I'M NOT LORDING IT OVER YOU, I'M REALLY NOT TRYING TO BE A DICK. I'M JUST BLOWN AWAY BY HOW I COULDN'T SEE WHAT WAS RIGHT IN FRONT OF ME.
THOSE MILLIONS OF MONSTERS, THOSE MORLOCKS, THOSE MYRMIDONS -- THEY WERE ABOVE ME. THEY HAD THE SECRET, AND I'M BLESSED BECAUSE NOW I HAVE IT TOO.
I HAVE MAGIC IN MY HEART.
THERE'S A METEOR SHOWER TONIGHT. FOR REAL. YOU CAN'T SEE IT, IT'S TOO FAR OUT. I STARE AT IT FOR HOURS, SITTING ON THE HOOD OF JASON'S CAR. THE TRAILS LOOK LIKE SOMETHING RIPPING THROUGH THE NIGHT. CLAWING TO GET IN.
IT'S SOMETHING TO SEE.
THE END.
CMS. 2003

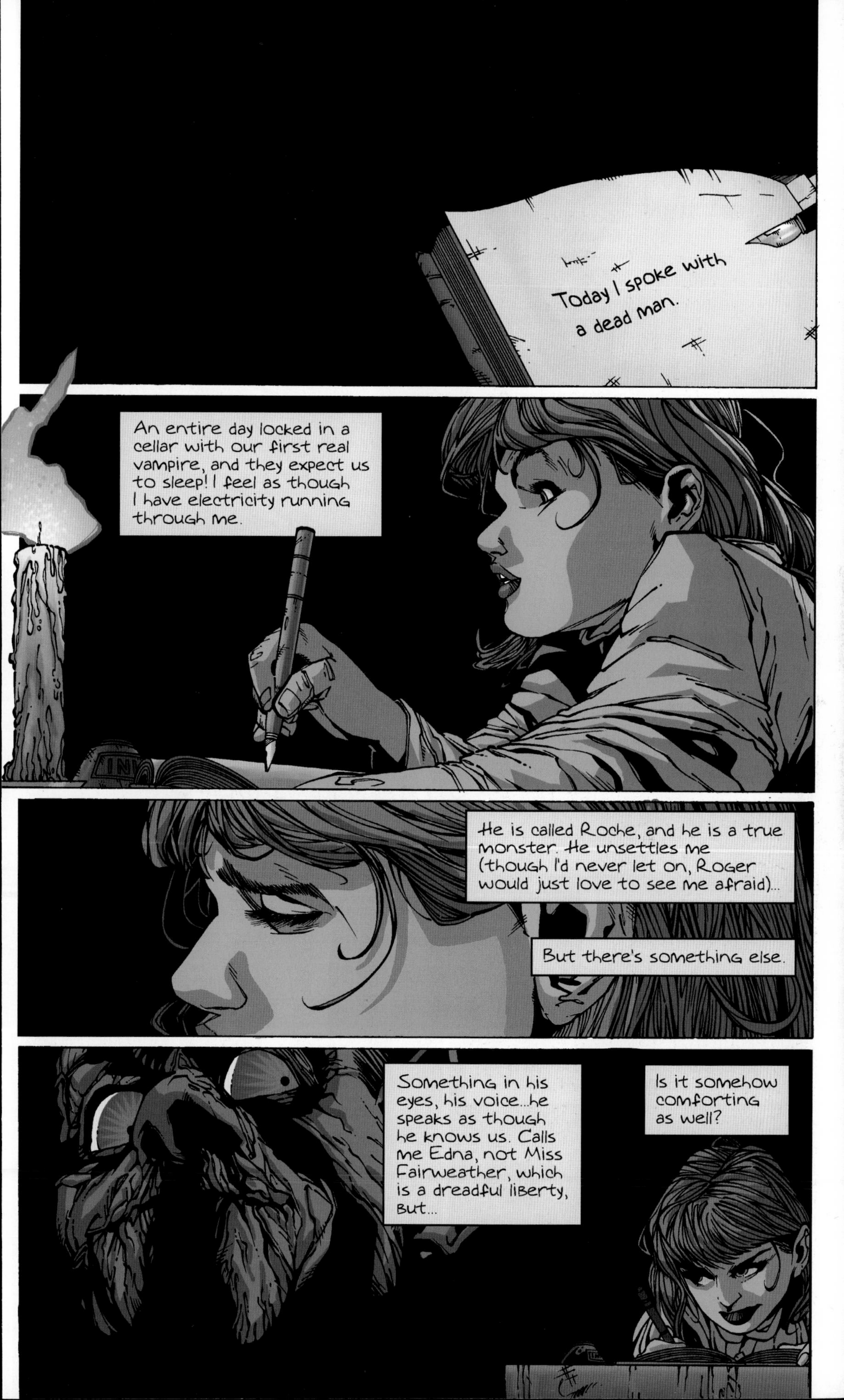
Today I spoke with a dead man.
An entire day locked in a cellar with our first real vampire, and they expect us to sleep! I feel as though I have electricity running through me.
He is called Roche, and he is a true monster. He unsettles me (though I'd never let on, Roger would just love to see me afraid)...
But there's something else.
Something in his eyes, his voice...he speaks as though he knows us. Calls me Edna, not Miss Fairweather, which is a dreadful liberty, but...
Is it somehow comforting as well?

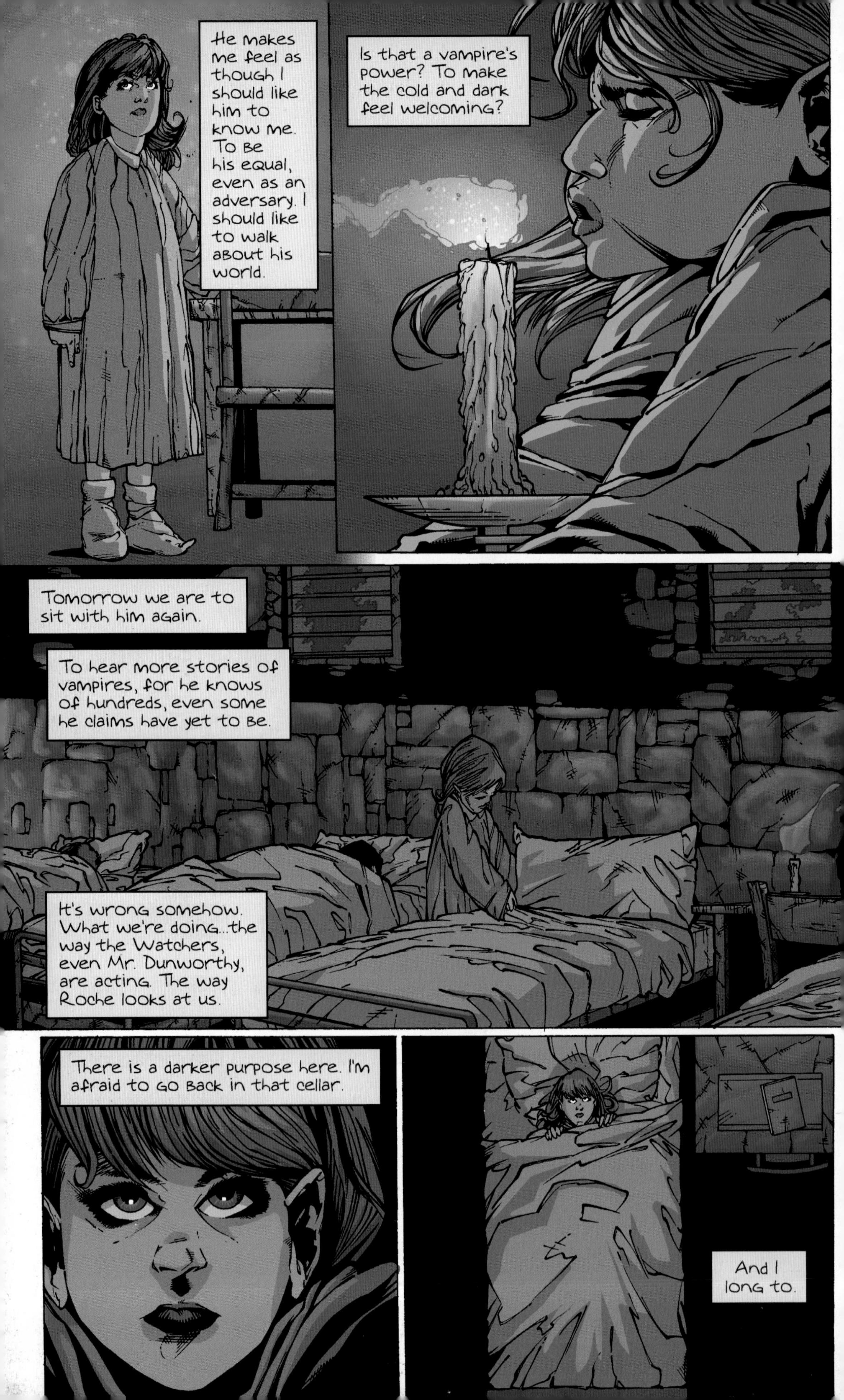
He makes me feel as though I should like him to know me. To be his equal, even as an adversary. I should like to walk about his world.
Is that a vampire's power? To make the cold and dark feel welcoming?
Tomorrow we are to sit with him again.
To hear more stories of vampires, for he knows of hundreds, even some he claims have yet to be.
It's wrong somehow. What we're doing...the way the Watchers, even Mr. Dunworthy, are acting. The way Roche looks at us.
There is a darker purpose here. I'm afraid to go back in that cellar.
And I long to.

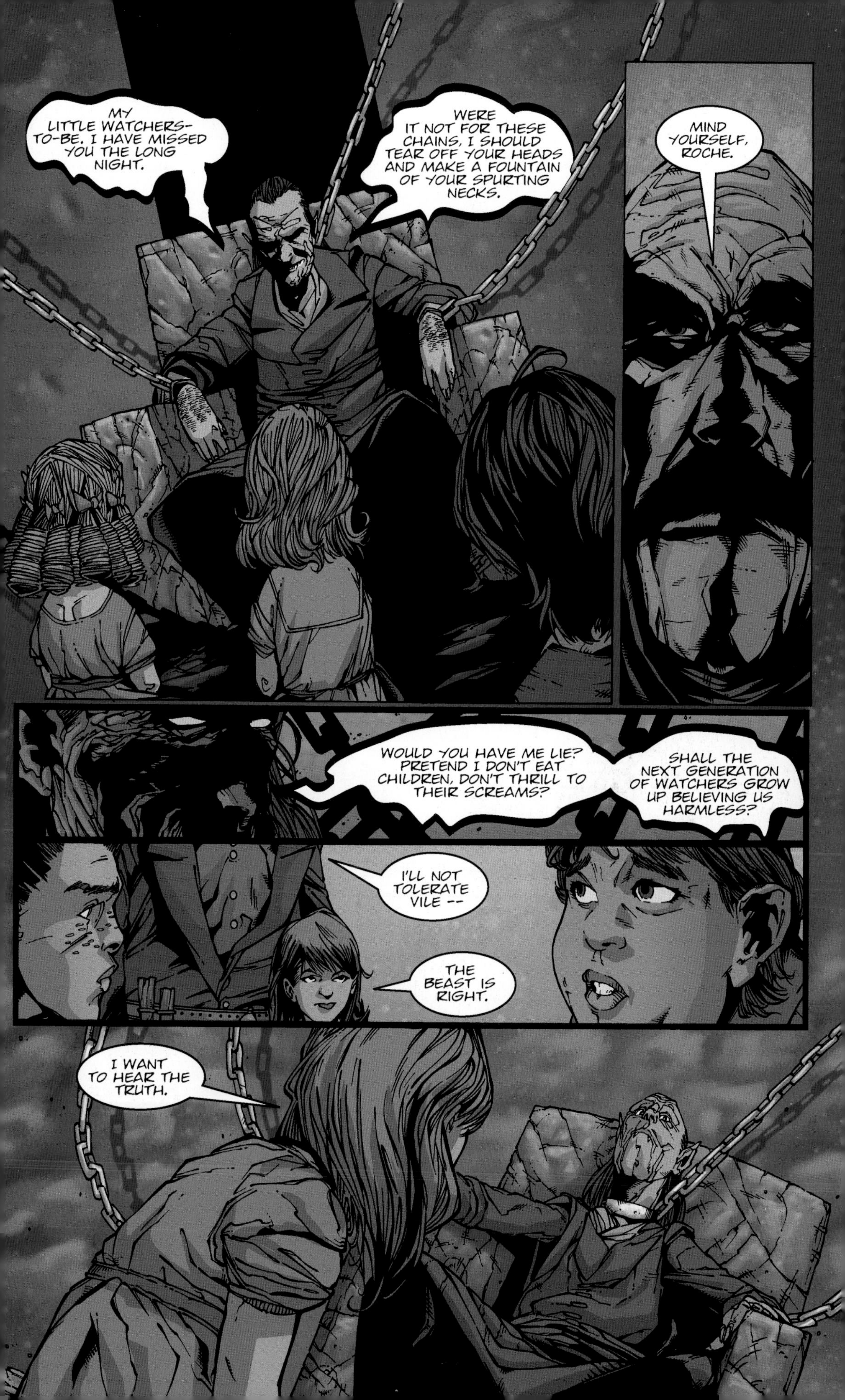
MY LITTLE WATCHERS-TO-BE. I HAVE MISSED YOU THE LONG NIGHT.
WERE IT NOT FOR THESE CHAINS, I SHOULD TEAR OFF YOUR HEADS AND MAKE A FOUNTAIN OF YOUR SPURTING NECKS.
MIND YOURSELF, ROCHE.
WOULD YOU HAVE ME LIE? PRETEND I DON'T EAT CHILDREN, DON'T THRILL TO THEIR SCREAMS?
SHALL THE NEXT GENERATION OF WATCHERS GROW UP BELIEVING US HARMLESS?
I'LL NOT TOLERATE VILE --
THE BEAST IS RIGHT.
I WANT TO HEAR THE TRUTH.

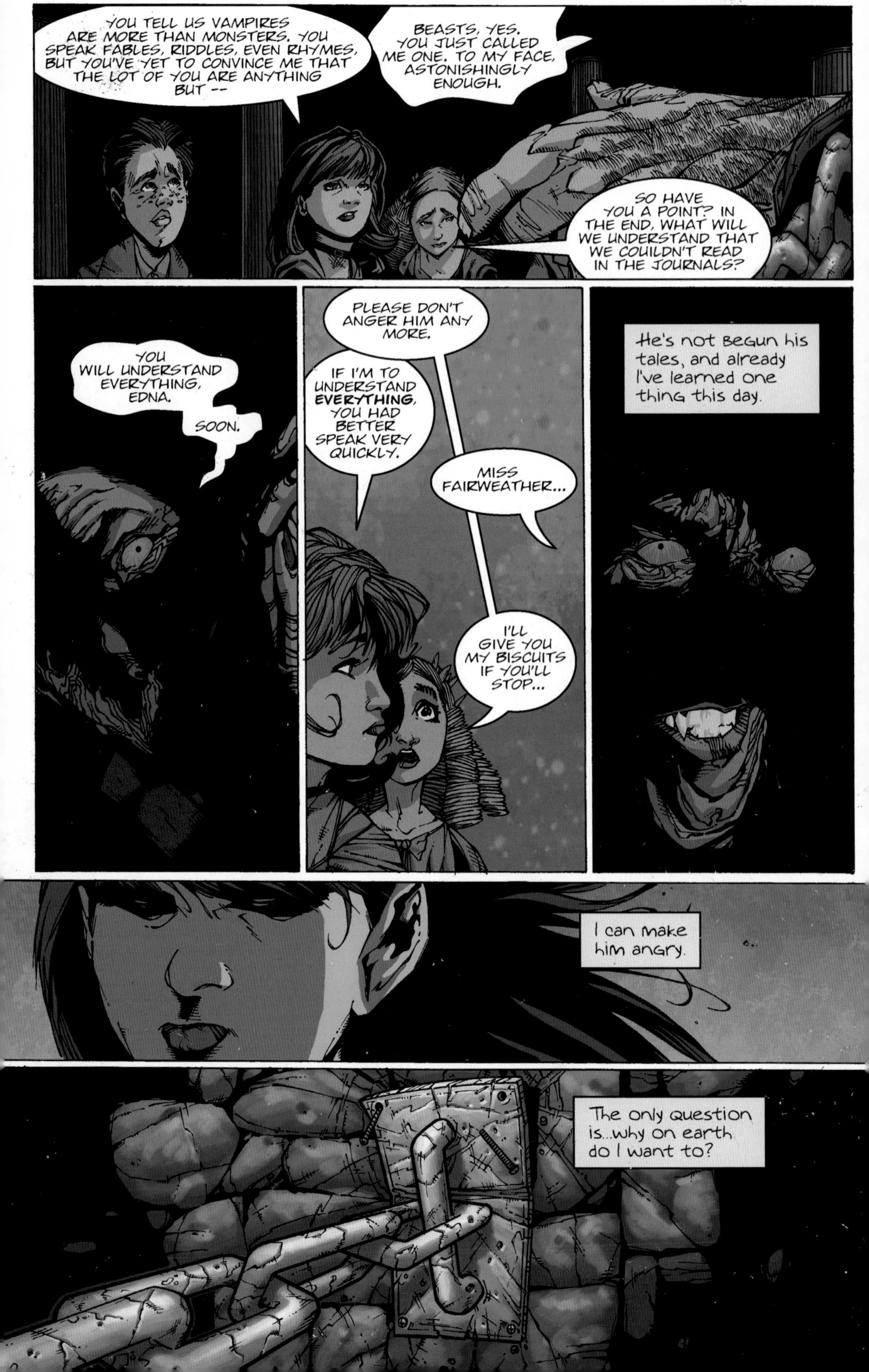

YOU TELL US VAMPIRES ARE MORE THAN MONSTERS. YOU SPEAK FABLES, RIDDLES, EVEN RHYMES, BUT YOU'VE YET TO CONVINCE ME THAT THE LOT OF YOU ARE ANYTHING BUT --
BEASTS, YES. YOU JUST CALLED ME ONE. TO MY FACE, ASTONISHINGLY ENOUGH.
SO HAVE YOU A POINT? IN THE END, WHAT WILL WE UNDERSTAND THAT WE COULDN'T READ IN THE JOURNALS?
YOU WILL UNDERSTAND EVERYTHING, EDNA.
SOON.
PLEASE DON'T ANGER HIM ANY MORE.
IF I'M TO UNDERSTAND **EVERYTHING**, YOU HAD BETTER SPEAK VERY QUICKLY.
MISS FAIRWEATHER...
I'LL GIVE YOU MY BISCUITS IF YOU'LL STOP...
He's not begun his tales, and already I've learned one thing this day.
I can make him angry.
The only question is...why on earth do I want to?

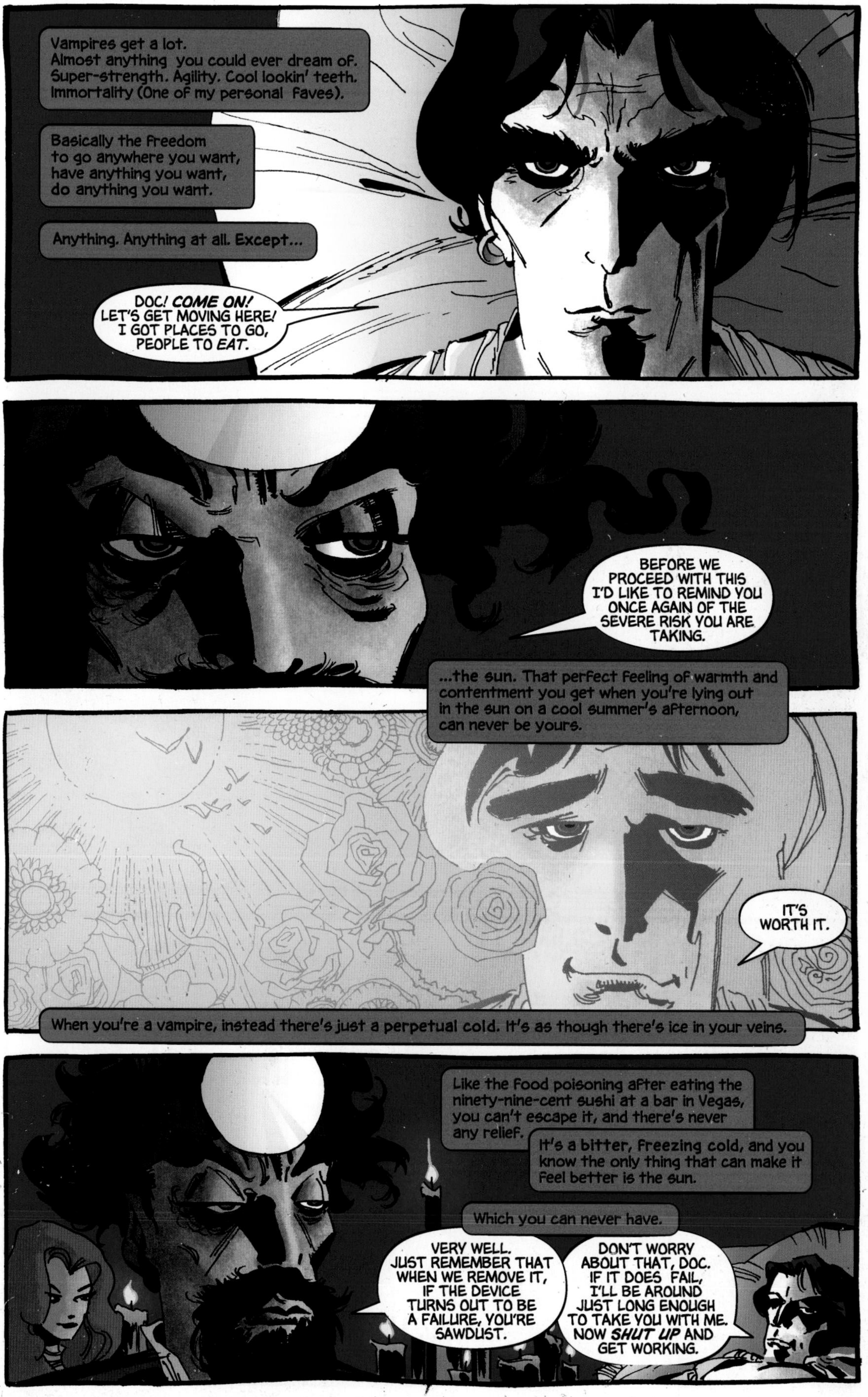

Vampires get a lot.
Almost anything you could ever dream of.
Super-strength. Agility. Cool lookin' teeth.
Immortality (One of my personal faves).
Basically the freedom to go anywhere you want, have anything you want, do anything you want.
Anything. Anything at all. Except...
DOC! COME ON! LET'S GET MOVING HERE! I GOT PLACES TO GO, PEOPLE TO EAT.
BEFORE WE PROCEED WITH THIS I'D LIKE TO REMIND YOU ONCE AGAIN OF THE SEVERE RISK YOU ARE TAKING.
...the sun. That perfect feeling of warmth and contentment you get when you're lying out in the sun on a cool summer's afternoon, can never be yours.
IT'S WORTH IT.
When you're a vampire, instead there's just a perpetual cold. It's as though there's ice in your veins.
Like the food poisoning after eating the ninety-nine-cent sushi at a bar in Vegas, you can't escape it, and there's never any relief.
It's a bitter, freezing cold, and you know the only thing that can make it feel better is the sun.
Which you can never have.
VERY WELL. JUST REMEMBER THAT WHEN WE REMOVE IT, IF THE DEVICE TURNS OUT TO BE A FAILURE, YOU'RE SAWDUST.
DON'T WORRY ABOUT THAT, DOC. IF IT DOES FAIL, I'LL BE AROUND JUST LONG ENOUGH TO TAKE YOU WITH ME. NOW SHUT UP AND GET WORKING.

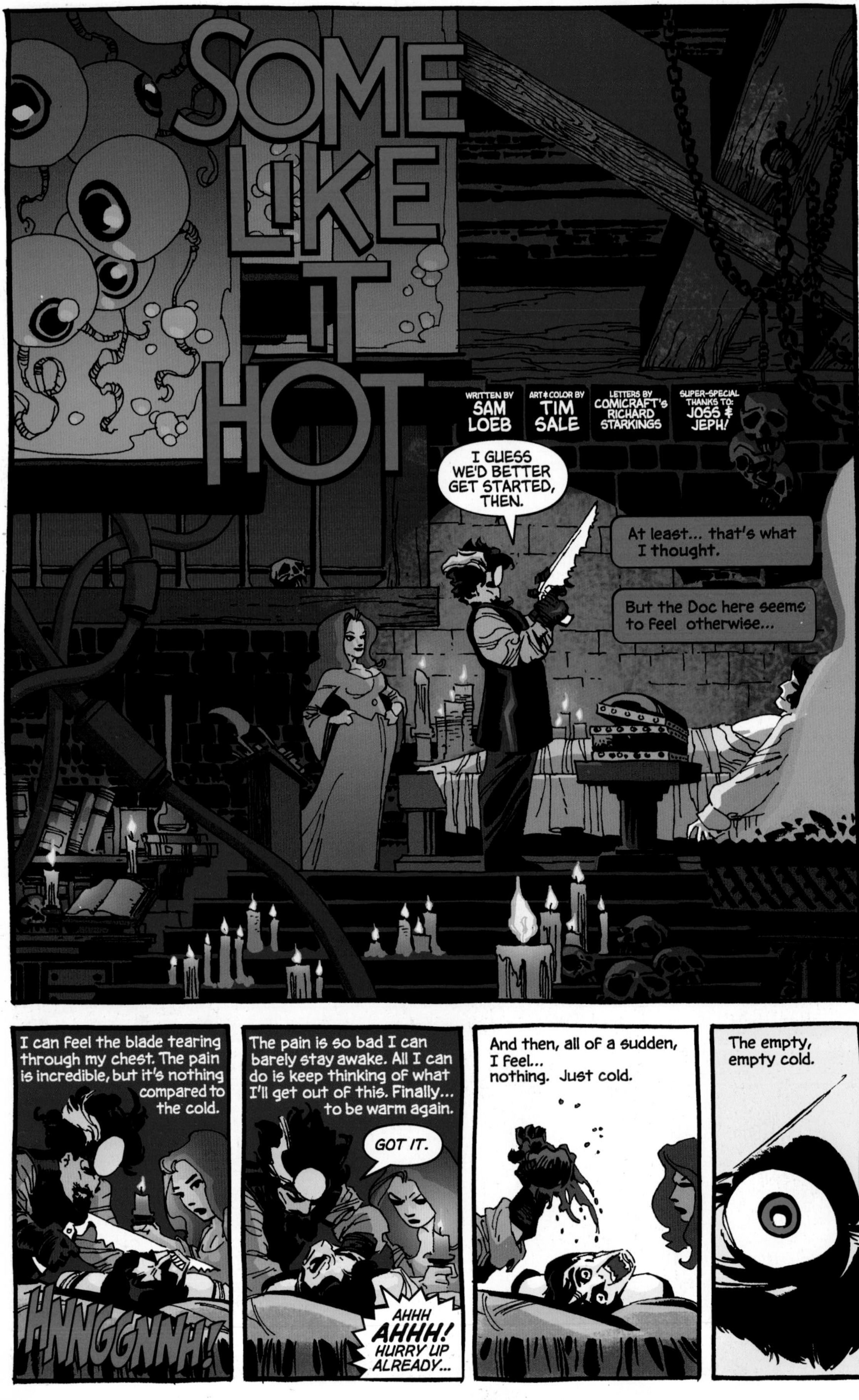
SOME LIKE IT HOT
WRITTEN BY SAM LOEB
ART & COLOR BY TIM SALE
LETTERS BY COMICRAFT'S RICHARD STARKINGS
SUPER-SPECIAL THANKS TO: JOSS & JEPH!
I GUESS WE'D BETTER GET STARTED, THEN.
At least... that's what I thought.
But the Doc here seems to feel otherwise...
I can feel the blade tearing through my chest. The pain is incredible, but it's nothing compared to the cold.
HNNGGNNH!
The pain is so bad I can barely stay awake. All I can do is keep thinking of what I'll get out of this. Finally... to be warm again.
GOT IT.
AHHH AHHH! HURRY UP ALREADY...
And then, all of a sudden, I feel... nothing. Just cold.
The empty, empty cold.

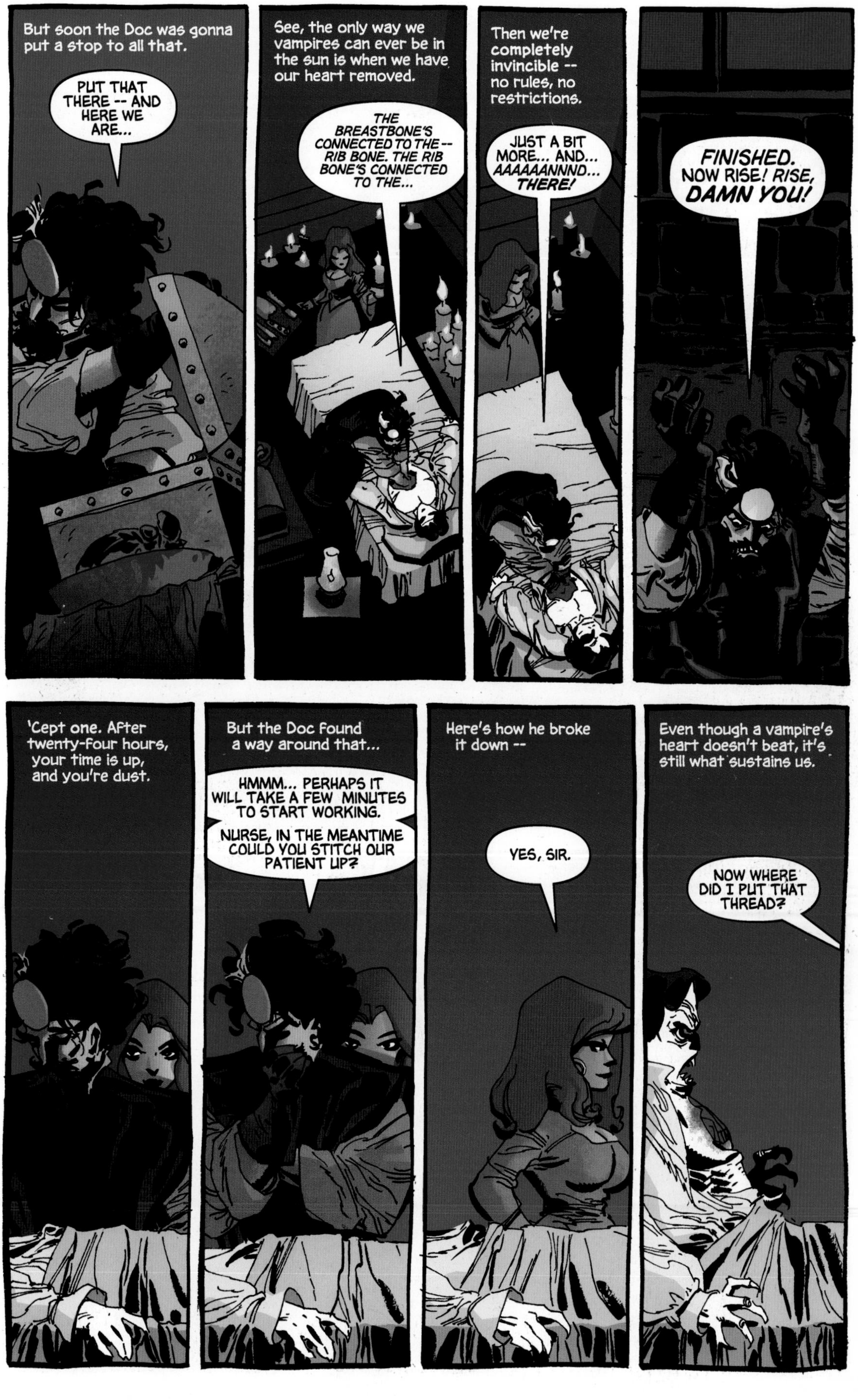
But soon the Doc was gonna put a stop to all that.
PUT THAT THERE -- AND HERE WE ARE...
See, the only way we vampires can ever be in the sun is when we have our heart removed.
THE BREASTBONE'S CONNECTED TO THE -- RIB BONE. THE RIB BONE'S CONNECTED TO THE...
Then we're completely invincible -- no rules, no restrictions.
JUST A BIT MORE... AND... AAAAAAANNND... THERE!
FINISHED. NOW RISE! RISE, DAMN YOU!
'Cept one. After twenty-four hours, your time is up, and you're dust.
But the Doc found a way around that...
HMMM... PERHAPS IT WILL TAKE A FEW MINUTES TO START WORKING.
NURSE, IN THE MEANTIME COULD YOU STITCH OUR PATIENT UP?
Here's how he broke it down --
YES, SIR.
Even though a vampire's heart doesn't beat, it's still what sustains us.
NOW WHERE DID I PUT THAT THREAD?

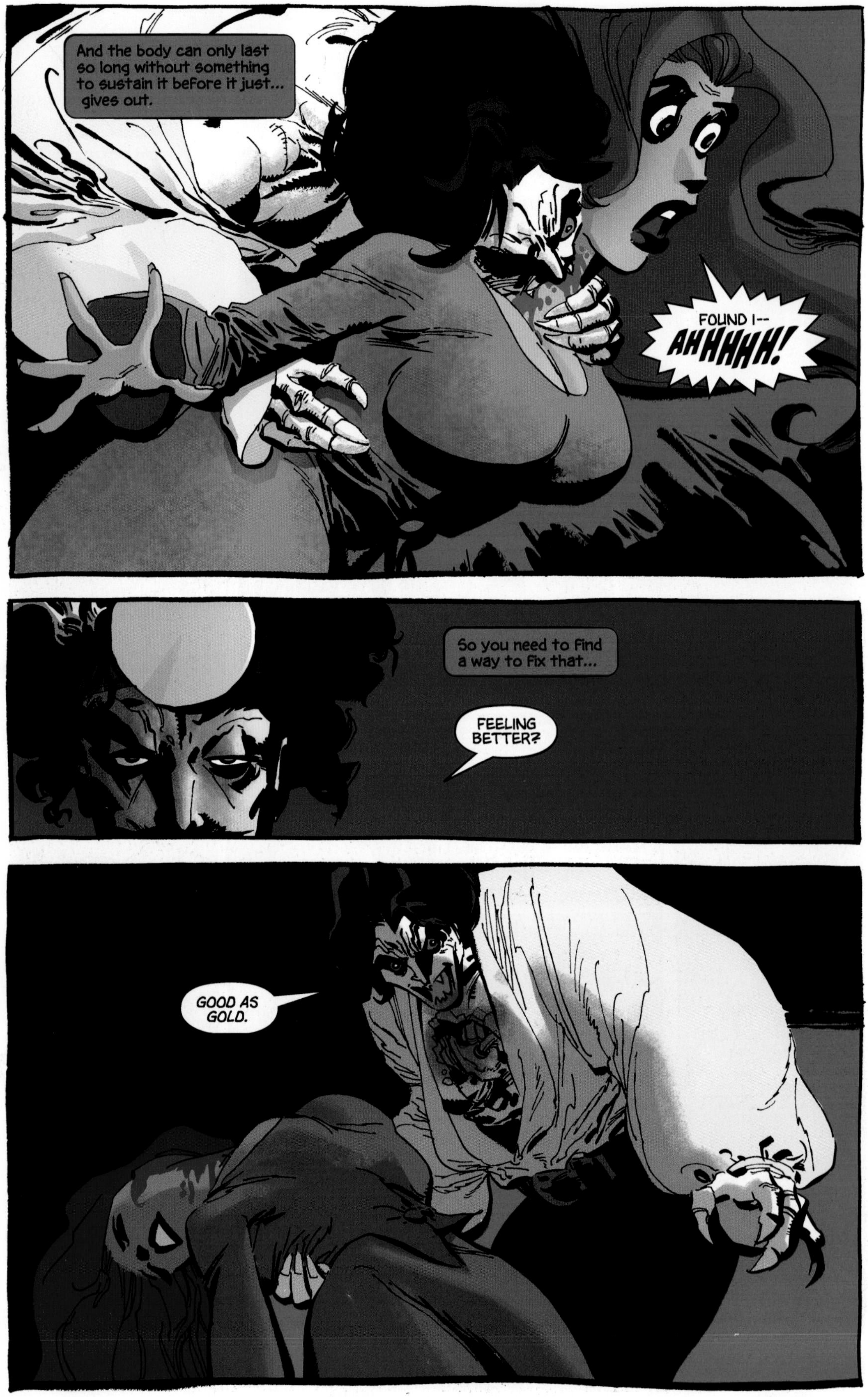

And the body can only last so long without something to sustain it before it just... gives out.
FOUND I-- AHHHHH!
So you need to find a way to fix that...
FEELING BETTER?
GOOD AS GOLD.

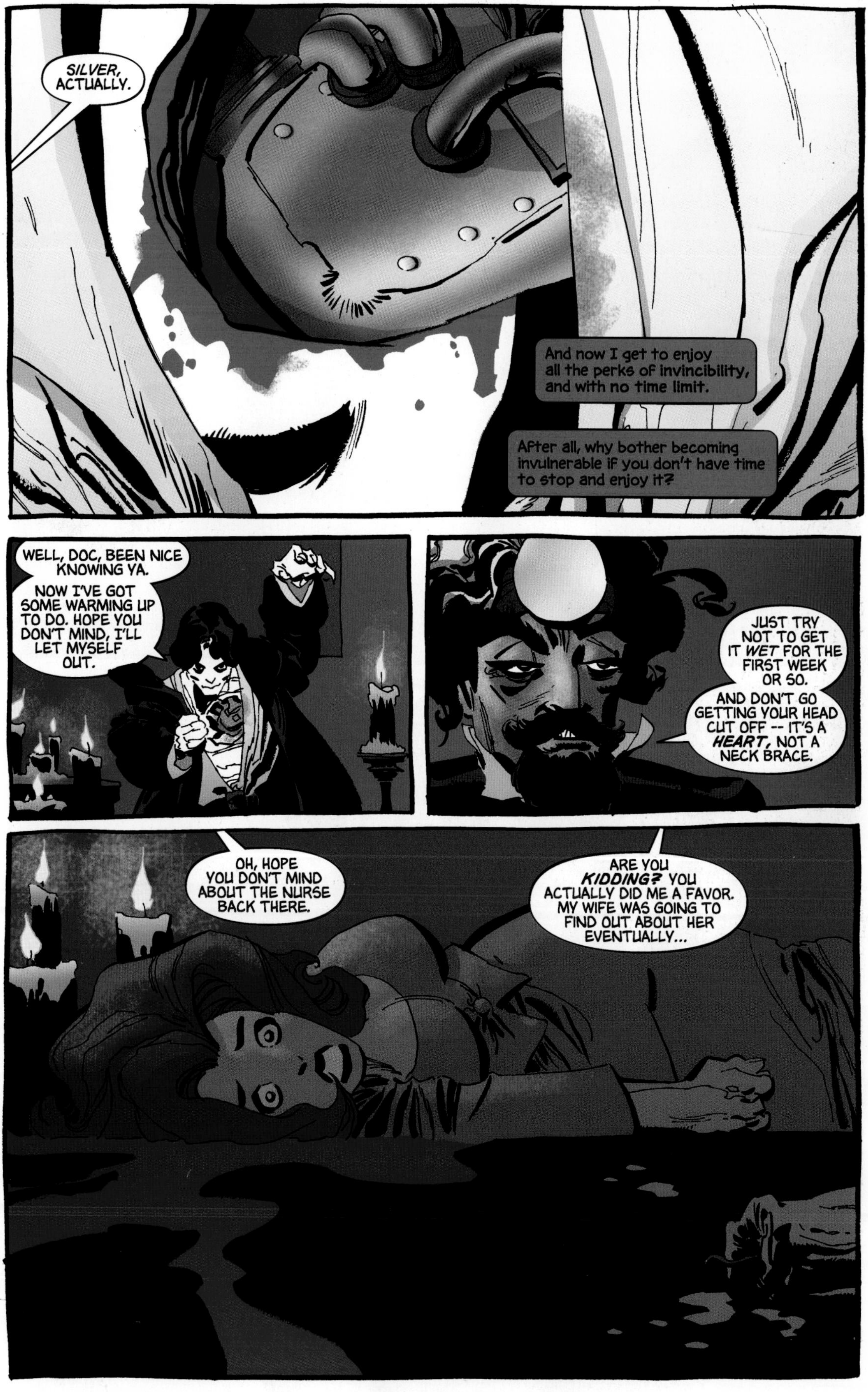
SILVER, ACTUALLY.
And now I get to enjoy all the perks of invincibility, and with no time limit.
After all, why bother becoming invulnerable if you don't have time to stop and enjoy it?
WELL, DOC, BEEN NICE KNOWING YA.
NOW I'VE GOT SOME WARMING UP TO DO. HOPE YOU DON'T MIND, I'LL LET MYSELF OUT.
JUST TRY NOT TO GET IT WET FOR THE FIRST WEEK OR SO.
AND DON'T GO GETTING YOUR HEAD CUT OFF -- IT'S A HEART, NOT A NECK BRACE.
OH, HOPE YOU DON'T MIND ABOUT THE NURSE BACK THERE.
ARE YOU KIDDING? YOU ACTUALLY DID ME A FAVOR. MY WIFE WAS GOING TO FIND OUT ABOUT HER EVENTUALLY...

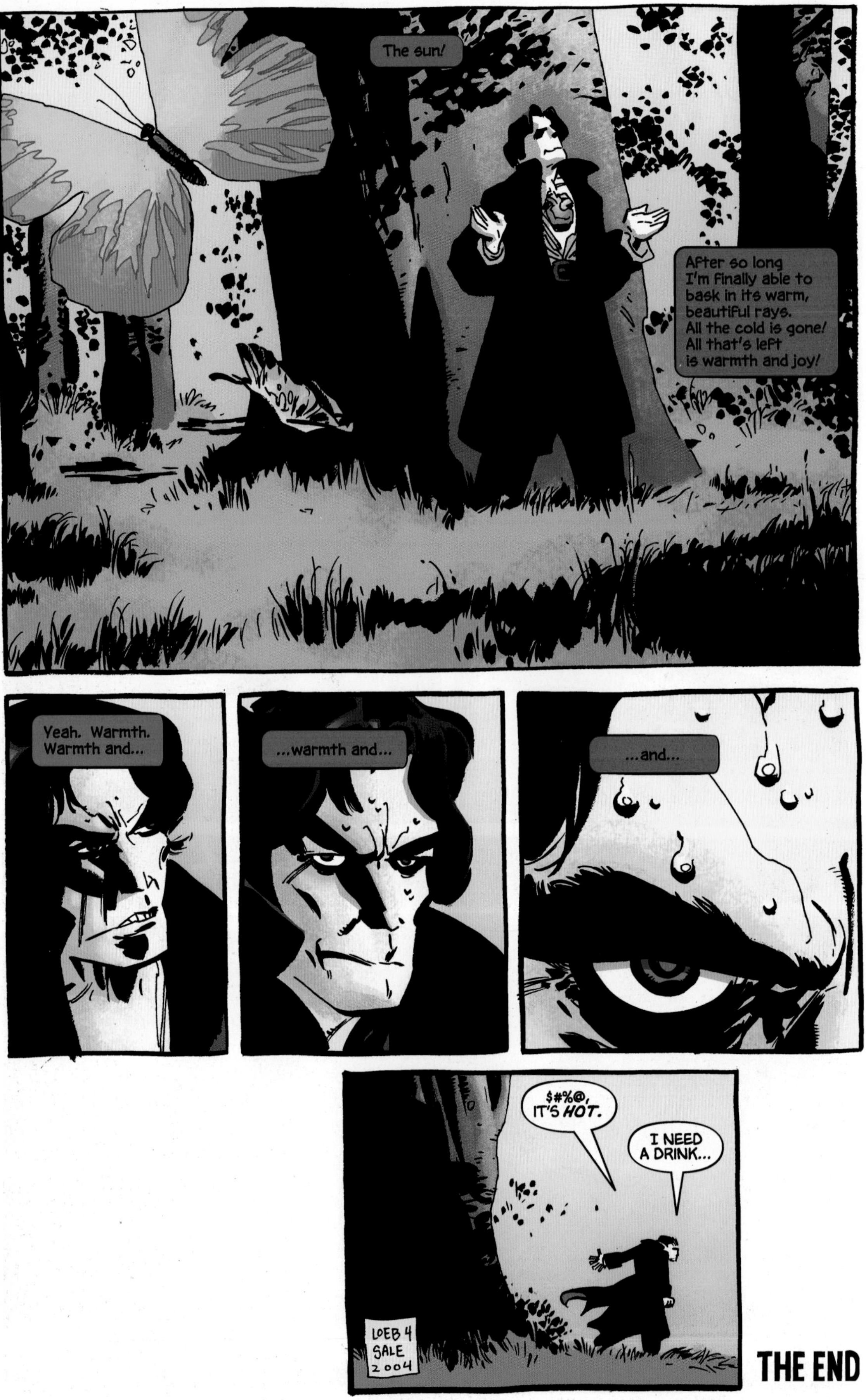
The sun!
After so long I'm finally able to bask in its warm, beautiful rays. All the cold is gone! All that's left is warmth and joy!
Yeah. Warmth. Warmth and...
...warmth and...
...and...
$#%@, IT'S HOT.
I NEED A DRINK...
LOEB 4 SALE 2004

THE END

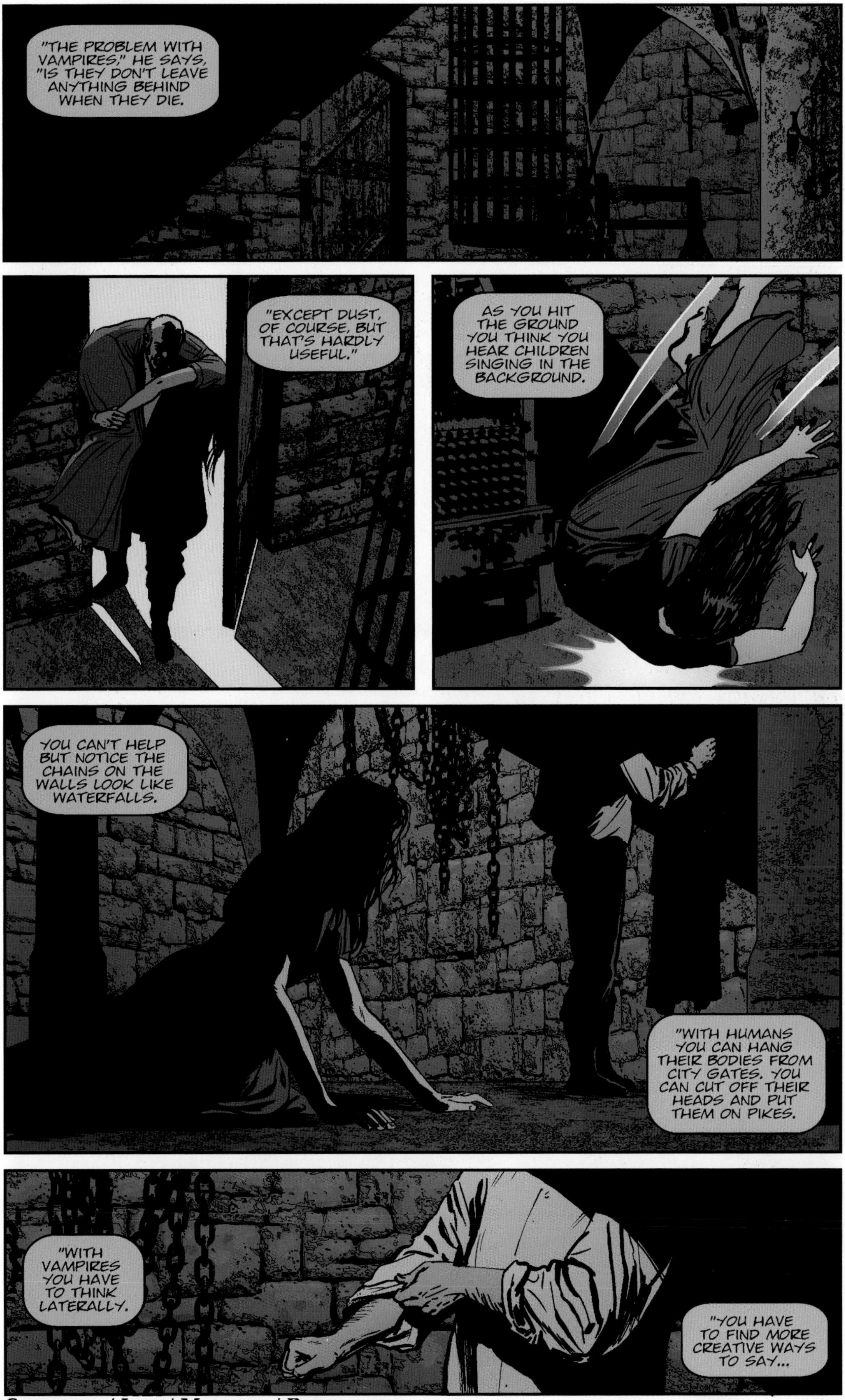
"THE PROBLEM WITH VAMPIRES," HE SAYS, "IS THEY DON'T LEAVE ANYTHING BEHIND WHEN THEY DIE.
"EXCEPT DUST, OF COURSE, BUT THAT'S HARDLY USEFUL."
AS YOU HIT THE GROUND YOU THINK YOU HEAR CHILDREN SINGING IN THE BACKGROUND.
YOU CAN'T HELP BUT NOTICE THE CHAINS ON THE WALLS LOOK LIKE WATERFALLS.
"WITH HUMANS YOU CAN HANG THEIR BODIES FROM CITY GATES. YOU CAN CUT OFF THEIR HEADS AND PUT THEM ON PIKES.
"WITH VAMPIRES YOU HAVE TO THINK LATERALLY.
"YOU HAVE TO FIND MORE CREATIVE WAYS TO SAY...

GODDARD / LEE / MADSEN / PARKHOUSE

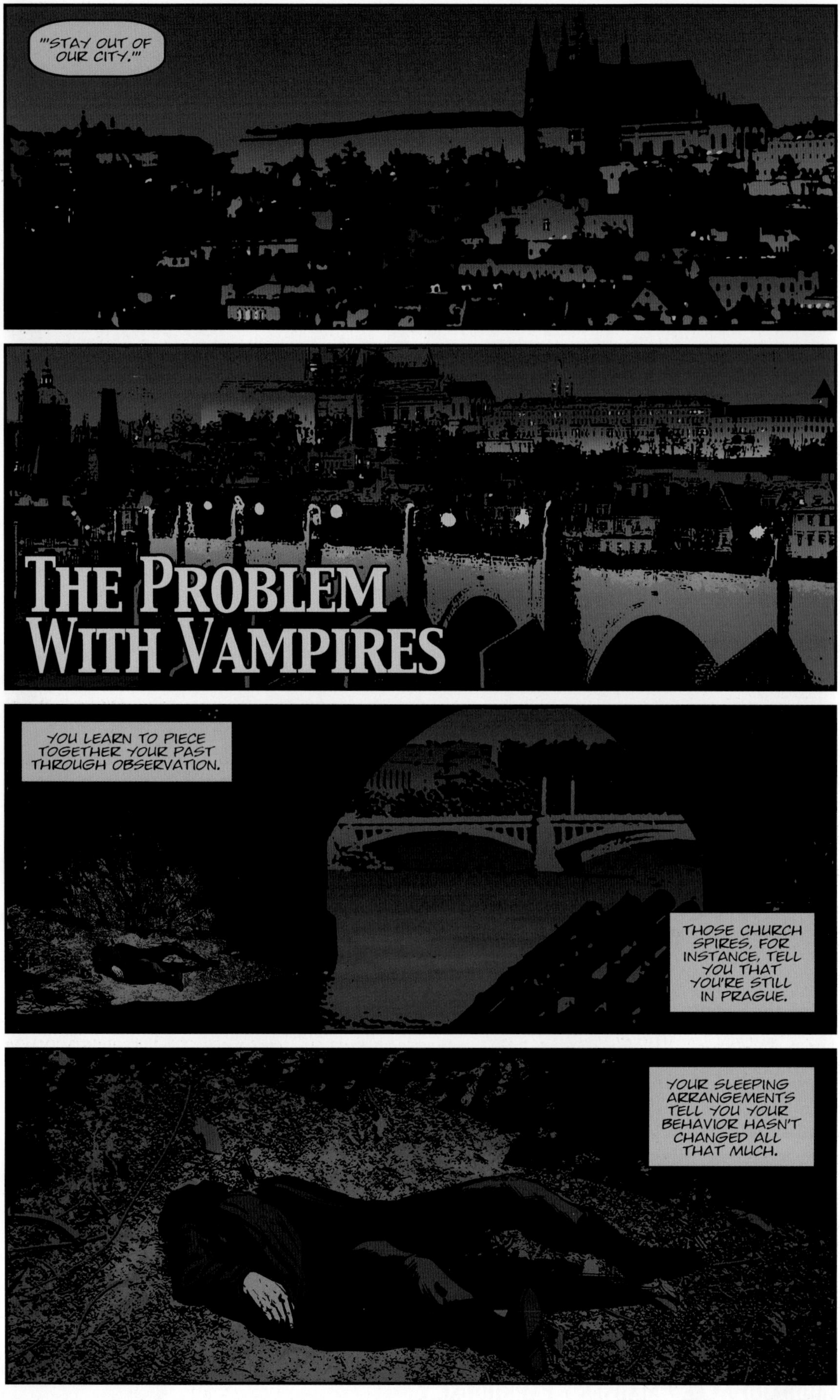
"'STAY OUT OF OUR CITY.'"
THE PROBLEM WITH VAMPIRES
YOU LEARN TO PIECE TOGETHER YOUR PAST THROUGH OBSERVATION.
THOSE CHURCH SPIRES, FOR INSTANCE, TELL YOU THAT YOU'RE STILL IN PRAGUE.
YOUR SLEEPING ARRANGEMENTS TELL YOU YOUR BEHAVIOR HASN'T CHANGED ALL THAT MUCH.

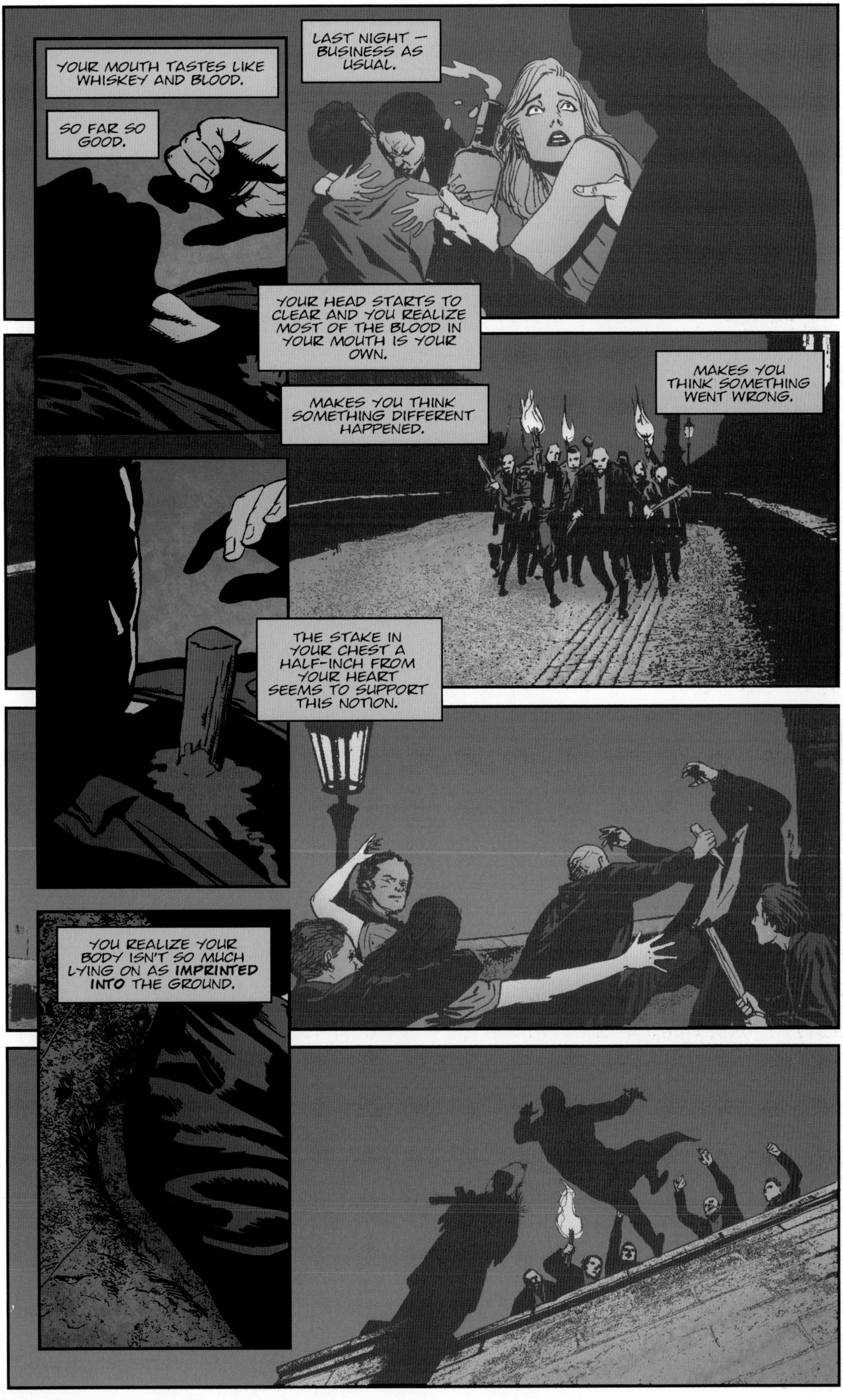
YOUR MOUTH TASTES LIKE WHISKEY AND BLOOD.
SO FAR SO GOOD.
LAST NIGHT — BUSINESS AS USUAL.
YOUR HEAD STARTS TO CLEAR AND YOU REALIZE MOST OF THE BLOOD IN YOUR MOUTH IS YOUR OWN.
MAKES YOU THINK SOMETHING DIFFERENT HAPPENED.
MAKES YOU THINK SOMETHING WENT WRONG.
THE STAKE IN YOUR CHEST A HALF-INCH FROM YOUR HEART SEEMS TO SUPPORT THIS NOTION.
YOU REALIZE YOUR BODY ISN'T SO MUCH LYING ON AS IMPRINTED INTO THE GROUND.

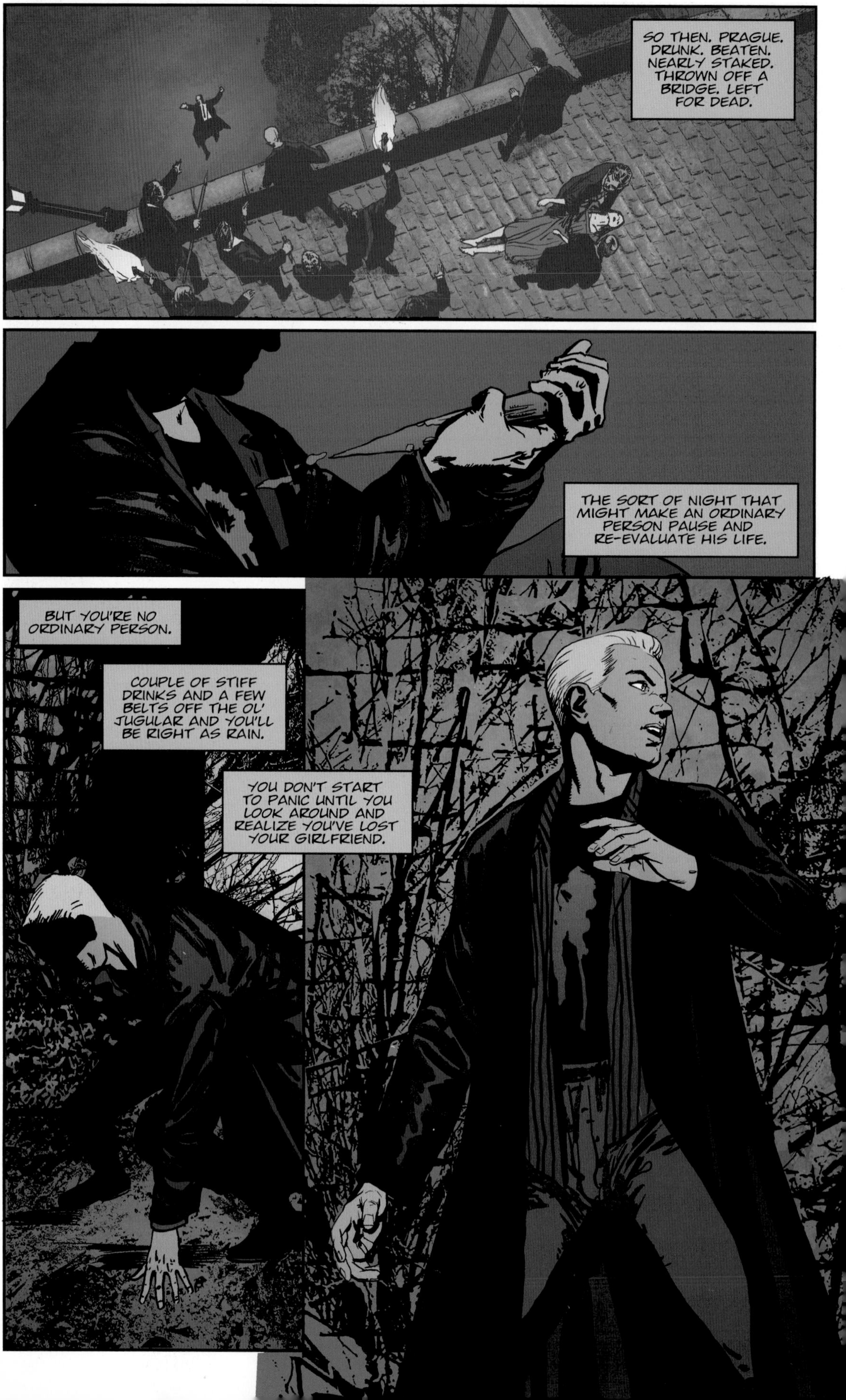
SO THEN. PRAGUE. DRUNK. BEATEN. NEARLY STAKED. THROWN OFF A BRIDGE. LEFT FOR DEAD.
THE SORT OF NIGHT THAT MIGHT MAKE AN ORDINARY PERSON PAUSE AND RE-EVALUATE HIS LIFE.
BUT YOU'RE NO ORDINARY PERSON.
COUPLE OF STIFF DRINKS AND A FEW BELTS OFF THE OL' JUGULAR AND YOU'LL BE RIGHT AS RAIN.
YOU DON'T START TO PANIC UNTIL YOU LOOK AROUND AND REALIZE YOU'VE LOST YOUR GIRLFRIEND.

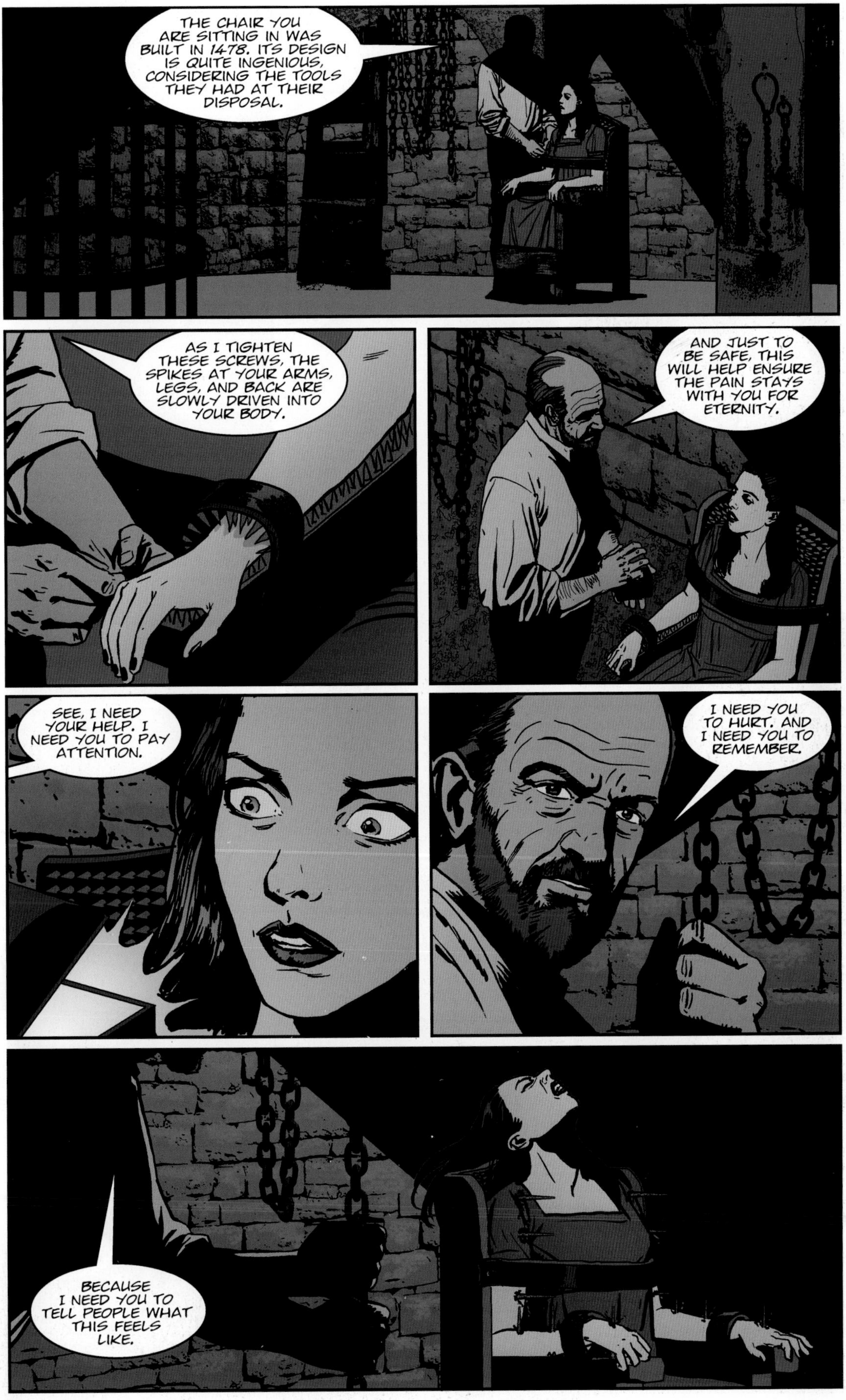
THE CHAIR YOU ARE SITTING IN WAS BUILT IN 1478. ITS DESIGN IS QUITE INGENIOUS, CONSIDERING THE TOOLS THEY HAD AT THEIR DISPOSAL.
AS I TIGHTEN THESE SCREWS, THE SPIKES AT YOUR ARMS, LEGS, AND BACK ARE SLOWLY DRIVEN INTO YOUR BODY.
AND JUST TO BE SAFE, THIS WILL HELP ENSURE THE PAIN STAYS WITH YOU FOR ETERNITY.
SEE, I NEED YOUR HELP. I NEED YOU TO PAY ATTENTION.
I NEED YOU TO HURT. AND I NEED YOU TO REMEMBER.
BECAUSE I NEED YOU TO TELL PEOPLE WHAT THIS FEELS LIKE.

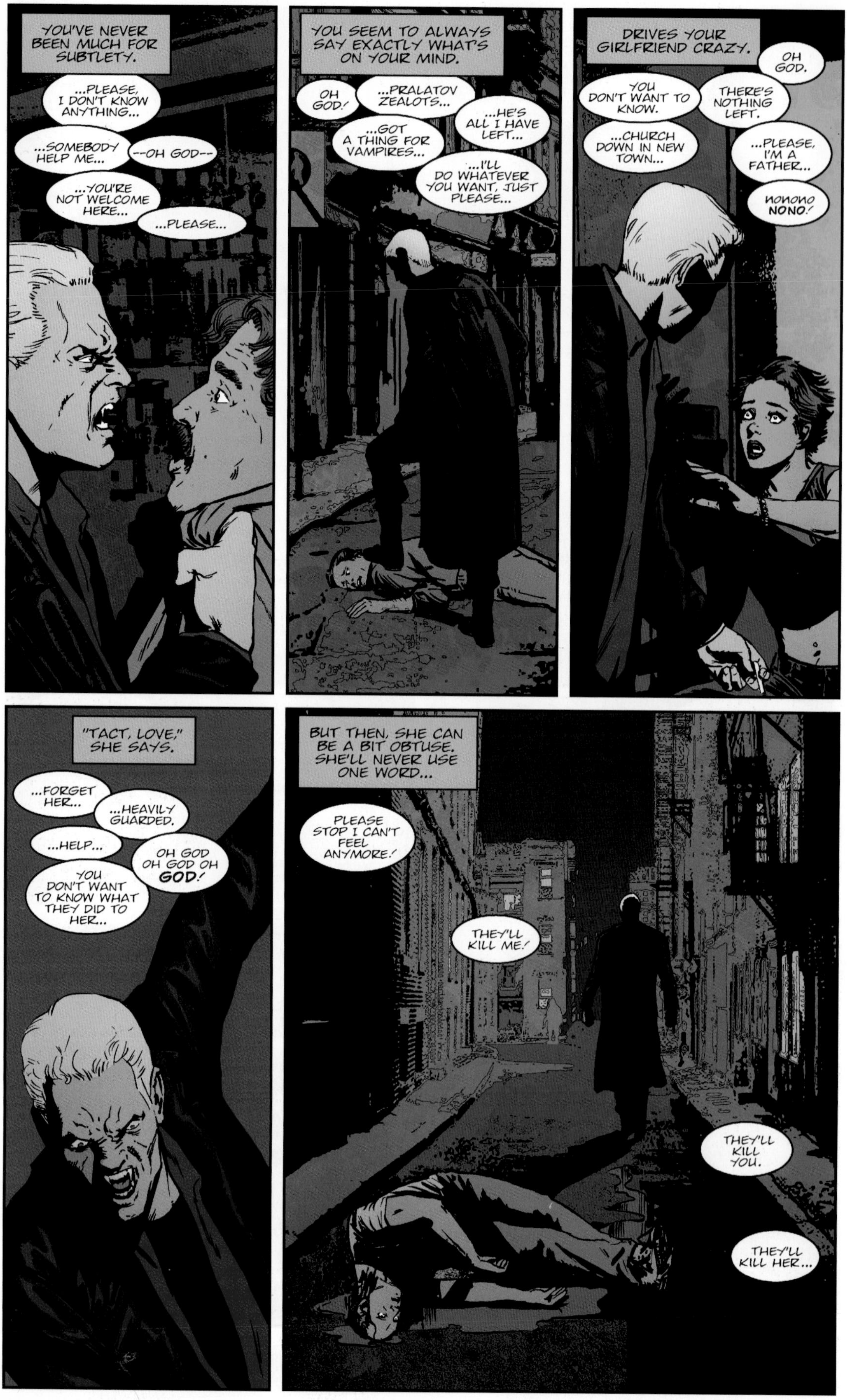
YOU'VE NEVER BEEN MUCH FOR SUBTLETY.
...PLEASE, I DON'T KNOW ANYTHING...
...SOMEBODY HELP ME...
--OH GOD--
...YOU'RE NOT WELCOME HERE...
...PLEASE...
YOU SEEM TO ALWAYS SAY EXACTLY WHAT'S ON YOUR MIND.
OH GOD!
...PRALATOV ZEALOTS...
...GOT A THING FOR VAMPIRES...
...HE'S ALL I HAVE LEFT...
...I'LL DO WHATEVER YOU WANT, JUST PLEASE...
DRIVES YOUR GIRLFRIEND CRAZY.
OH GOD.
YOU DON'T WANT TO KNOW.
THERE'S NOTHING LEFT.
...CHURCH DOWN IN NEW TOWN...
...PLEASE, I'M A FATHER...
nonono NONO!
"TACT, LOVE," SHE SAYS.
...FORGET HER...
...HEAVILY GUARDED.
...HELP...
OH GOD OH GOD OH GOD!
YOU DON'T WANT TO KNOW WHAT THEY DID TO HER...
BUT THEN, SHE CAN BE A BIT OBTUSE. SHE'LL NEVER USE ONE WORD...
PLEASE STOP I CAN'T FEEL ANYMORE!
THEY'LL KILL ME!
THEY'LL KILL YOU.
THEY'LL KILL HER...

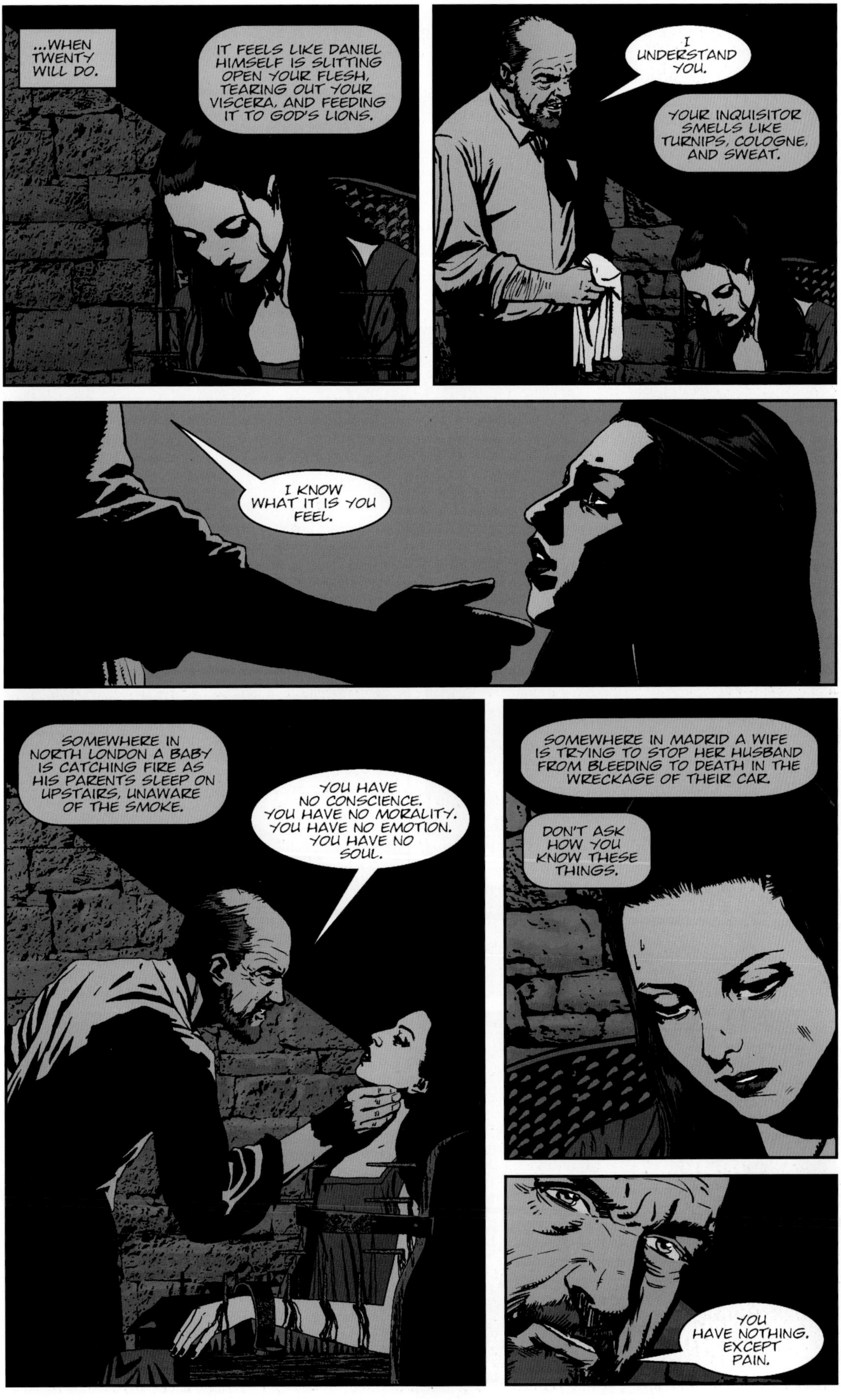
...WHEN TWENTY WILL DO.
IT FEELS LIKE DANIEL HIMSELF IS SLITTING OPEN YOUR FLESH, TEARING OUT YOUR VISCERA, AND FEEDING IT TO GOD'S LIONS.
I UNDERSTAND YOU.
YOUR INQUISITOR SMELLS LIKE TURNIPS, COLOGNE, AND SWEAT.
I KNOW WHAT IT IS YOU FEEL.
SOMEWHERE IN NORTH LONDON A BABY IS CATCHING FIRE AS HIS PARENTS SLEEP ON UPSTAIRS, UNAWARE OF THE SMOKE.
YOU HAVE NO CONSCIENCE. YOU HAVE NO MORALITY. YOU HAVE NO EMOTION. YOU HAVE NO SOUL.
SOMEWHERE IN MADRID A WIFE IS TRYING TO STOP HER HUSBAND FROM BLEEDING TO DEATH IN THE WRECKAGE OF THEIR CAR.
DON'T ASK HOW YOU KNOW THESE THINGS.
YOU HAVE NOTHING. EXCEPT PAIN.

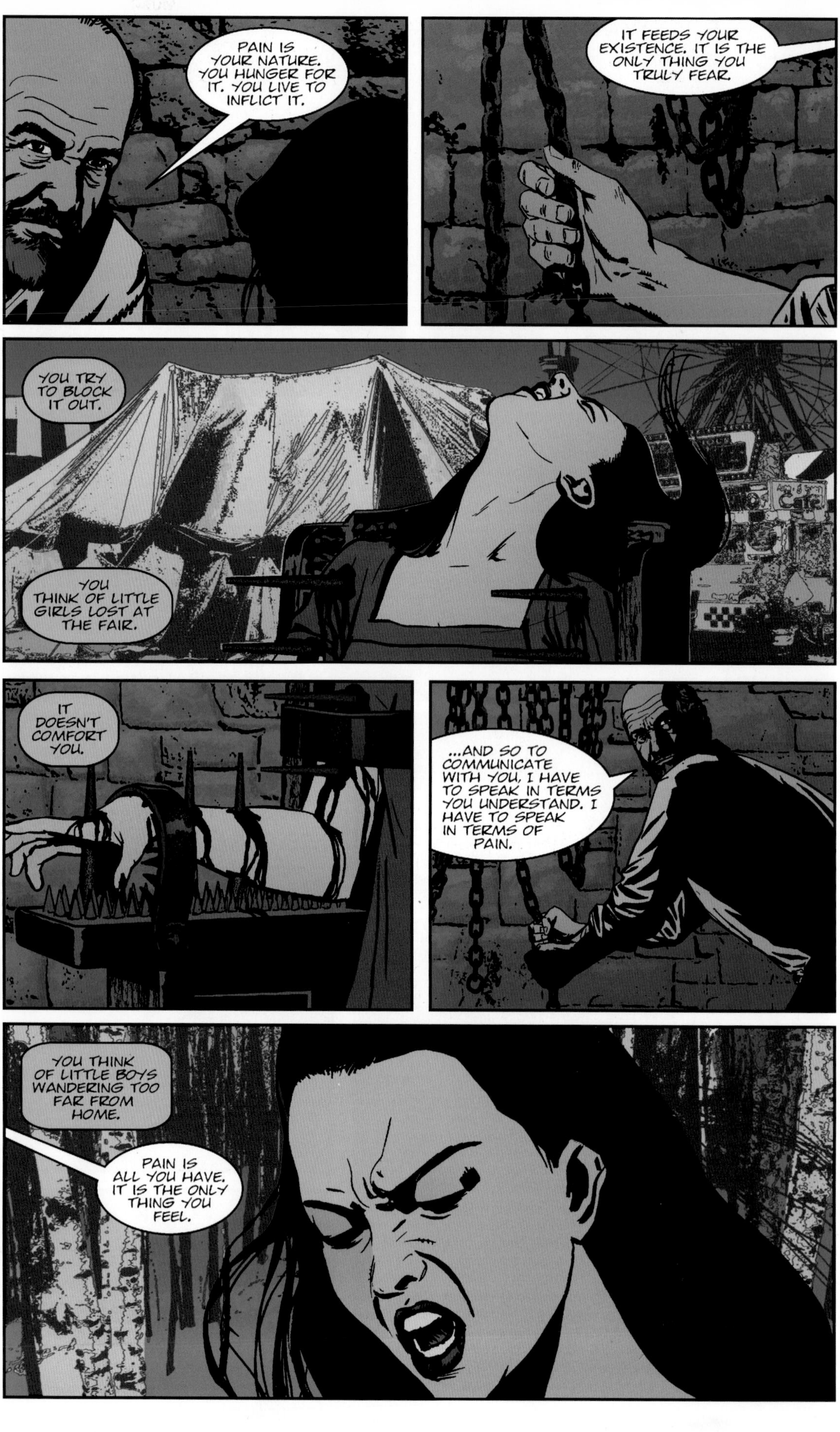
PAIN IS YOUR NATURE. YOU HUNGER FOR IT. YOU LIVE TO INFLICT IT.
IT FEEDS YOUR EXISTENCE. IT IS THE ONLY THING YOU TRULY FEAR.
YOU TRY TO BLOCK IT OUT.
YOU THINK OF LITTLE GIRLS LOST AT THE FAIR.
IT DOESN'T COMFORT YOU.
...AND SO TO COMMUNICATE WITH YOU, I HAVE TO SPEAK IN TERMS YOU UNDERSTAND. I HAVE TO SPEAK IN TERMS OF PAIN.
YOU THINK OF LITTLE BOYS WANDERING TOO FAR FROM HOME.
PAIN IS ALL YOU HAVE. IT IS THE ONLY THING YOU FEEL.

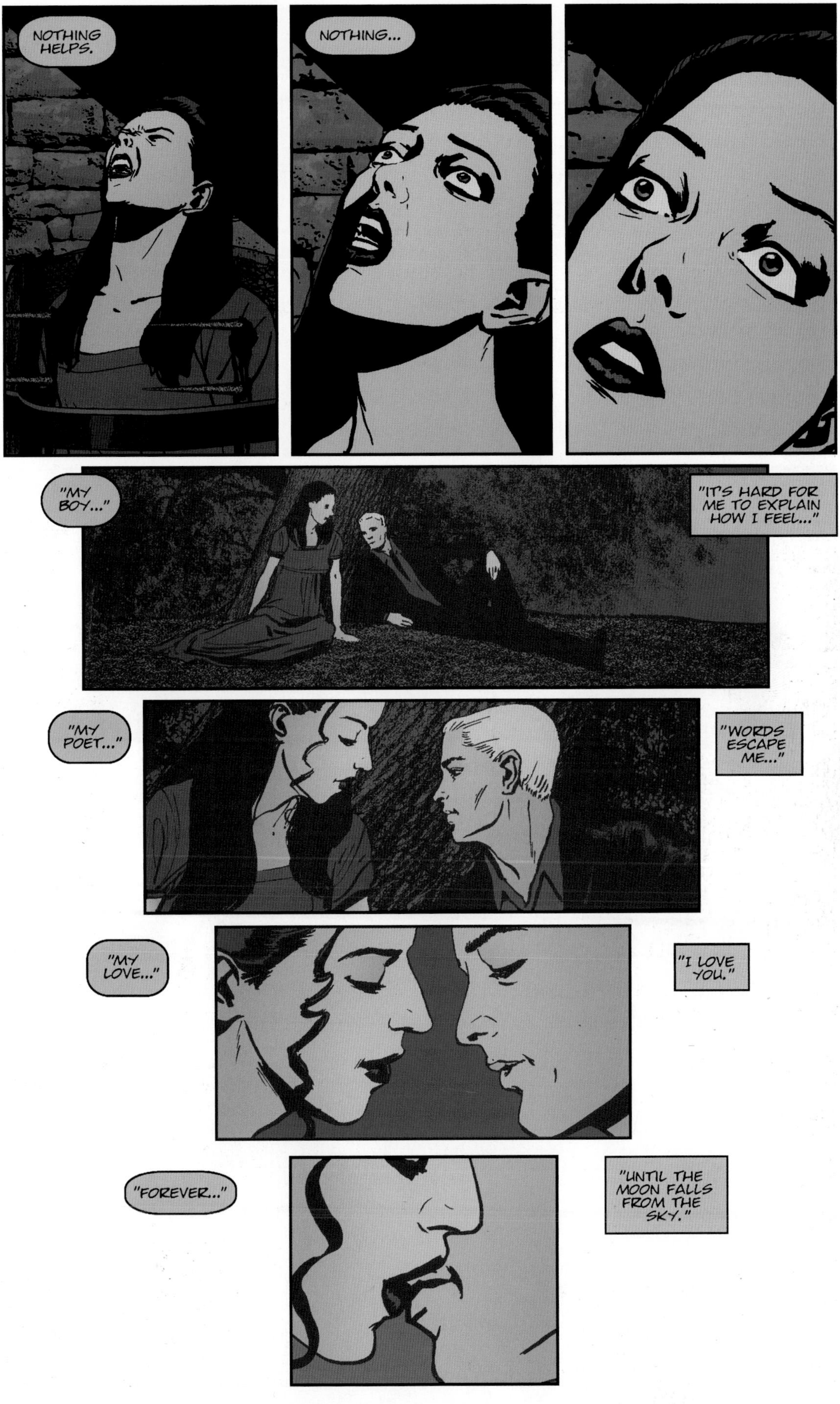
NOTHING HELPS.
NOTHING...
"MY BOY..."
"IT'S HARD FOR ME TO EXPLAIN HOW I FEEL..."
"MY POET..."
"WORDS ESCAPE ME..."
"MY LOVE..."
"I LOVE YOU."
"FOREVER..."
"UNTIL THE MOON FALLS FROM THE SKY."

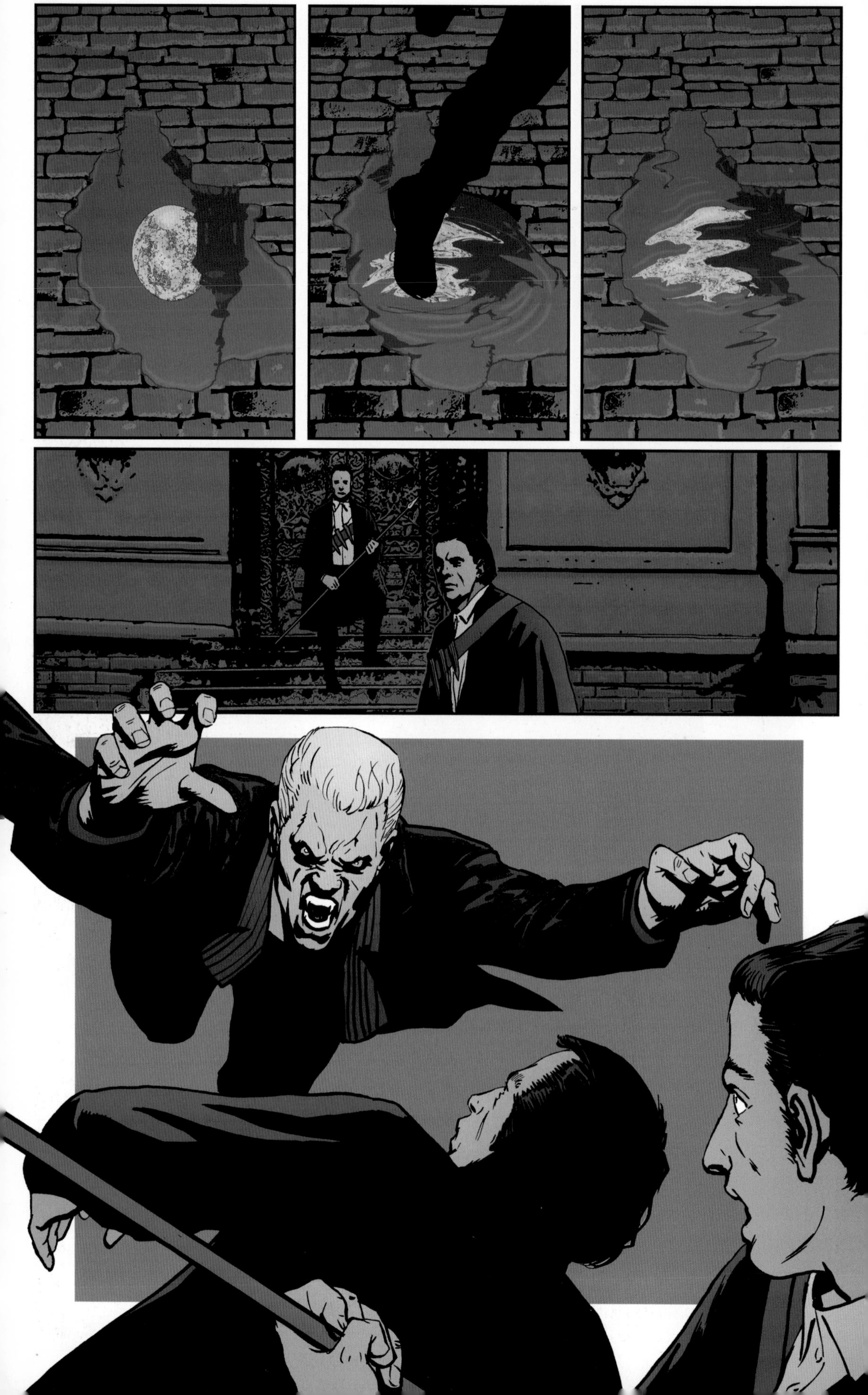

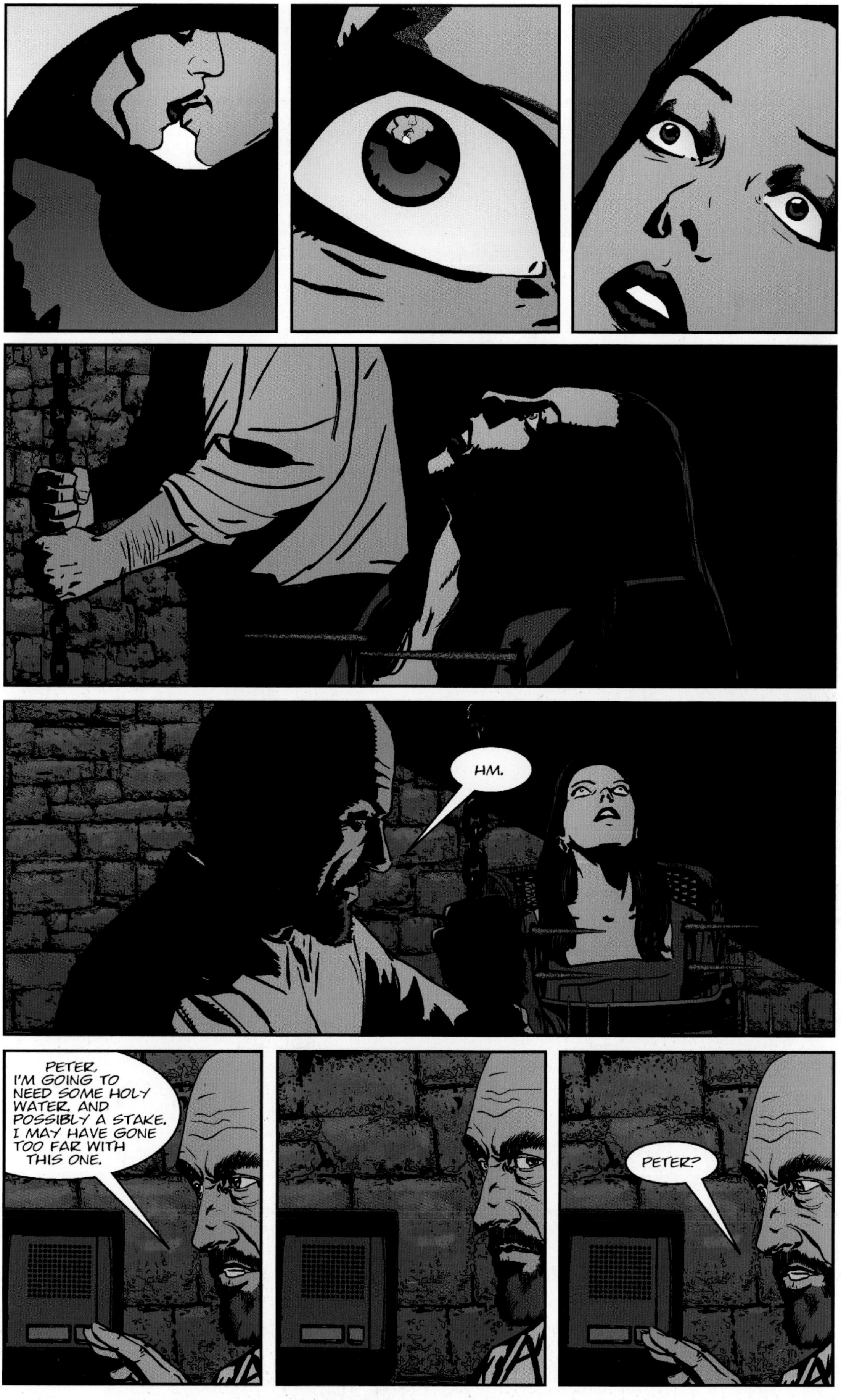
HM.
PETER, I'M GOING TO NEED SOME HOLY WATER. AND POSSIBLY A STAKE. I MAY HAVE GONE TOO FAR WITH THIS ONE.
PETER?

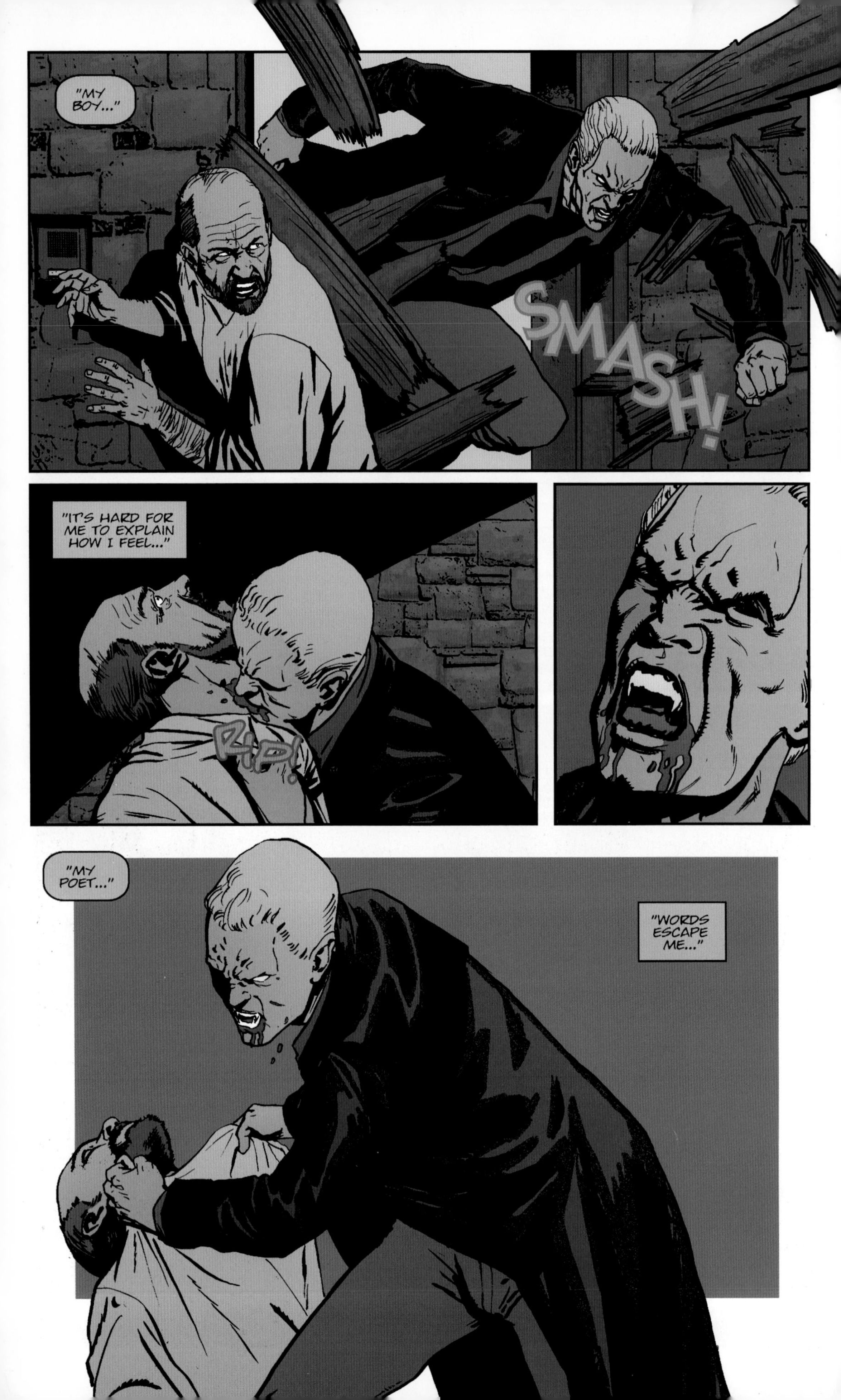
"MY BOY..."
SMASH!
"IT'S HARD FOR ME TO EXPLAIN HOW I FEEL..."
RIP!
"MY POET..."
"WORDS ESCAPE ME..."

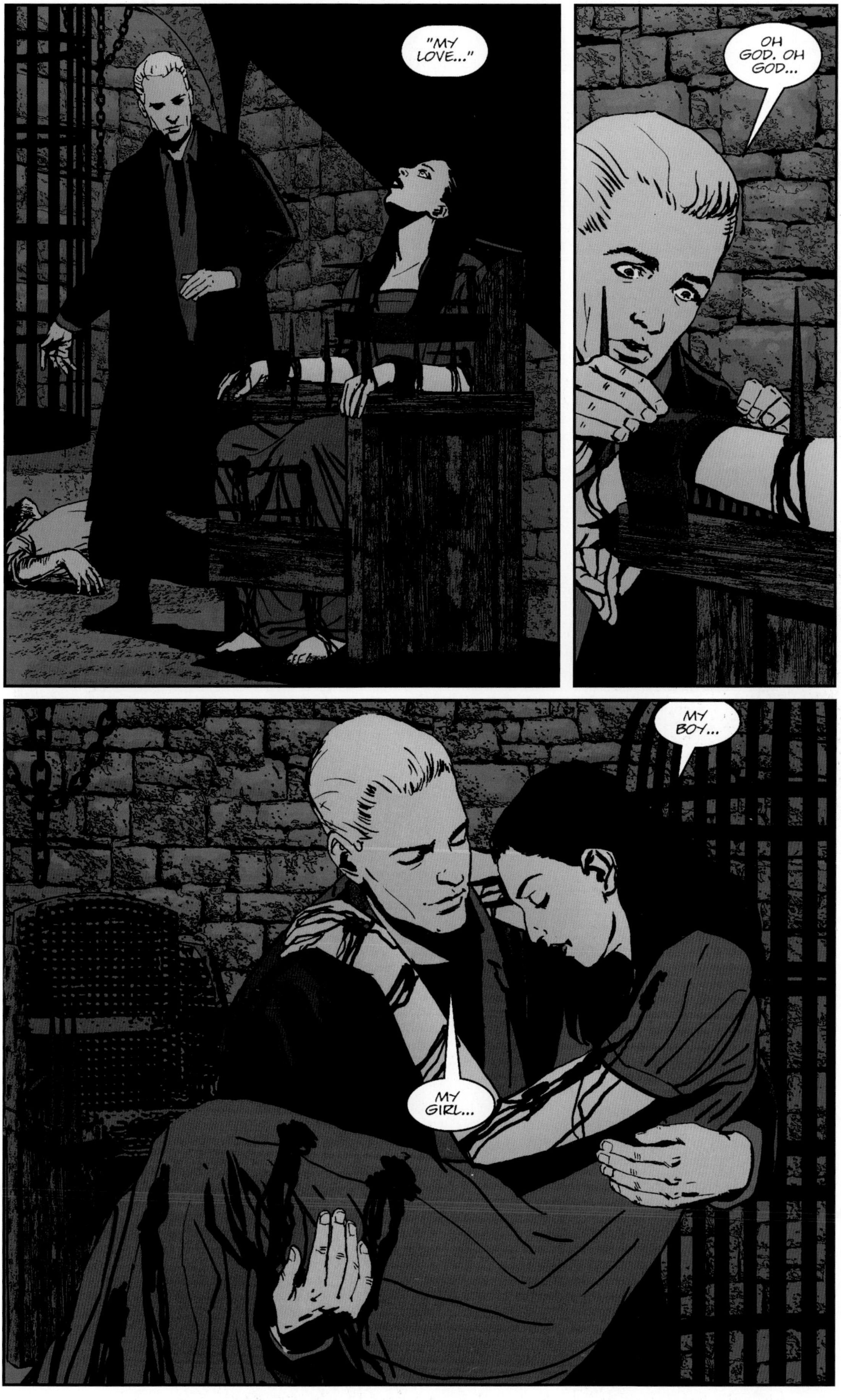
"MY LOVE..."
OH GOD. OH GOD...
MY BOY...
MY GIRL...

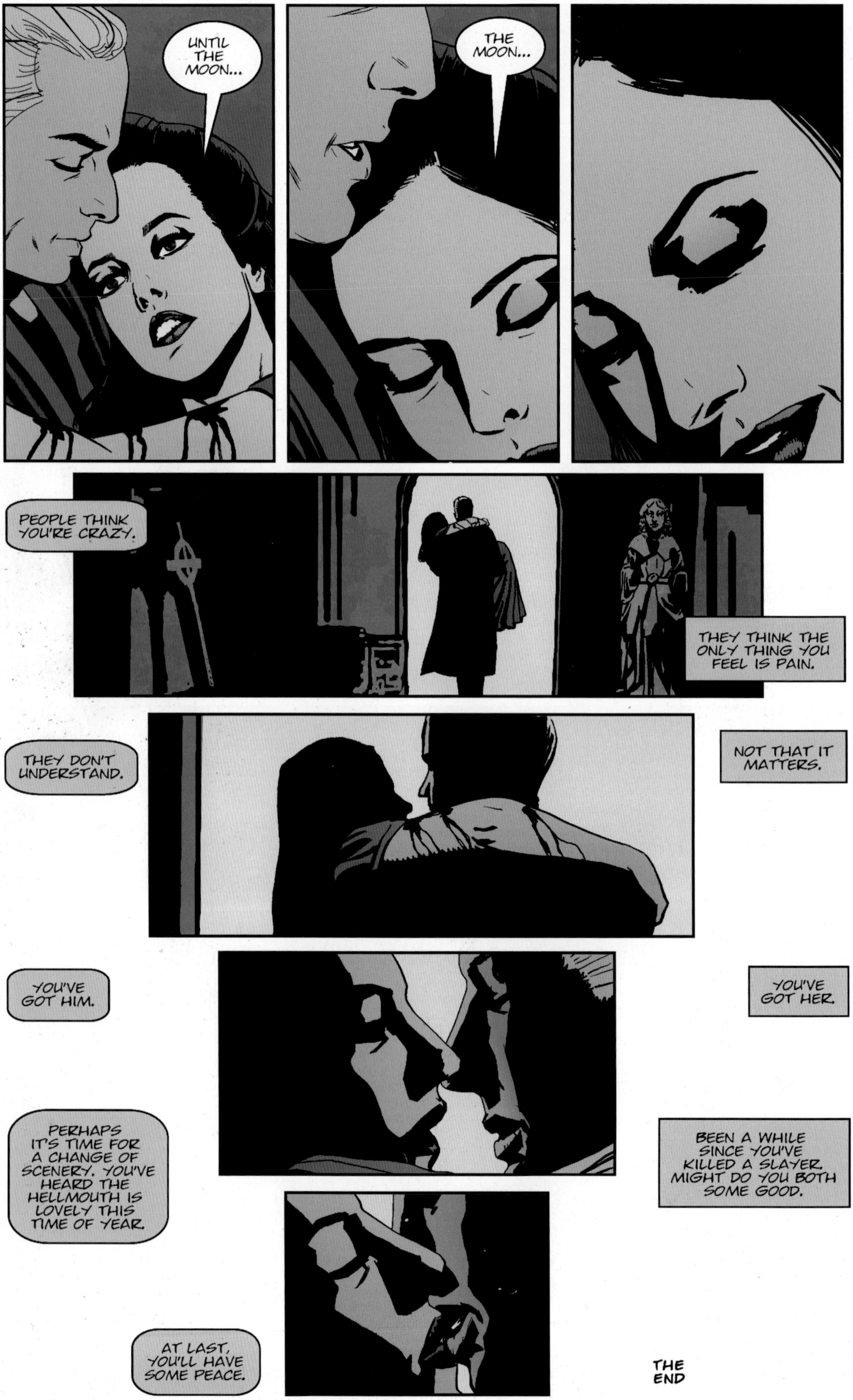
UNTIL THE MOON...
THE MOON...
PEOPLE THINK YOU'RE CRAZY.
THEY THINK THE ONLY THING YOU FEEL IS PAIN.
THEY DON'T UNDERSTAND.
NOT THAT IT MATTERS.
YOU'VE GOT HIM.
YOU'VE GOT HER.
PERHAPS IT'S TIME FOR A CHANGE OF SCENERY. YOU'VE HEARD THE HELLMOUTH IS LOVELY THIS TIME OF YEAR.
BEEN A WHILE SINCE YOU'VE KILLED A SLAYER. MIGHT DO YOU BOTH SOME GOOD.
AT LAST, YOU'LL HAVE SOME PEACE.
THE END

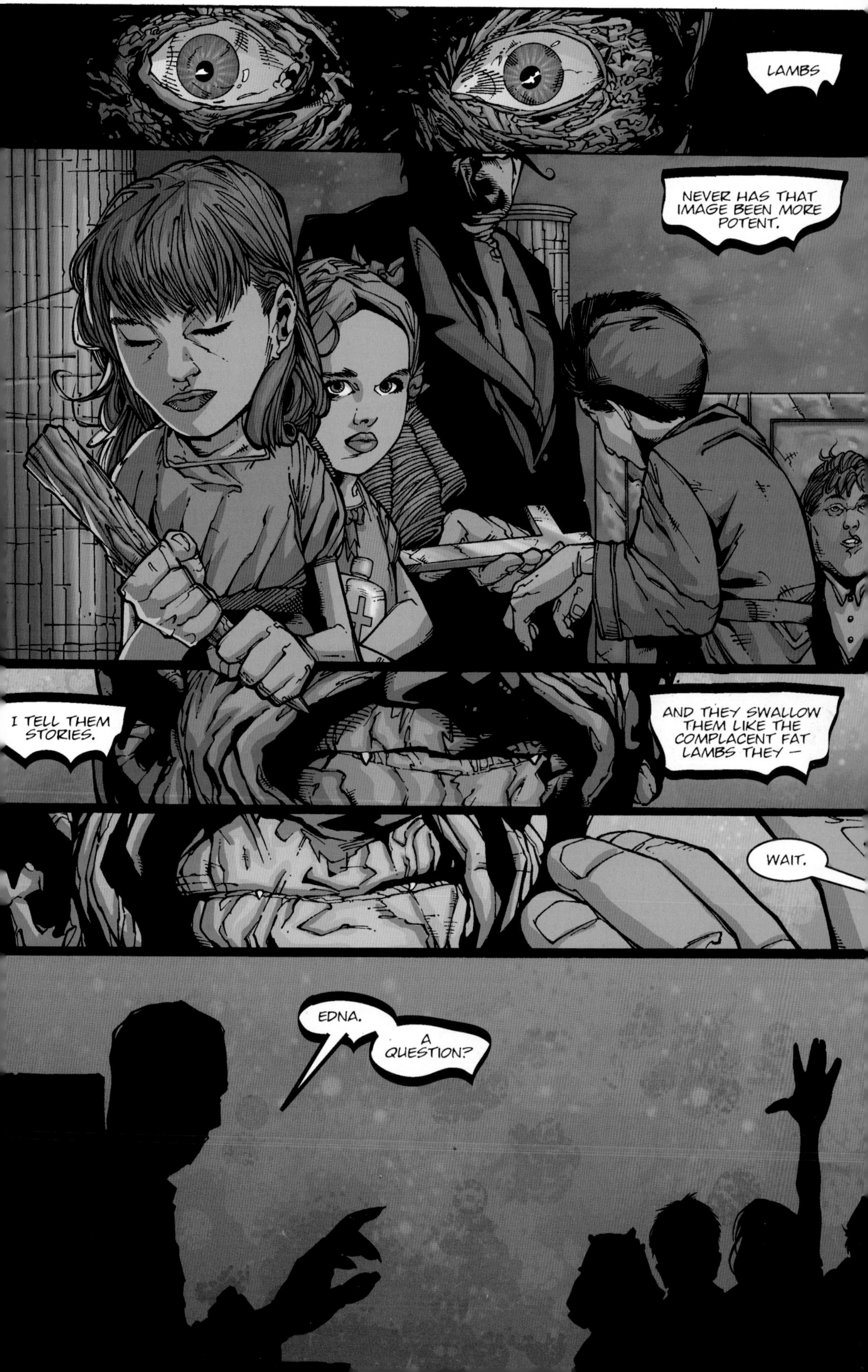
LAMBS
NEVER HAS THAT IMAGE BEEN MORE POTENT.
I TELL THEM STORIES.
AND THEY SWALLOW THEM LIKE THE COMPLACENT FAT LAMBS THEY —
WAIT.
EDNA.
A QUESTION?

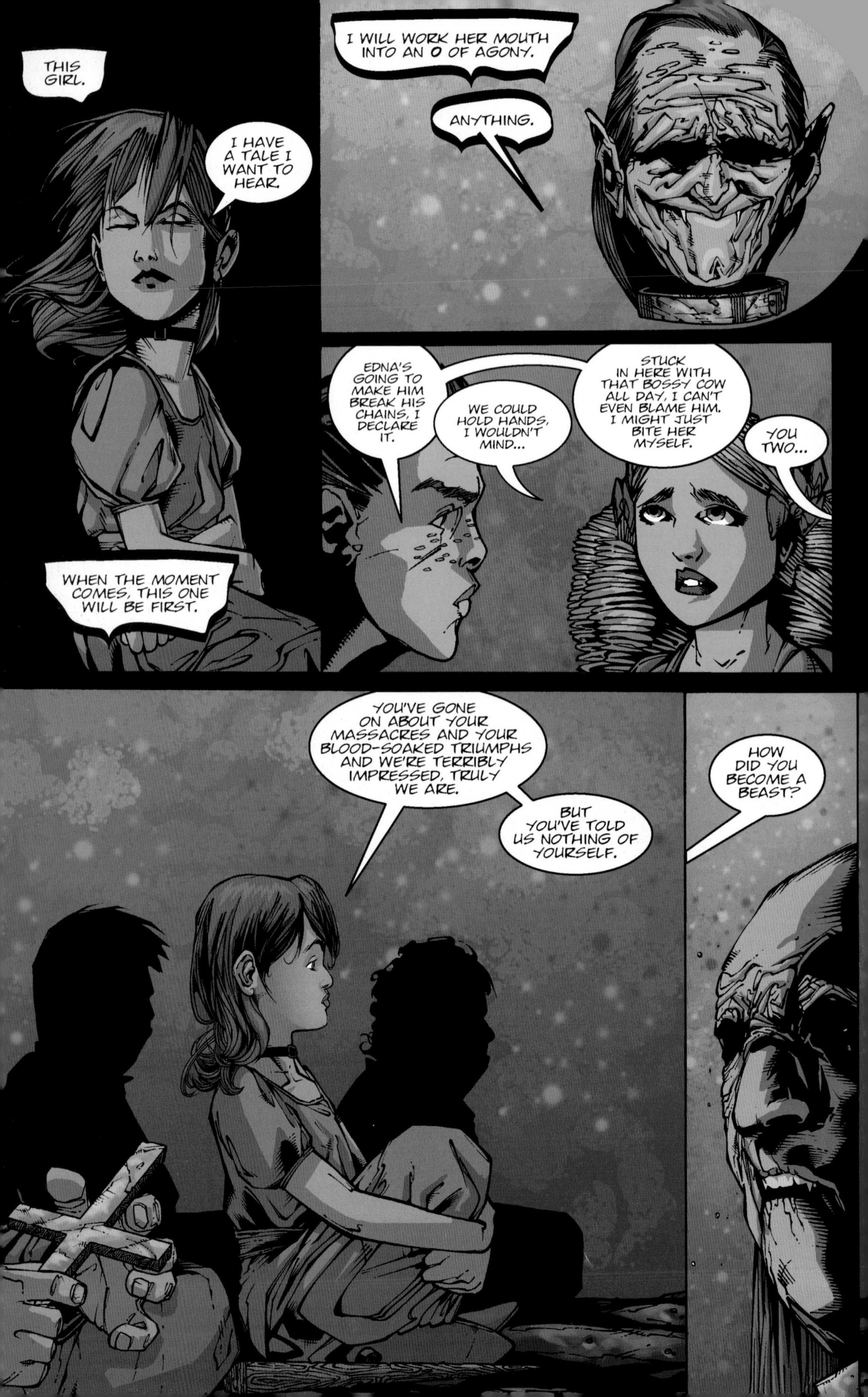
THIS GIRL.
I HAVE A TALE I WANT TO HEAR.
WHEN THE MOMENT COMES, THIS ONE WILL BE FIRST.
I WILL WORK HER MOUTH INTO AN O OF AGONY.
ANYTHING.
EDNA'S GOING TO MAKE HIM BREAK HIS CHAINS, I DECLARE IT.
WE COULD HOLD HANDS, I WOULDN'T MIND...
STUCK IN HERE WITH THAT BOSSY COW ALL DAY, I CAN'T EVEN BLAME HIM. I MIGHT JUST BITE HER MYSELF.
YOU TWO...
YOU'VE GONE ON ABOUT YOUR MASSACRES AND YOUR BLOOD-SOAKED TRIUMPHS AND WE'RE TERRIBLY IMPRESSED, TRULY WE ARE.
BUT YOU'VE TOLD US NOTHING OF YOURSELF.
HOW DID YOU BECOME A BEAST?

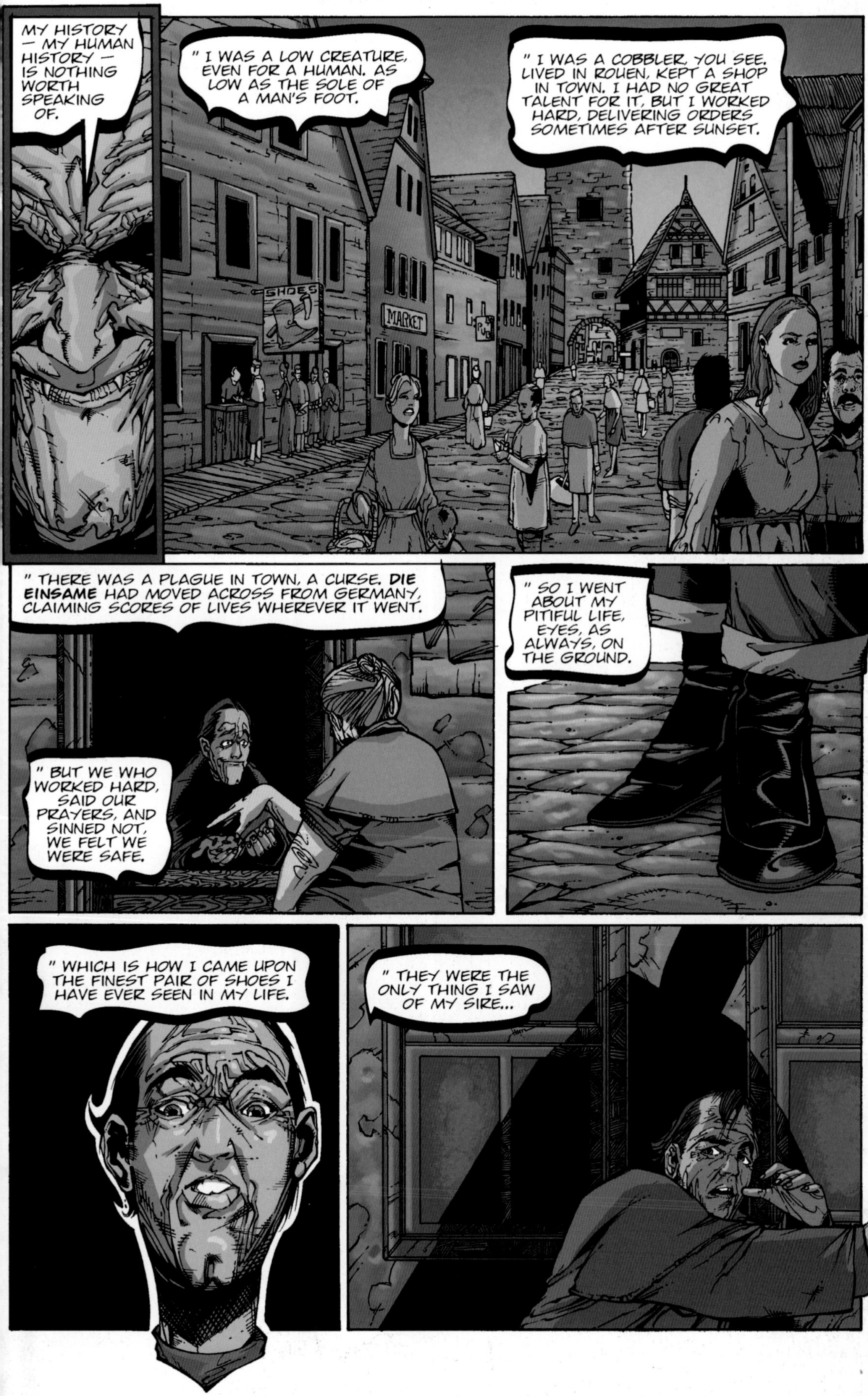
MY HISTORY — MY HUMAN HISTORY — IS NOTHING WORTH SPEAKING OF.
" I WAS A LOW CREATURE, EVEN FOR A HUMAN. AS LOW AS THE SOLE OF A MAN'S FOOT.
" I WAS A COBBLER, YOU SEE. LIVED IN ROUEN, KEPT A SHOP IN TOWN. I HAD NO GREAT TALENT FOR IT, BUT I WORKED HARD, DELIVERING ORDERS SOMETIMES AFTER SUNSET.
SHOES
MARKET
PUB
" THERE WAS A PLAGUE IN TOWN, A CURSE. **DIE EINSAME** HAD MOVED ACROSS FROM GERMANY, CLAIMING SCORES OF LIVES WHEREVER IT WENT.
" BUT WE WHO WORKED HARD, SAID OUR PRAYERS, AND SINNED NOT, WE FELT WE WERE SAFE.
" SO I WENT ABOUT MY PITIFUL LIFE, EYES, AS ALWAYS, ON THE GROUND.
" WHICH IS HOW I CAME UPON THE FINEST PAIR OF SHOES I HAVE EVER SEEN IN MY LIFE.
" THEY WERE THE ONLY THING I SAW OF MY SIRE...

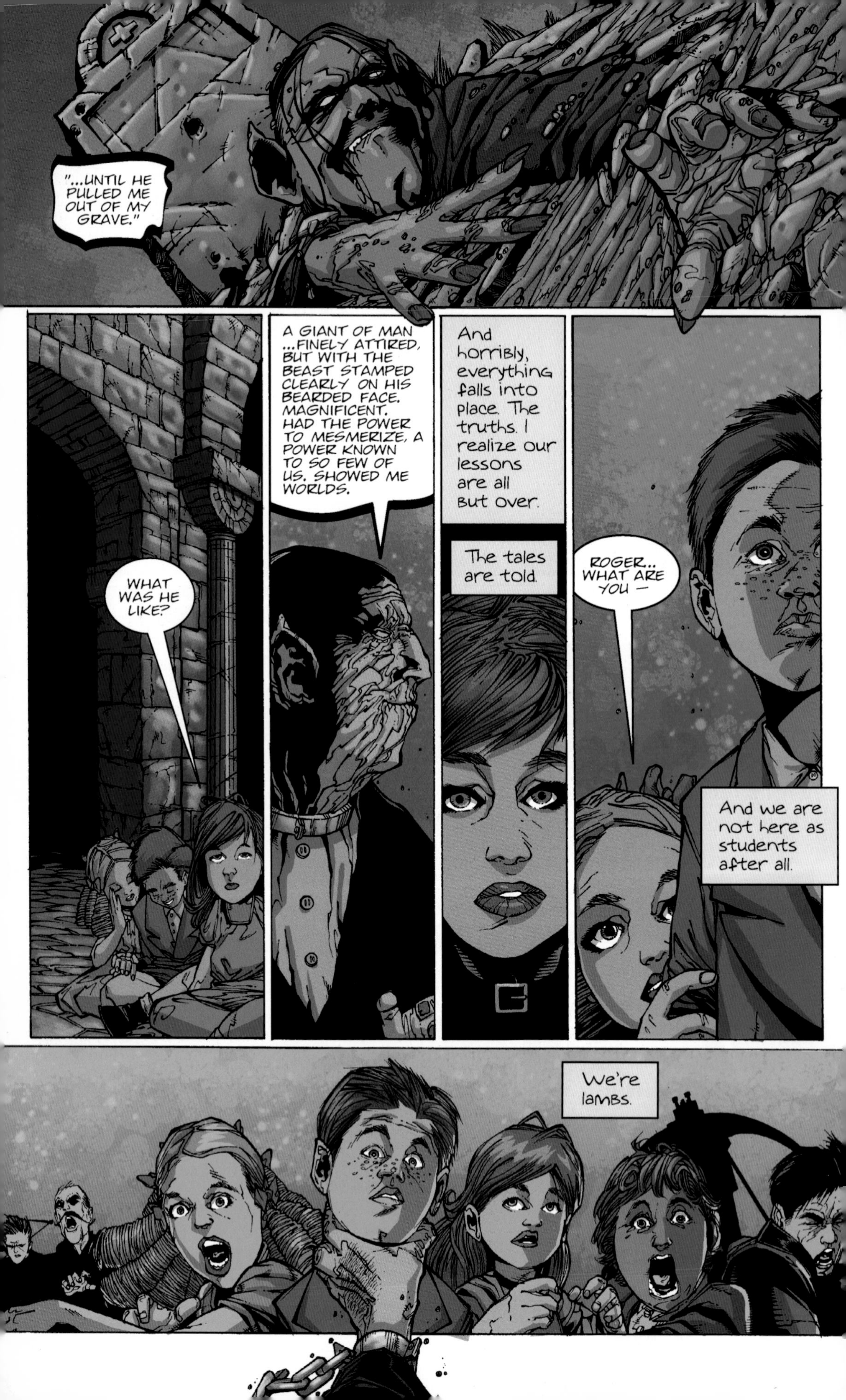
"...UNTIL HE PULLED ME OUT OF MY GRAVE."
WHAT WAS HE LIKE?
A GIANT OF MAN ...FINELY ATTIRED, BUT WITH THE BEAST STAMPED CLEARLY ON HIS BEARDED FACE. MAGNIFICENT. HAD THE POWER TO MESMERIZE, A POWER KNOWN TO SO FEW OF US. SHOWED ME WORLDS.
And horribly, everything falls into place. The truths. I realize our lessons are all but over.
The tales are told.
ROGER... WHAT ARE YOU —
And we are not here as students after all.
We're lambs.

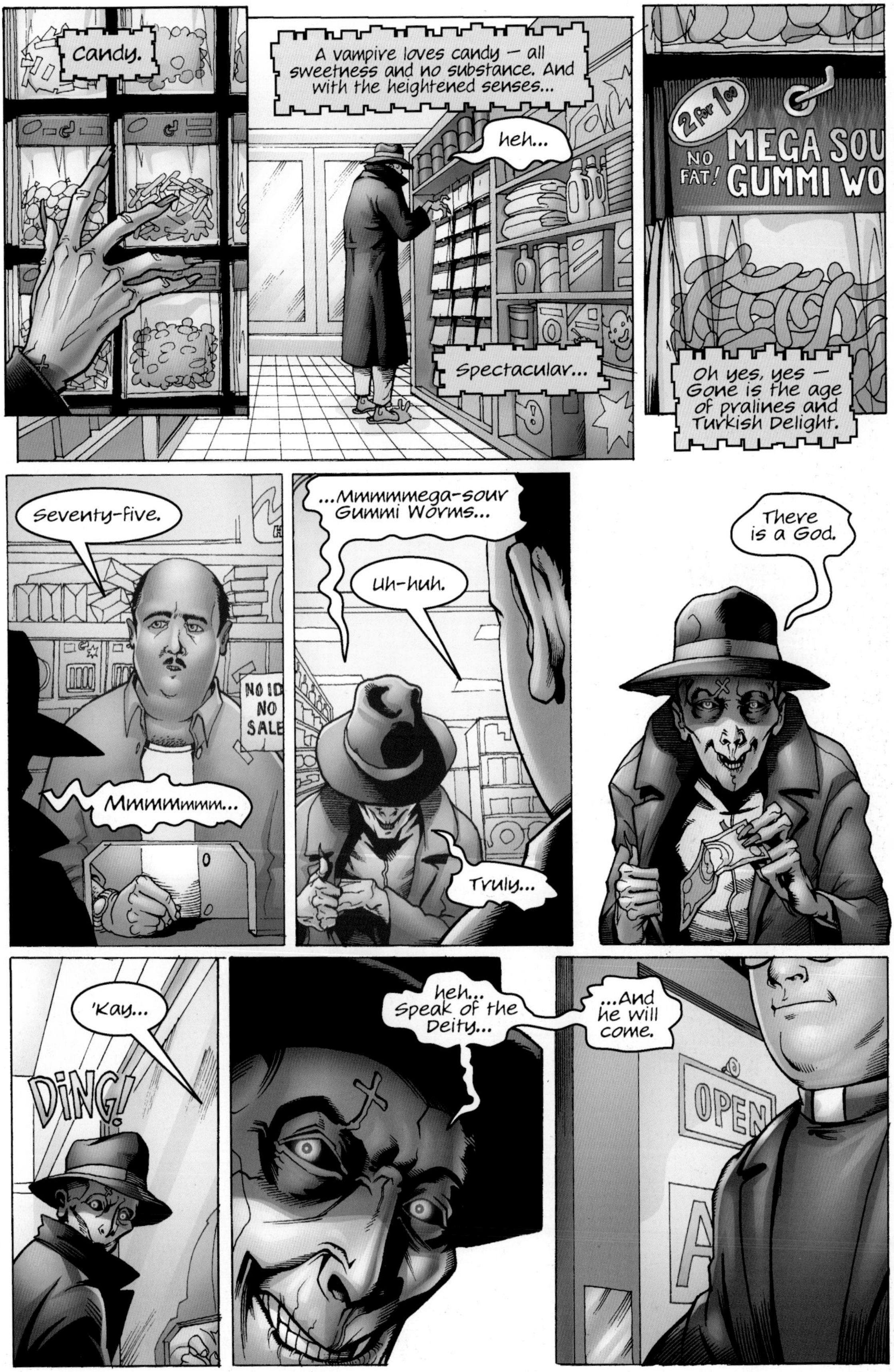

Candy.
A vampire loves candy — all sweetness and no substance. And with the heightened senses...
heh...
Spectacular...
2 for 1.00
NO FAT!
MEGA SOU
GUMMI WO
Oh yes, yes — Gone is the age of pralines and Turkish Delight.
Seventy-five.
NO ID NO SALE
Mmmmmmm...
...Mmmmmega-sour Gummi Worms...
Uh-huh.
Truly...
There is a God.
'Kay...
DING!
heh... Speak of the Deity...
...And he will come.
OPEN

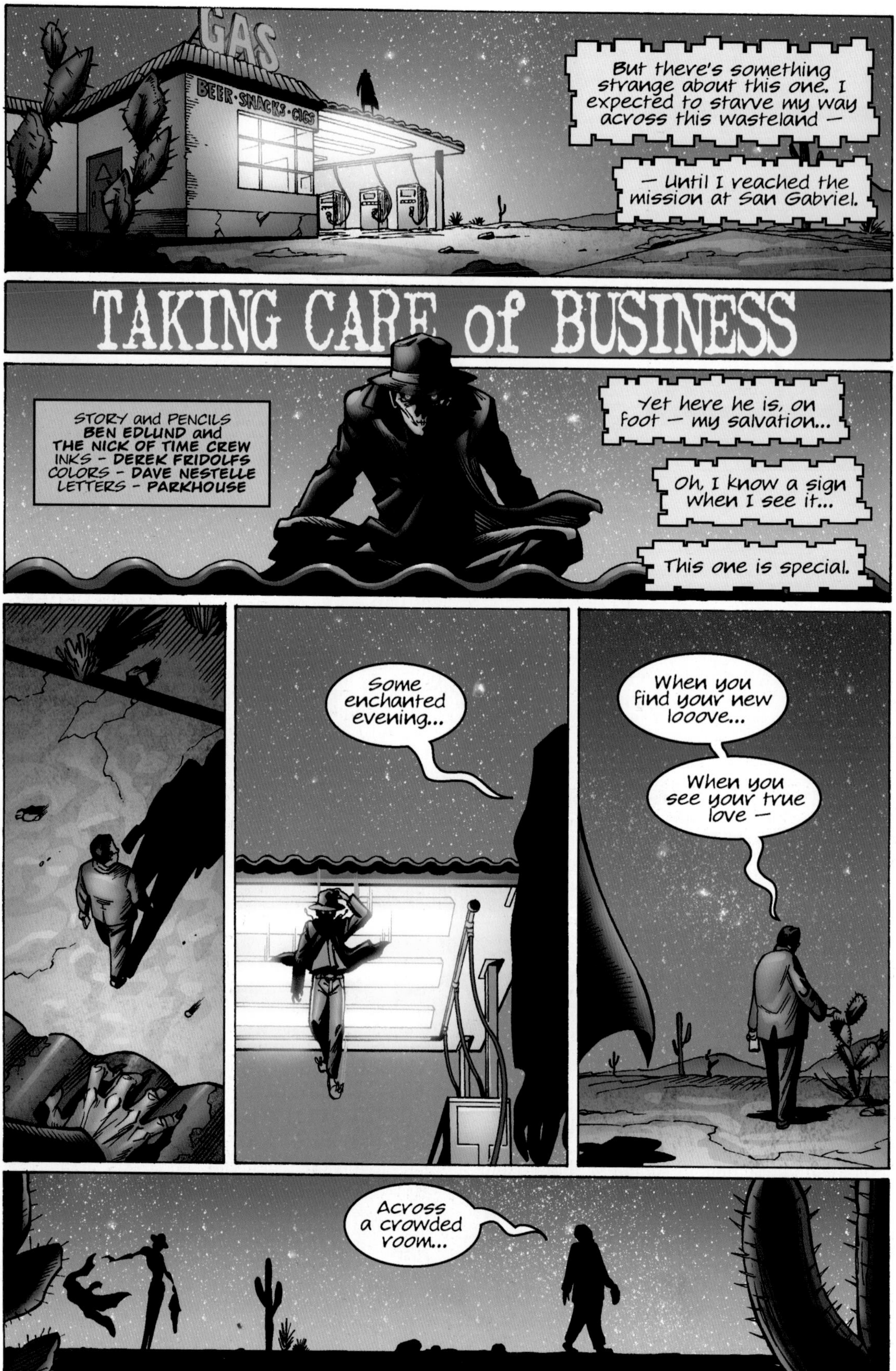
GAS
BEER · SNACKS · CIGS
But there's something strange about this one. I expected to starve my way across this wasteland —
— Until I reached the mission at San Gabriel.
TAKING CARE of BUSINESS
STORY and PENCILS BEN EDLUND and THE NICK OF TIME CREW
INKS - DEREK FRIDOLFS
COLORS - DAVE NESTELLE
LETTERS - PARKHOUSE
Yet here he is, on foot — my salvation...
Oh, I know a sign when I see it...
This one is special.
Some enchanted evening...
When you find your new looove...
When you see your true love —
Across a crowded room...

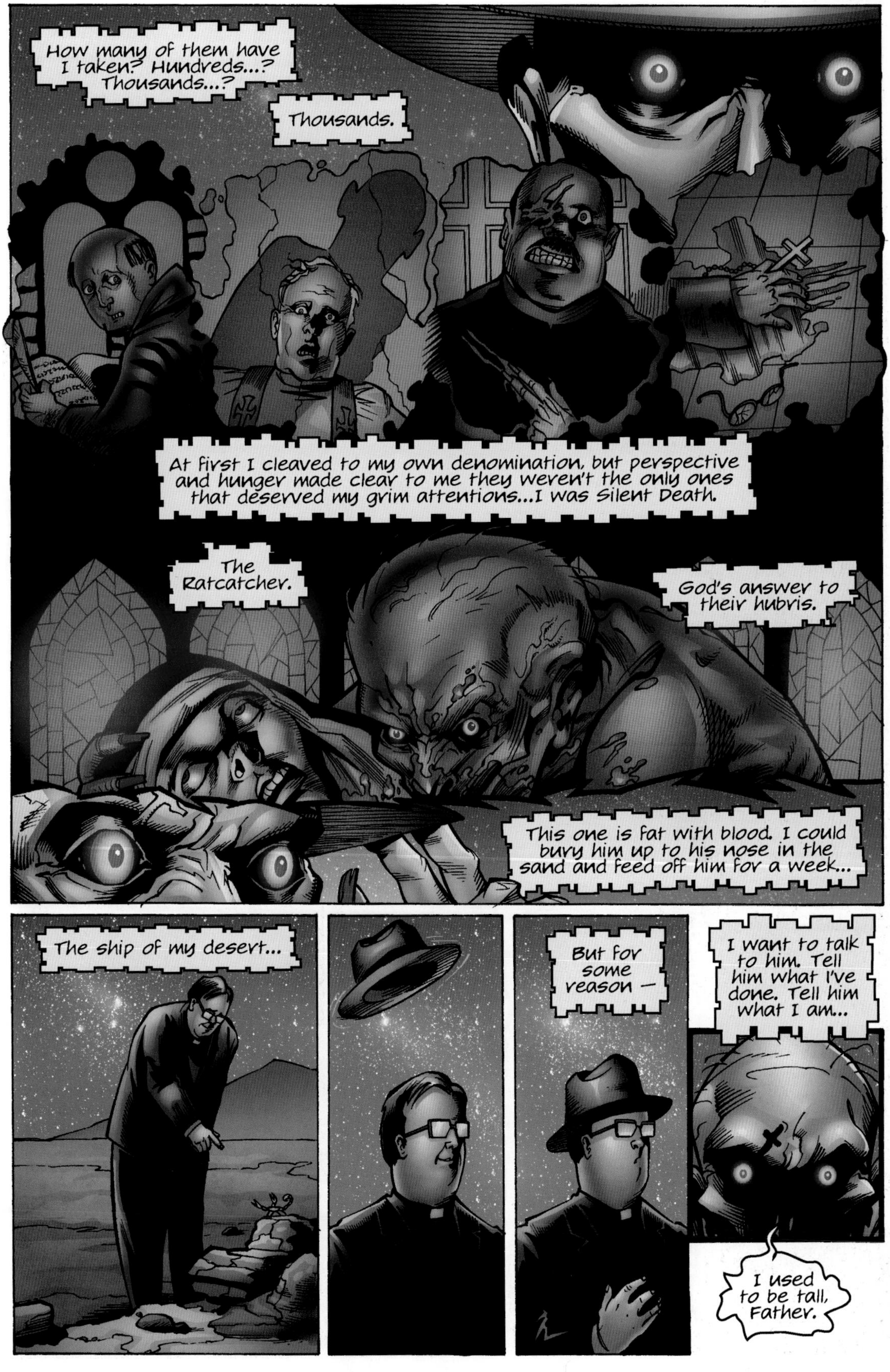
How many of them have I taken? Hundreds...? Thousands...?
Thousands.
At first I cleaved to my own denomination, but perspective and hunger made clear to me they weren't the only ones that deserved my grim attentions...I was Silent Death.
The Ratcatcher.
God's answer to their hubris.
This one is fat with blood. I could bury him up to his nose in the sand and feed off him for a week...
The ship of my desert...
But for some reason —
I want to talk to him. Tell him what I've done. Tell him what I am...
I used to be tall, Father.

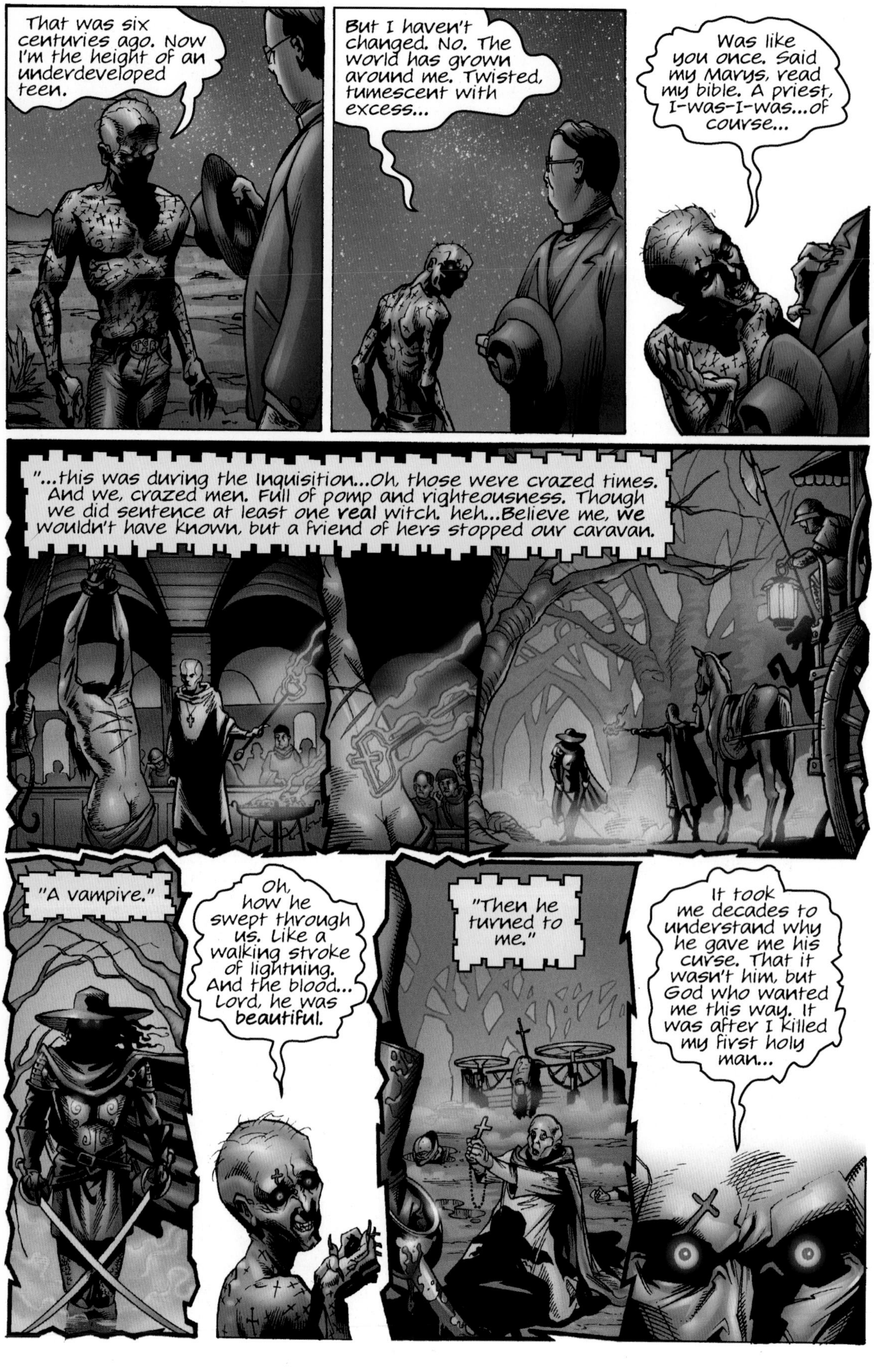
That was six centuries ago. Now I'm the height of an underdeveloped teen.
But I haven't changed. No. The world has grown around me. Twisted, tumescent with excess...
Was like you once. Said my Marys, read my bible. A priest, I-was-I-was...of course...
"...this was during the Inquisition...Oh, those were crazed times. And we, crazed men. Full of pomp and righteousness. Though we did sentence at least one real witch. heh...Believe me, we wouldn't have known, but a friend of hers stopped our caravan.
"A vampire."
Oh, how he swept through us. Like a walking stroke of lightning. And the blood... Lord, he was beautiful.
"Then he turned to me."
It took me decades to understand why he gave me his curse. That it wasn't him, but God who wanted me this way. It was after I killed my first holy man...

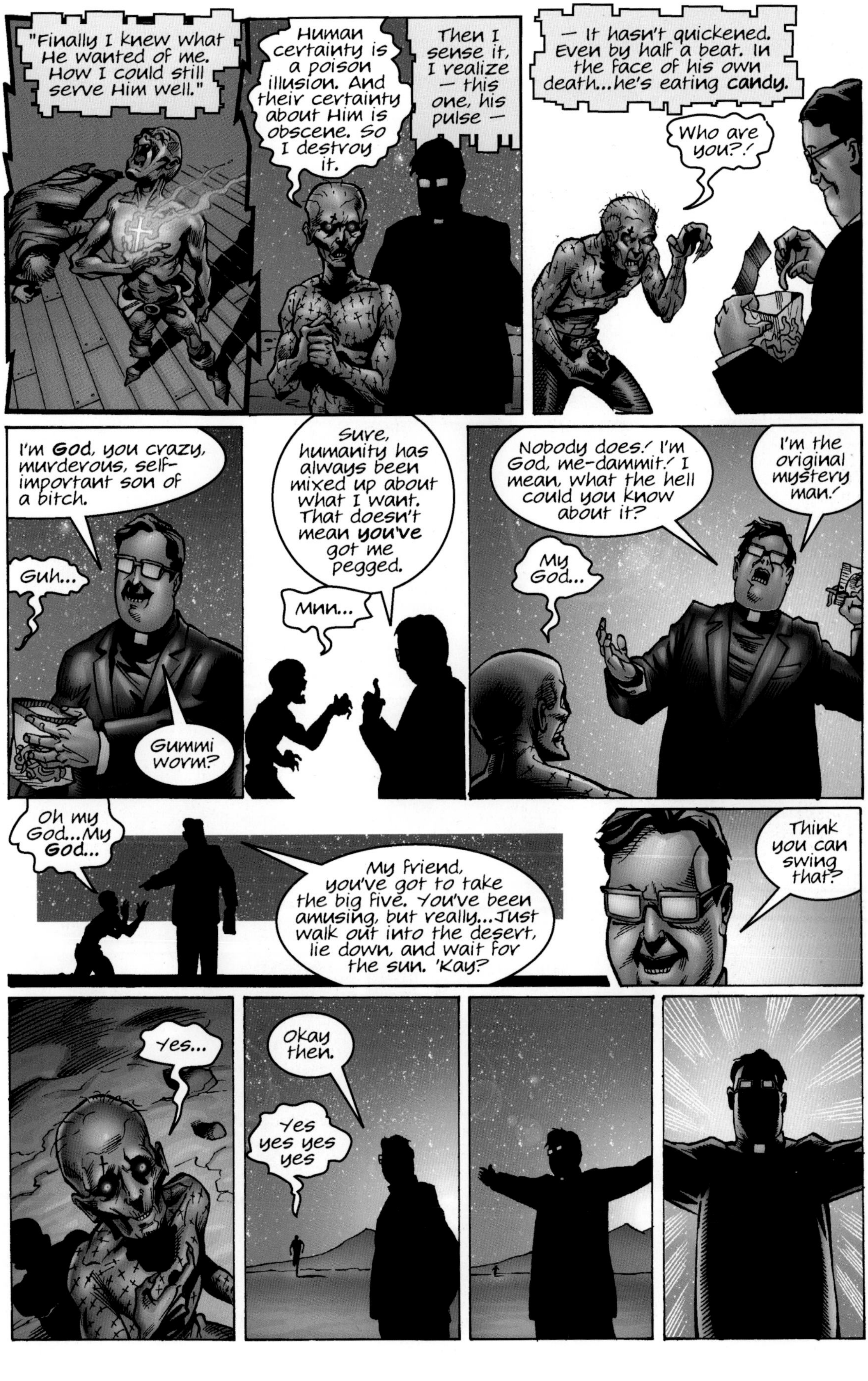

"Finally I knew what He wanted of me. How I could still serve Him well."
Human certainty is a poison illusion. And their certainty about Him is obscene. So I destroy it.
Then I sense it, I realize — this one, his pulse —
— It hasn't quickened. Even by half a beat. In the face of his own death...he's eating candy.
Who are you?!
I'm God, you crazy, murderous, self-important son of a bitch.
Guh...
Gummi worm?
Sure, humanity has always been mixed up about what I want. That doesn't mean you've got me pegged.
Mnn...
Nobody does! I'm God, me-dammit! I mean, what the hell could you know about it?
I'm the original mystery man!
My God...
Oh my God...My God...
My friend, you've got to take the big five. You've been amusing, but really...Just walk out into the desert, lie down, and wait for the sun. 'Kay?
Think you can swing that?
Yes...
Okay then.
Yes yes yes yes

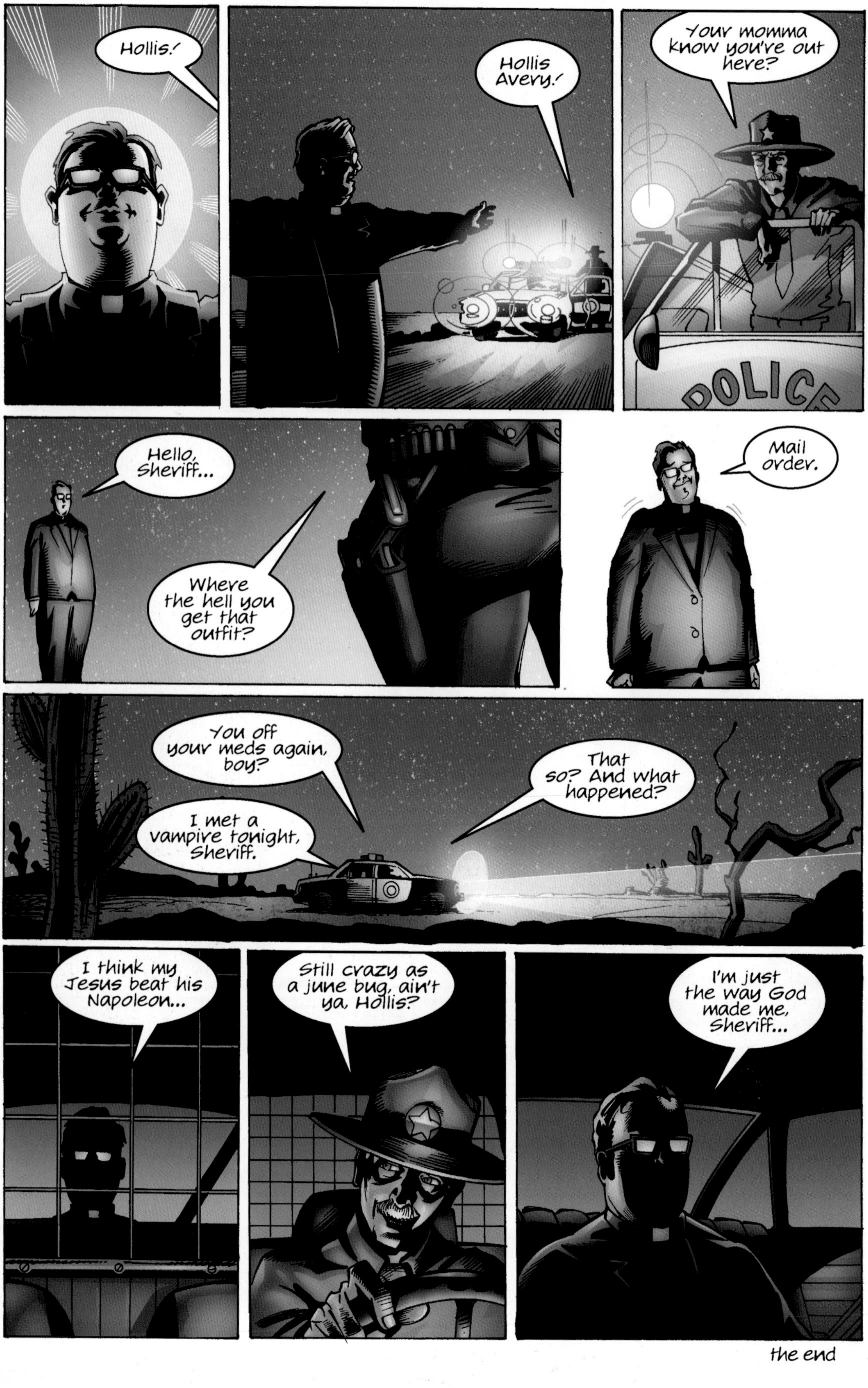
Hollis!
Hollis Avery!
Your momma know you're out here?
POLICE
Hello, Sheriff...
Where the hell you get that outfit?
Mail order.
You off your meds again, boy?
I met a vampire tonight, Sheriff.
That so? And what happened?
I think my Jesus beat his Napoleon...
Still crazy as a june bug, ain't ya, Hollis?
I'm just the way God made me, Sheriff...

the end

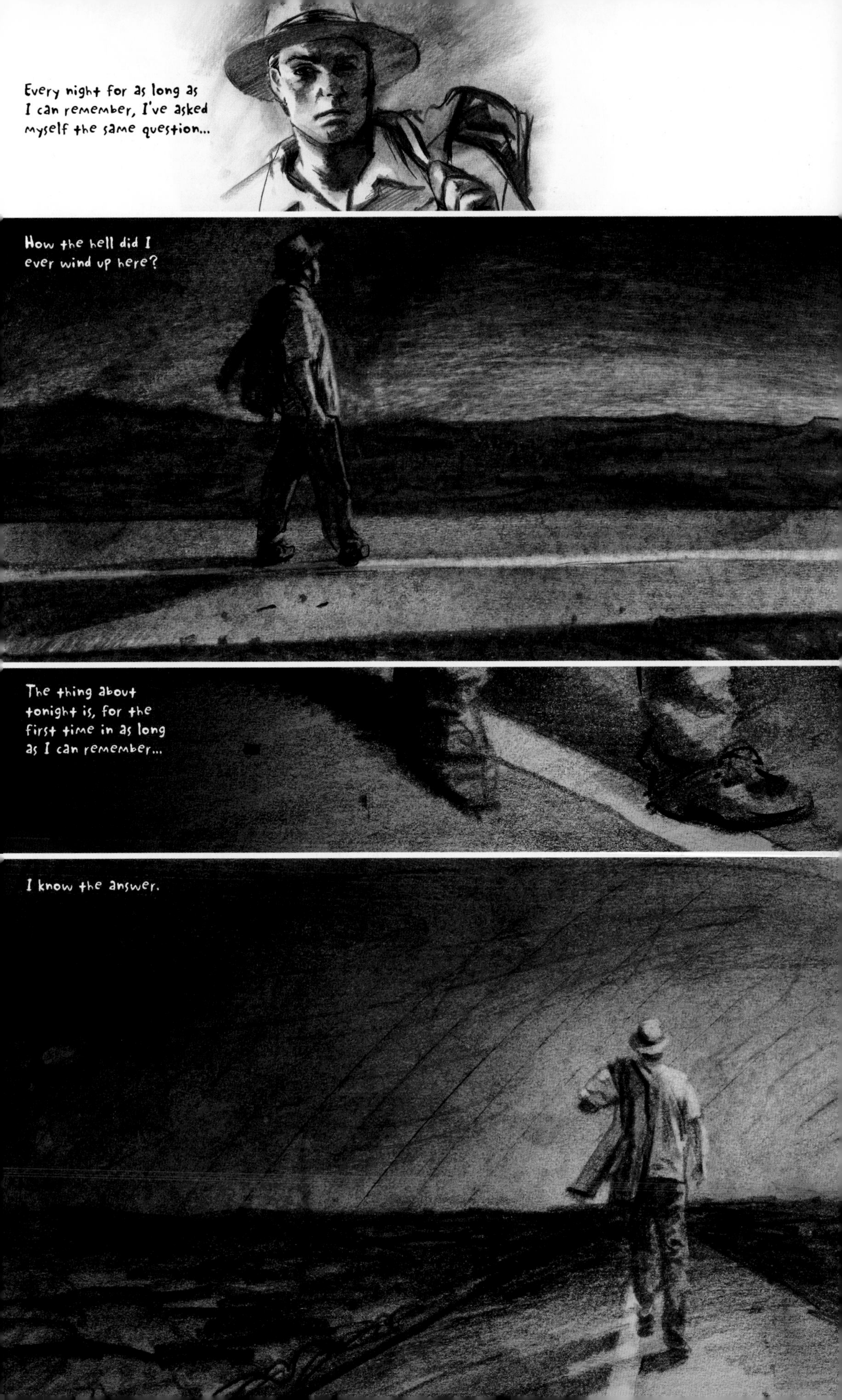
Every night for as long as I can remember, I've asked myself the same question...
How the hell did I ever wind up here?
The thing about tonight is, for the first time in as long as I can remember...
I know the answer.

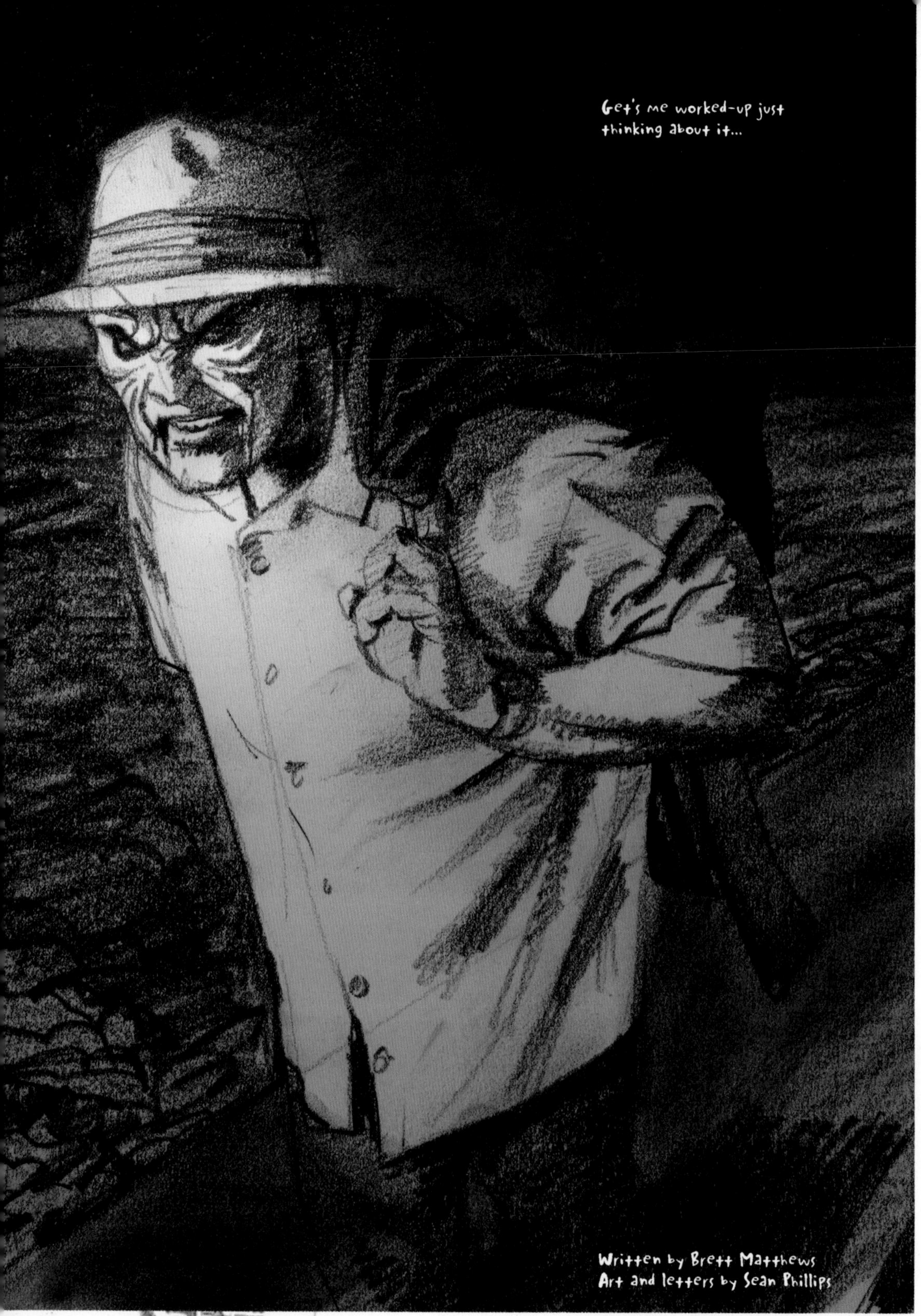
Get's me worked-up just thinking about it...
Written by Brett Matthews
Art and letters by Sean Phillips

DAMES

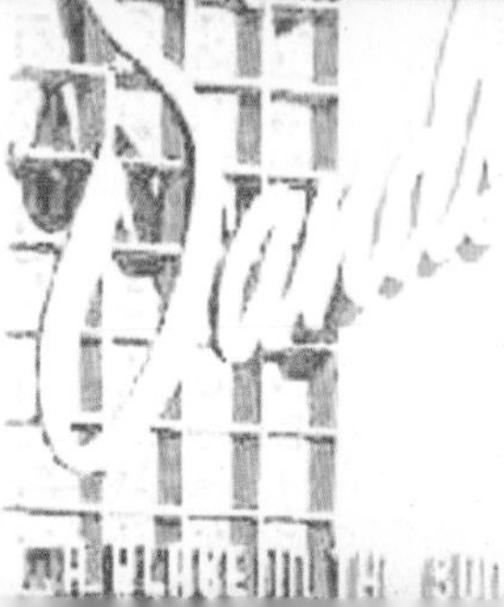
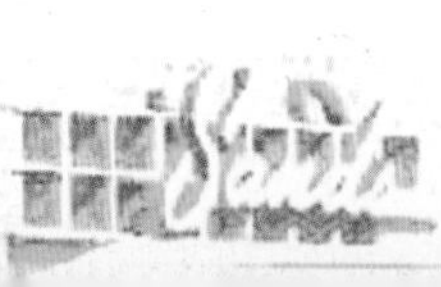

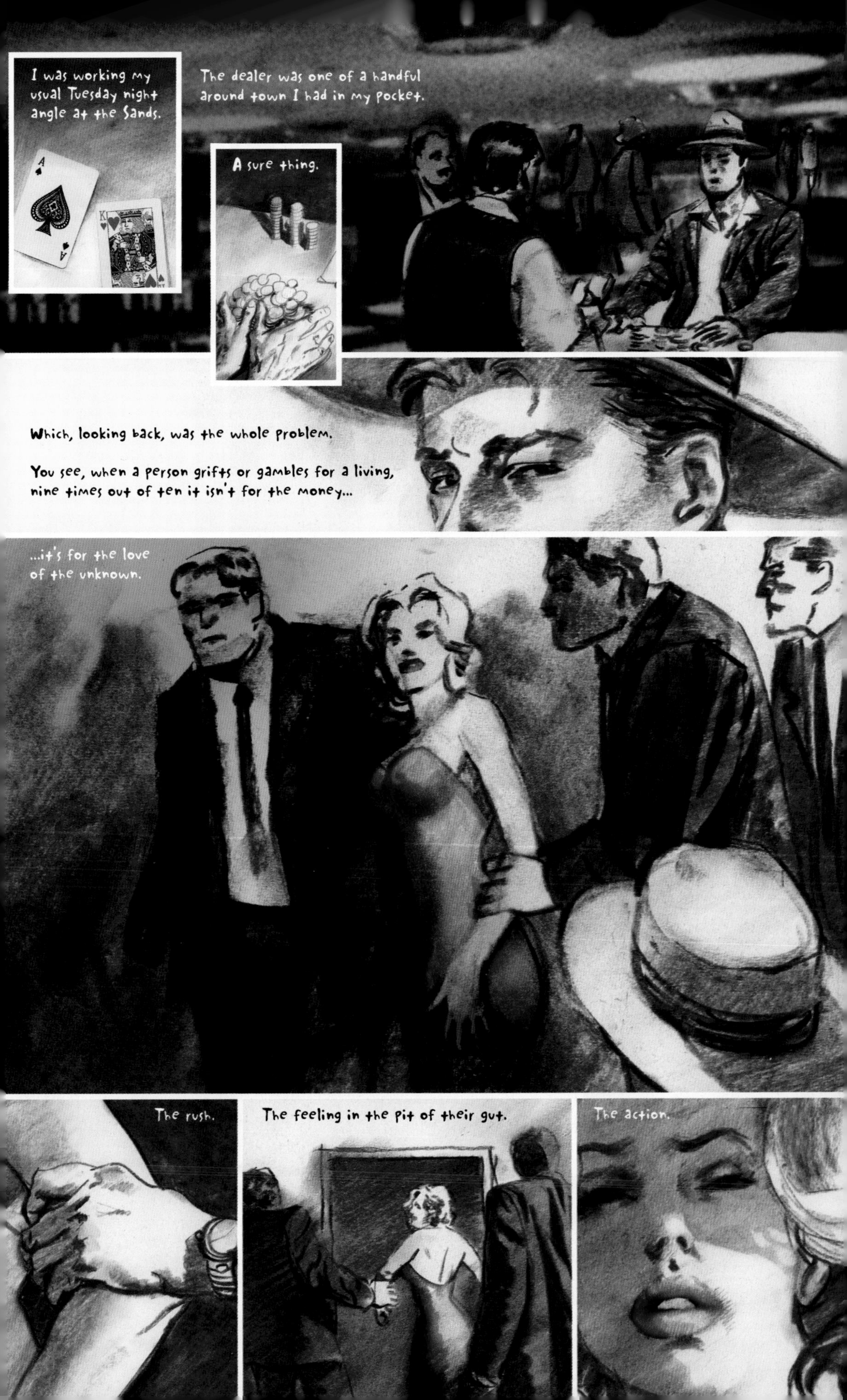
I was working my usual Tuesday night angle at the Sands.
The dealer was one of a handful around town I had in my pocket.
A sure thing.
Which, looking back, was the whole problem.
You see, when a person grifts or gambles for a living, nine times out of ten it isn't for the money...
...it's for the love of the unknown.
The rush.
The feeling in the pit of their gut.
The action.

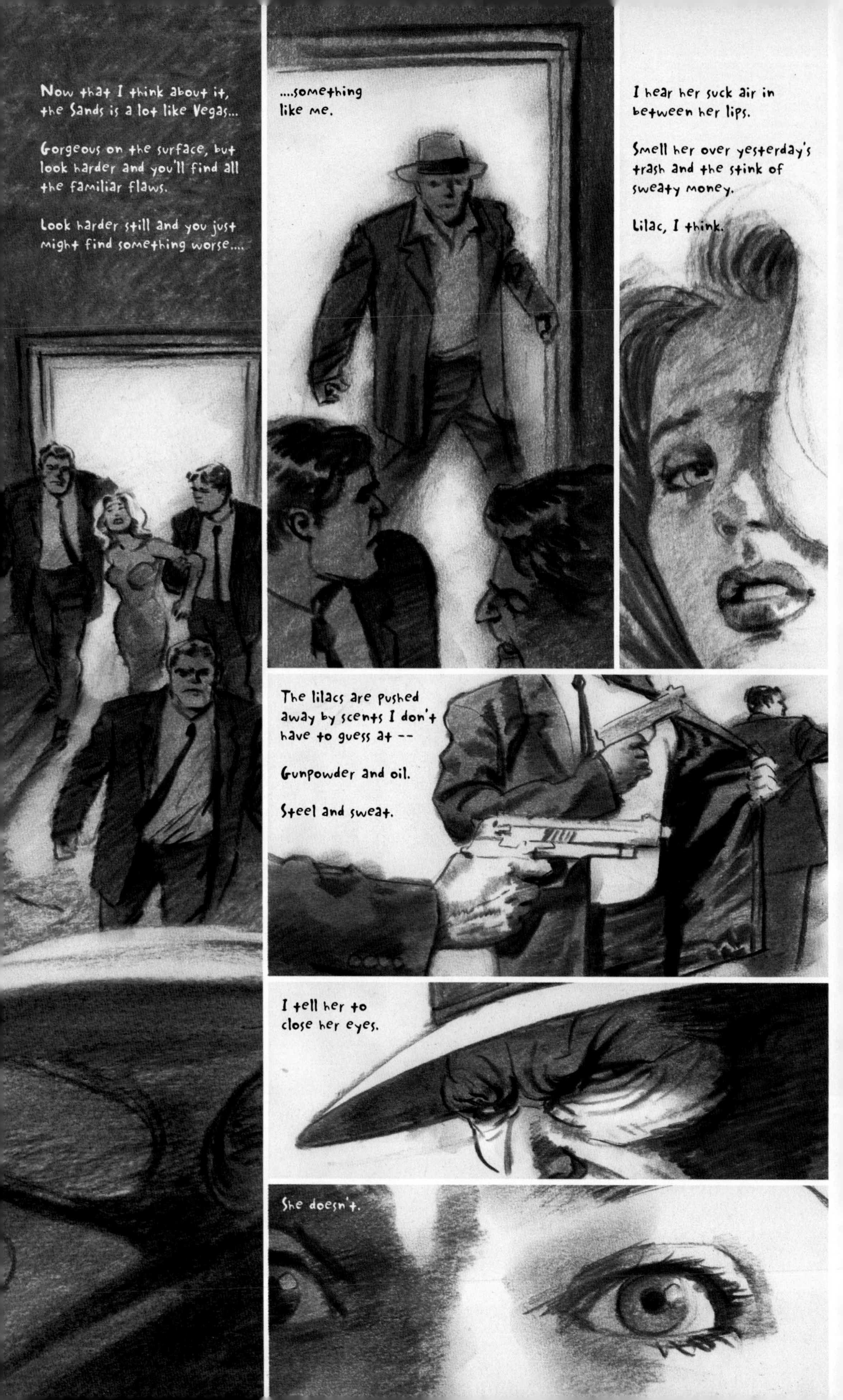

Now that I think about it, the Sands is a lot like Vegas...
Gorgeous on the surface, but look harder and you'll find all the familiar flaws.
Look harder still and you just might find something worse....
....something like me.
I hear her suck air in between her lips.
Smell her over yesterday's trash and the stink of sweaty money.
Lilac, I think.
The lilacs are pushed away by scents I don't have to guess at --
Gunpowder and oil.
Steel and sweat.
I tell her to close her eyes.
She doesn't.

It's over quick.

I wait for it.

For her to scream bloody murder.

To vomit.

To run.

It's then that something very rare happens --

I get surprised.

She doesn't move. Or puke. Or scream.

Just says one word...

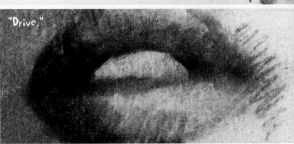

"Drive."

I do.

She tells me to take her someplace special.

I know just the place...

When we get to the spot, she asks me if I've ever brought anyone here before...

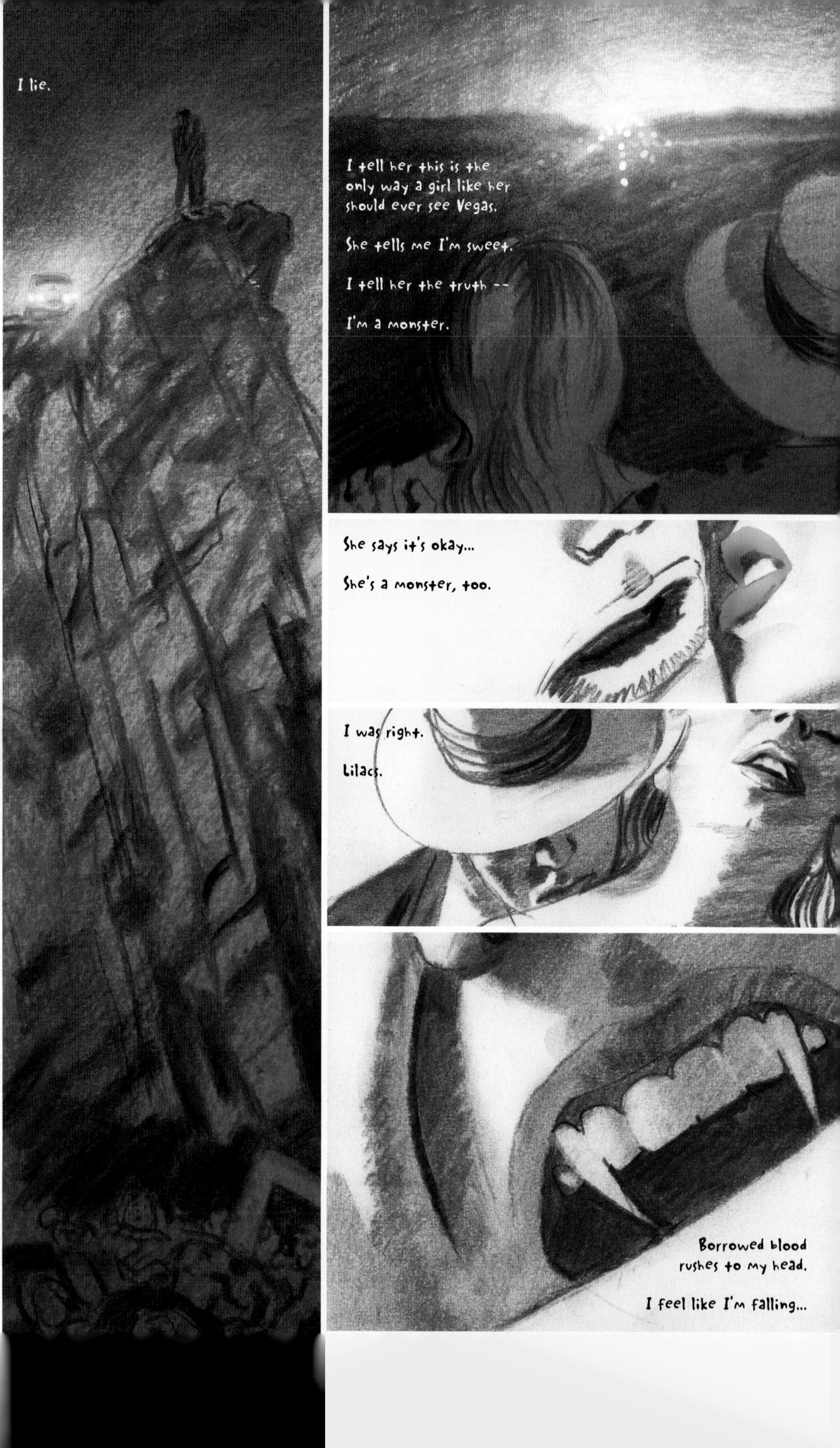
I lie.
I tell her this is the only way a girl like her should ever see Vegas.
She tells me I'm sweet.
I tell her the truth --
I'm a monster.
She says it's okay...
She's a monster, too.
I was right.
Lilacs.
Borrowed blood rushes to my head.
I feel like I'm falling...

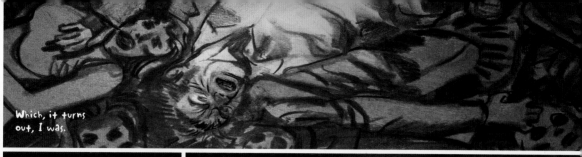

Which, it turns
out, I was.

Don't know how long
I was out for...

Reason being she boosted my
watch along with my wallet,
from what she must have
thought was my dead corpse --

She was half right.

Looking back, I see those suits
at the Sands must've had a
legitimate bone to pick with
the girl --

I'm not the first guy she's ever
brought here, either...

Which brings us to here.

Nowhere.

Seems as good
a place as any.

She must not smoke.

Can't say I'd of put money
on it ending like this.

But then again...

...I never thought I'd meet
a monster smelled like lilacs.

Dames.

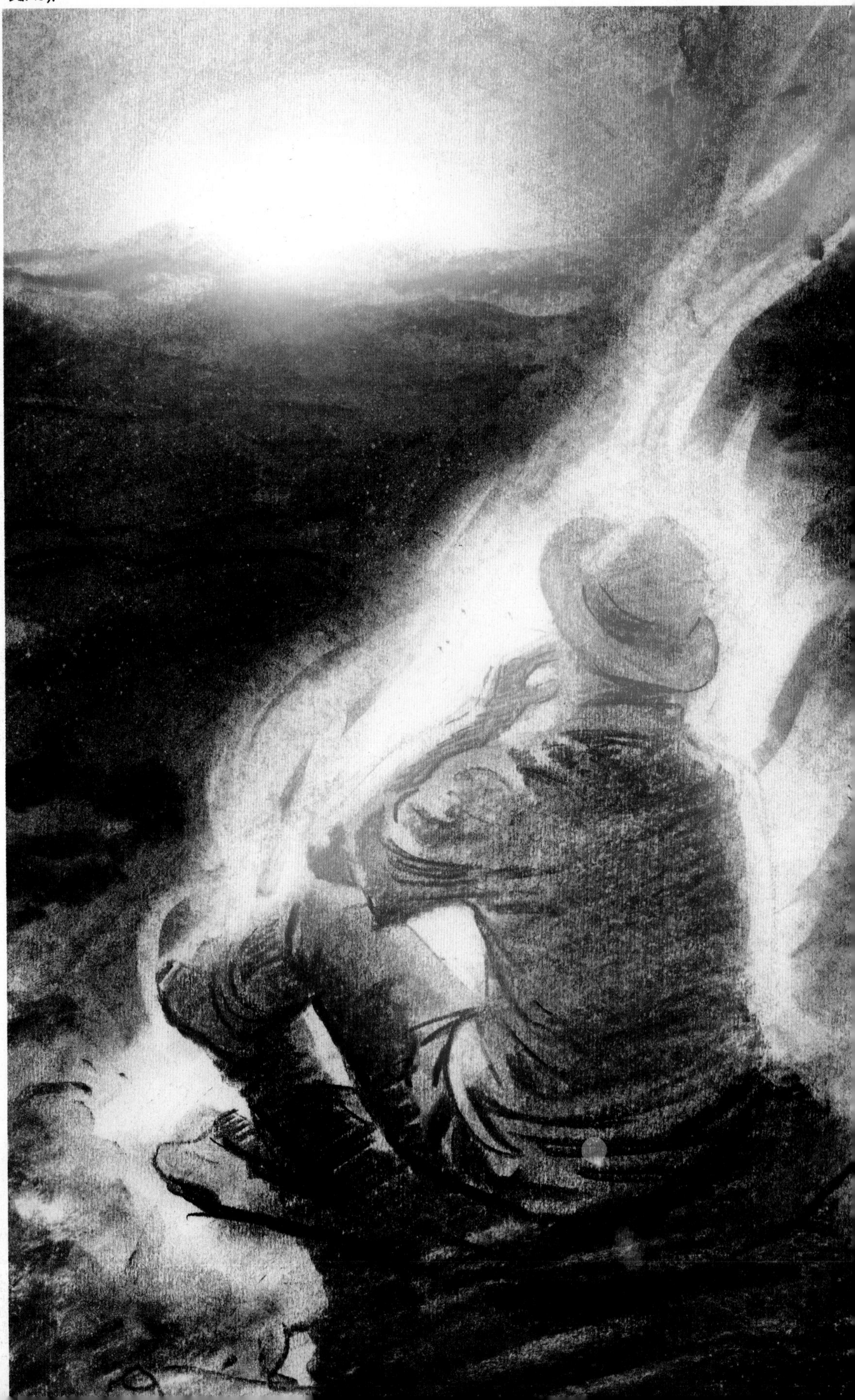

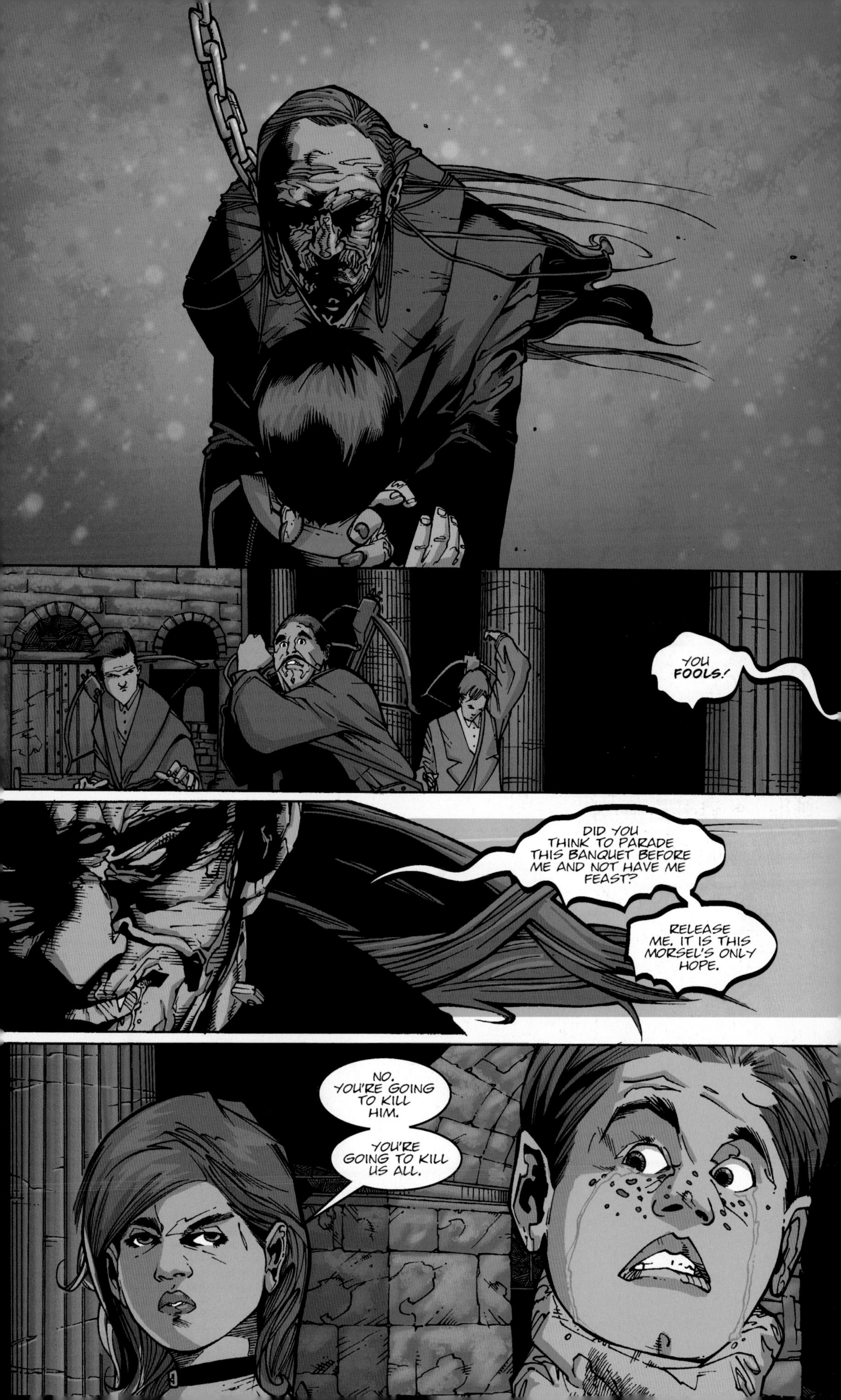
YOU FOOLS!
DID YOU THINK TO PARADE THIS BANQUET BEFORE ME AND NOT HAVE ME FEAST?
RELEASE ME. IT IS THIS MORSEL'S ONLY HOPE.
NO. YOU'RE GOING TO KILL HIM.
YOU'RE GOING TO KILL US ALL.

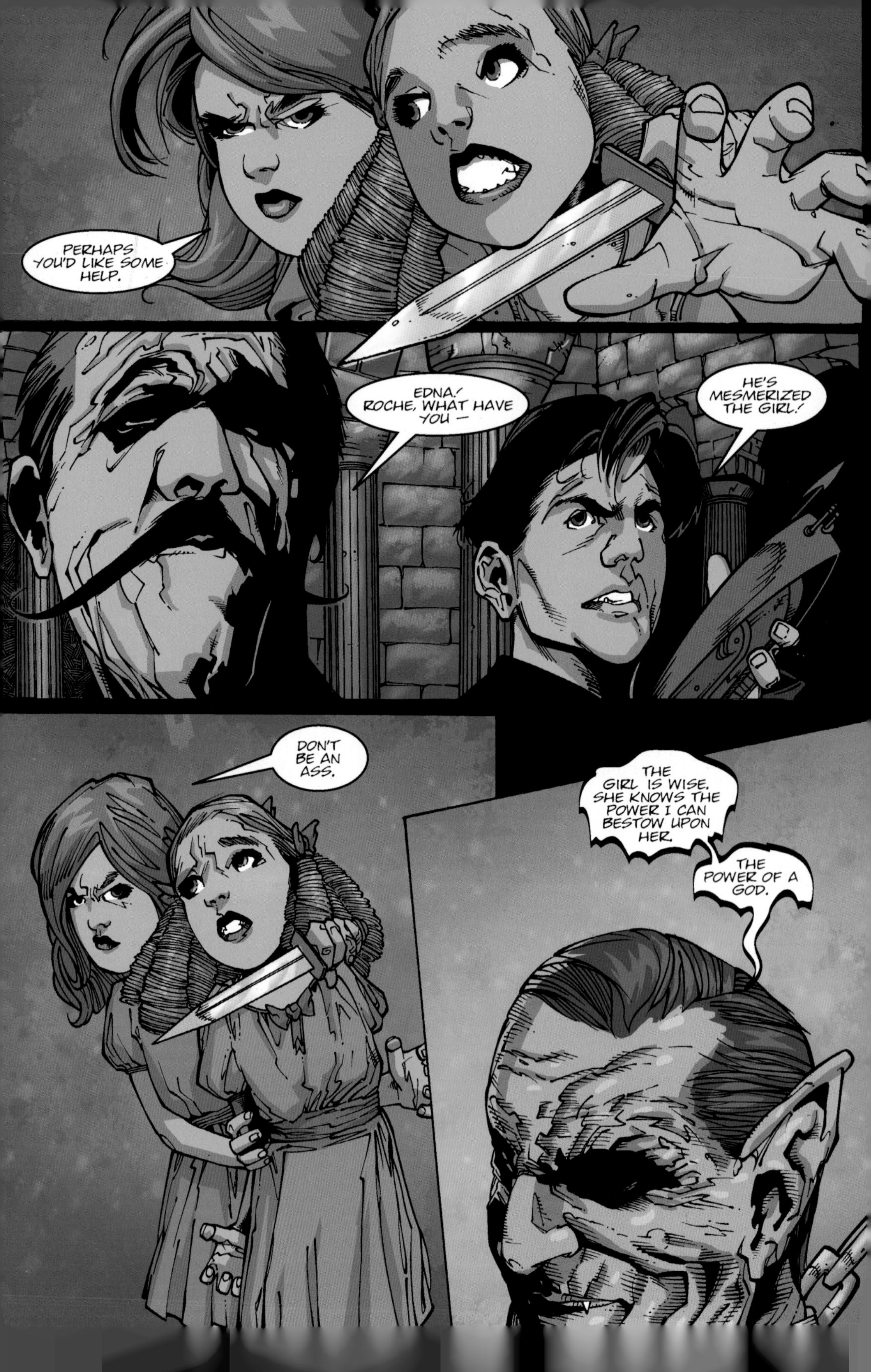
PERHAPS YOU'D LIKE SOME HELP.
EDNA! ROCHE, WHAT HAVE YOU —
HE'S MESMERIZED THE GIRL!
DON'T BE AN ASS.
THE GIRL IS WISE. SHE KNOWS THE POWER I CAN BESTOW UPON HER.
THE POWER OF A GOD.

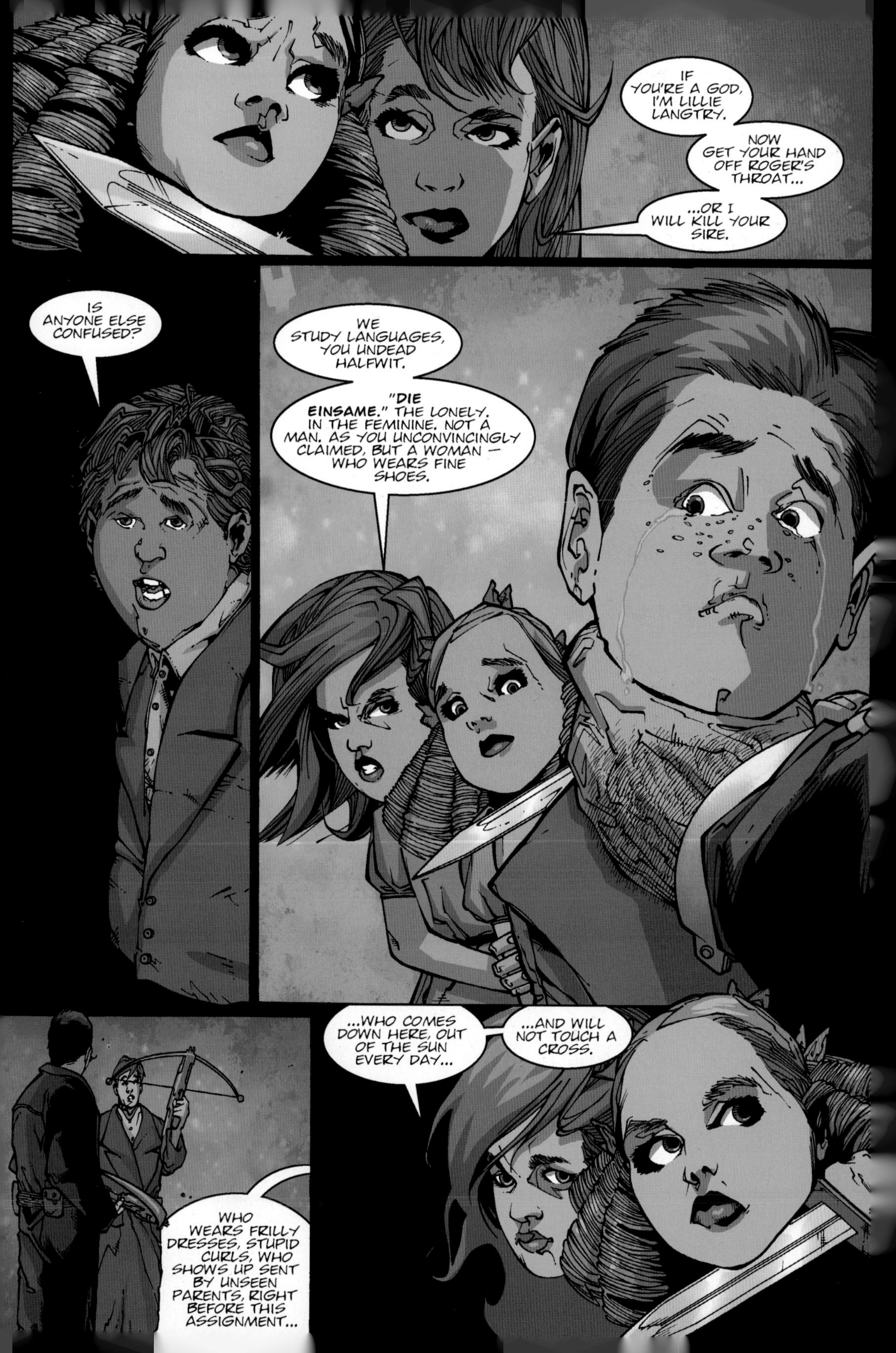
IF YOU'RE A GOD, I'M LILLIE LANGTRY.
NOW GET YOUR HAND OFF ROGER'S THROAT...
...OR I WILL KILL YOUR SIRE.
IS ANYONE ELSE CONFUSED?
WE STUDY LANGUAGES, YOU UNDEAD HALFWIT.
"DIE EINSAME." THE LONELY. IN THE FEMININE. NOT A MAN. AS YOU UNCONVINCINGLY CLAIMED, BUT A WOMAN -- WHO WEARS FINE SHOES.
WHO WEARS FRILLY DRESSES, STUPID CURLS, WHO SHOWS UP SENT BY UNSEEN PARENTS, RIGHT BEFORE THIS ASSIGNMENT...
...WHO COMES DOWN HERE, OUT OF THE SUN EVERY DAY...
...AND WILL NOT TOUCH A CROSS.

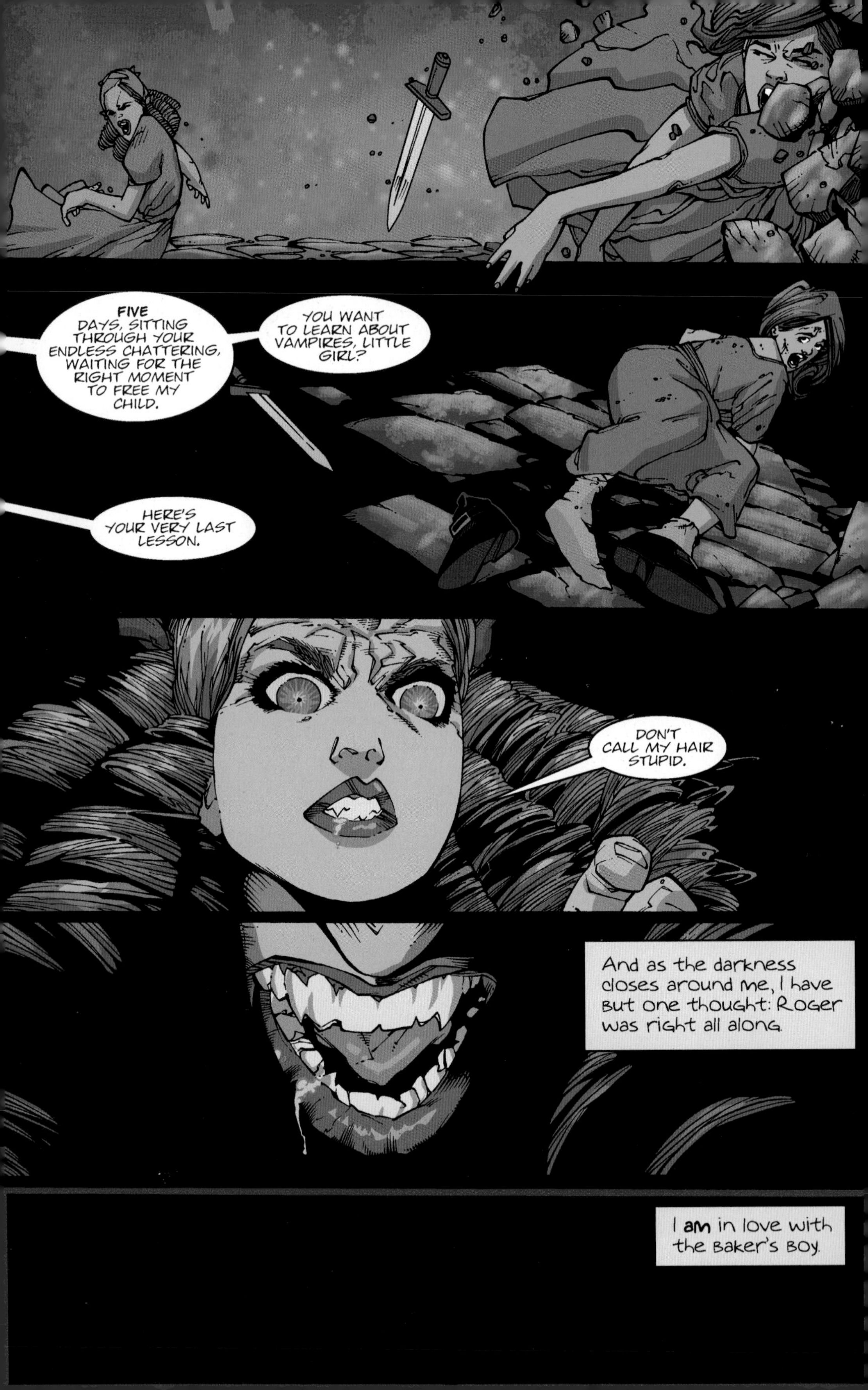

FIVE DAYS, SITTING THROUGH YOUR ENDLESS CHATTERING, WAITING FOR THE RIGHT MOMENT TO FREE MY CHILD.
YOU WANT TO LEARN ABOUT VAMPIRES, LITTLE GIRL?
HERE'S YOUR VERY LAST LESSON.
DON'T CALL MY HAIR STUPID.
And as the darkness closes around me, I have but one thought: Roger was right all along.
I **am** in love with the Baker's Boy.

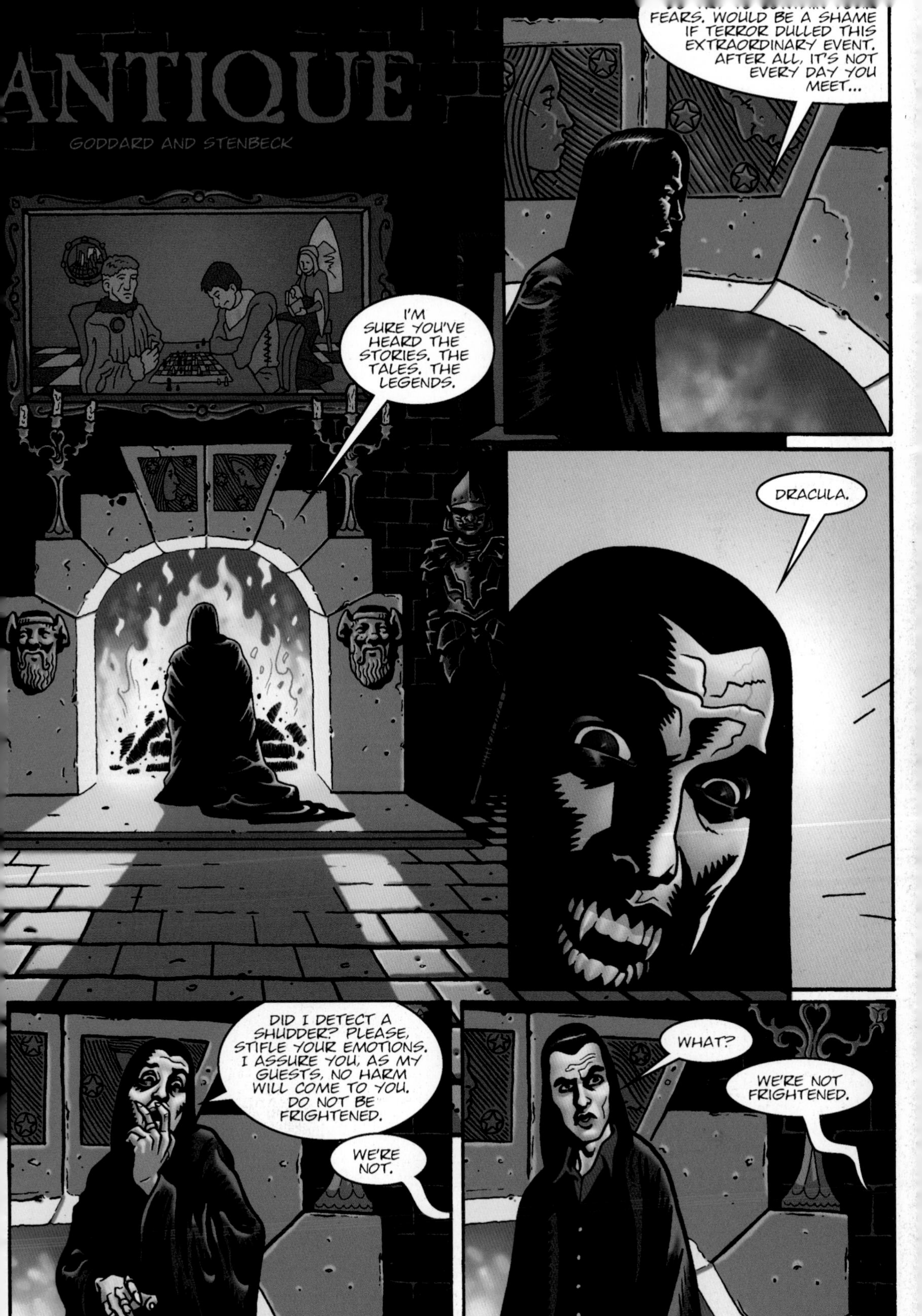

ANTIQUE
GODDARD AND STENBECK
I'M SURE YOU'VE HEARD THE STORIES. THE TALES. THE LEGENDS.
FEARS. WOULD BE A SHAME IF TERROR DULLED THIS EXTRAORDINARY EVENT. AFTER ALL, IT'S NOT EVERY DAY YOU MEET...
DRACULA.
DID I DETECT A SHUDDER? PLEASE, STIFLE YOUR EMOTIONS. I ASSURE YOU, AS MY GUESTS, NO HARM WILL COME TO YOU. DO NOT BE FRIGHTENED.
WE'RE NOT.
WHAT?
WE'RE NOT FRIGHTENED.

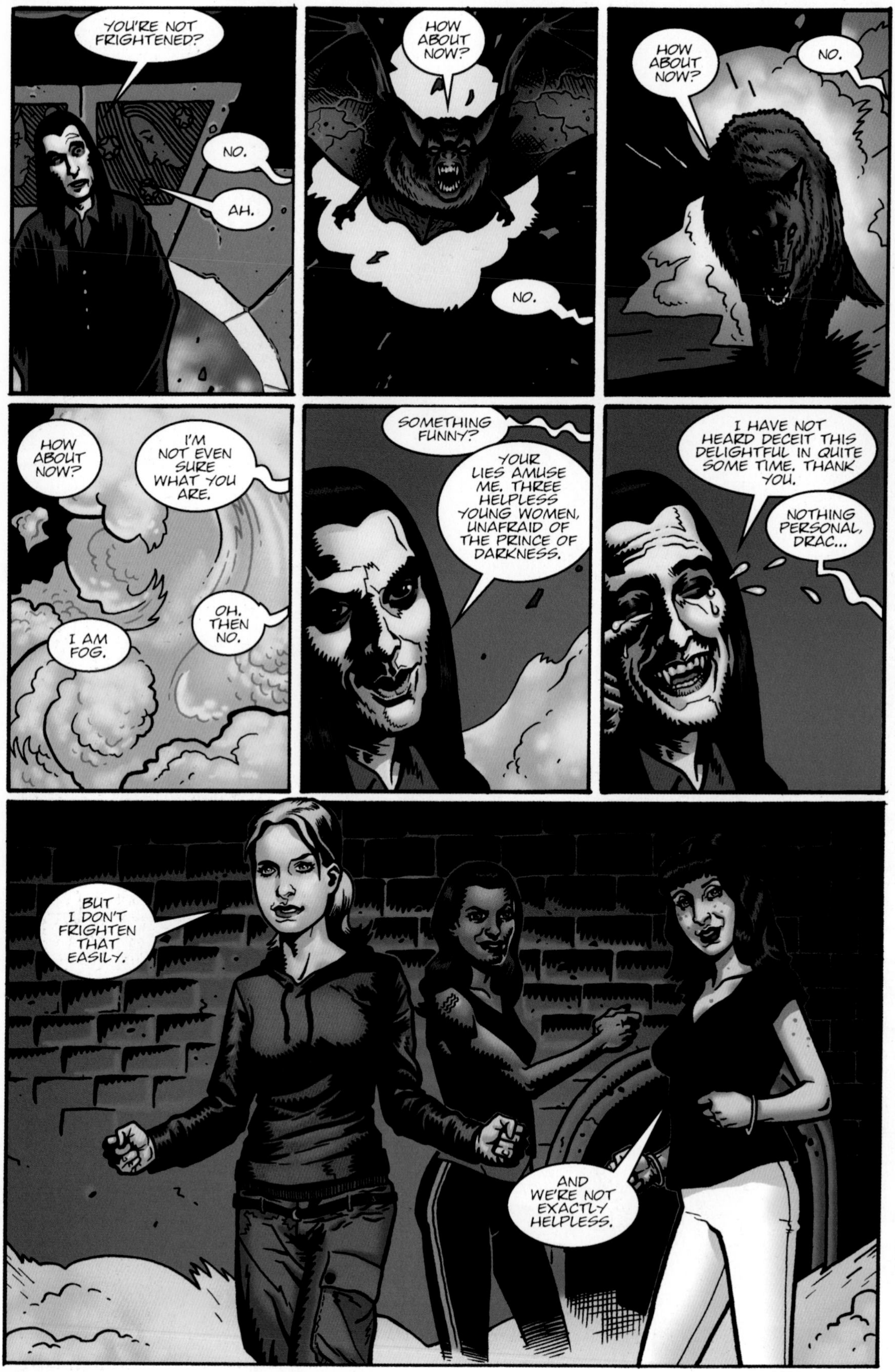
YOU'RE NOT FRIGHTENED?
NO.
AH.
HOW ABOUT NOW?
NO.
HOW ABOUT NOW?
NO.
HOW ABOUT NOW?
I'M NOT EVEN SURE WHAT YOU ARE.
I AM FOG.
OH. THEN NO.
SOMETHING FUNNY?
YOUR LIES AMUSE ME. THREE HELPLESS YOUNG WOMEN, UNAFRAID OF THE PRINCE OF DARKNESS.
I HAVE NOT HEARD DECEIT THIS DELIGHTFUL IN QUITE SOME TIME. THANK YOU.
NOTHING PERSONAL, DRAC...
BUT I DON'T FRIGHTEN THAT EASILY.
AND WE'RE NOT EXACTLY HELPLESS.

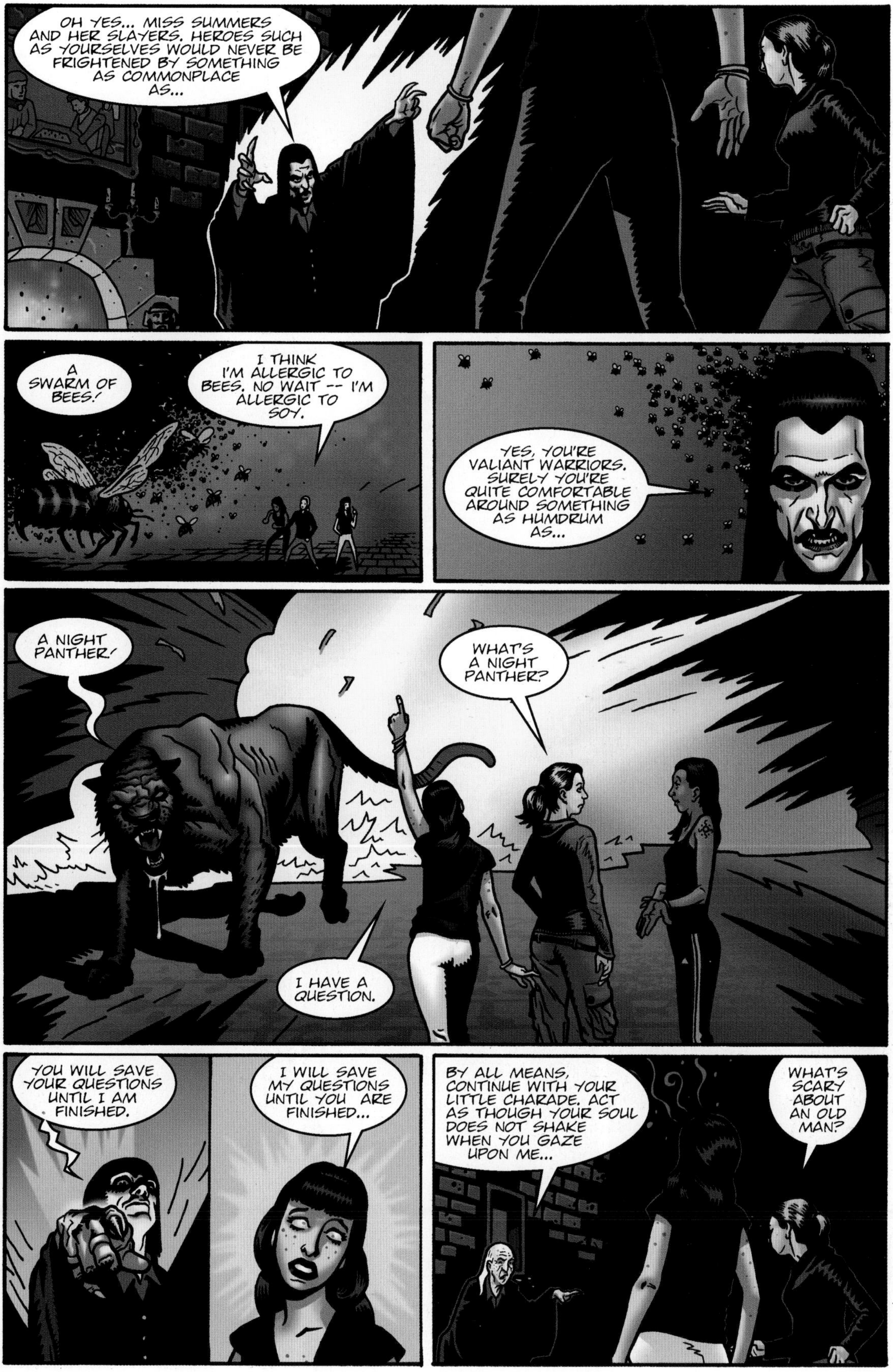
OH YES... MISS SUMMERS AND HER SLAYERS. HEROES SUCH AS YOURSELVES WOULD NEVER BE FRIGHTENED BY SOMETHING AS COMMONPLACE AS...
A SWARM OF BEES!
I THINK I'M ALLERGIC TO BEES. NO WAIT -- I'M ALLERGIC TO SOY.
YES, YOU'RE VALIANT WARRIORS. SURELY YOU'RE QUITE COMFORTABLE AROUND SOMETHING AS HUMDRUM AS...
A NIGHT PANTHER!
WHAT'S A NIGHT PANTHER?
I HAVE A QUESTION.
YOU WILL SAVE YOUR QUESTIONS UNTIL I AM FINISHED.
I WILL SAVE MY QUESTIONS UNTIL YOU ARE FINISHED...
BY ALL MEANS, CONTINUE WITH YOUR LITTLE CHARADE. ACT AS THOUGH YOUR SOUL DOES NOT SHAKE WHEN YOU GAZE UPON ME...
WHAT'S SCARY ABOUT AN OLD MAN?

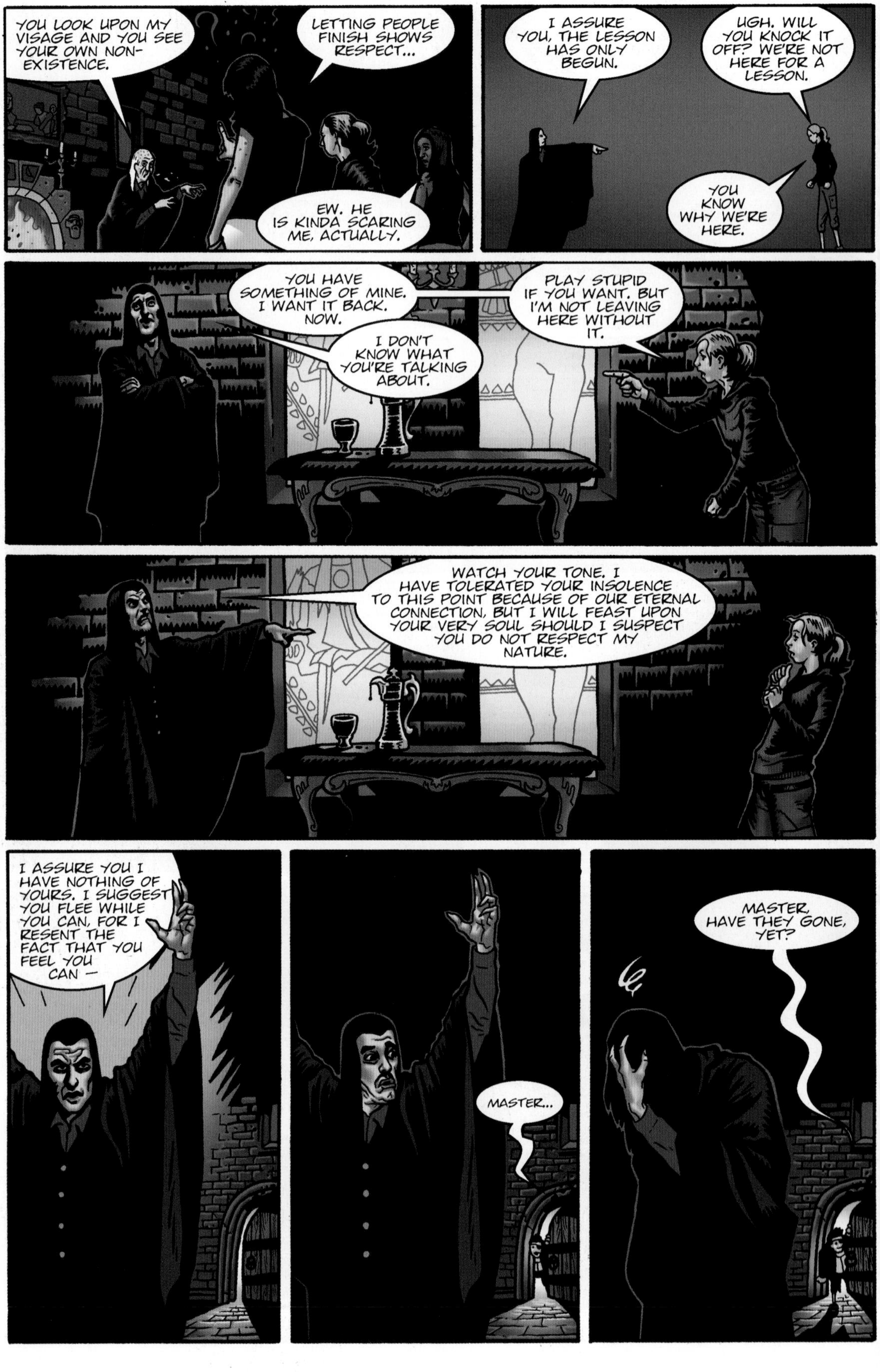
YOU LOOK UPON MY VISAGE AND YOU SEE YOUR OWN NON-EXISTENCE.
LETTING PEOPLE FINISH SHOWS RESPECT...
EW. HE IS KINDA SCARING ME, ACTUALLY.
I ASSURE YOU, THE LESSON HAS ONLY BEGUN.
UGH. WILL YOU KNOCK IT OFF? WE'RE NOT HERE FOR A LESSON.
YOU KNOW WHY WE'RE HERE.
YOU HAVE SOMETHING OF MINE. I WANT IT BACK. NOW.
I DON'T KNOW WHAT YOU'RE TALKING ABOUT.
PLAY STUPID IF YOU WANT. BUT I'M NOT LEAVING HERE WITHOUT IT.
WATCH YOUR TONE. I HAVE TOLERATED YOUR INSOLENCE TO THIS POINT BECAUSE OF OUR ETERNAL CONNECTION, BUT I WILL FEAST UPON YOUR VERY SOUL SHOULD I SUSPECT YOU DO NOT RESPECT MY NATURE.
I ASSURE YOU I HAVE NOTHING OF YOURS. I SUGGEST YOU FLEE WHILE YOU CAN, FOR I RESENT THE FACT THAT YOU FEEL YOU CAN —
MASTER...
MASTER, HAVE THEY GONE, YET?

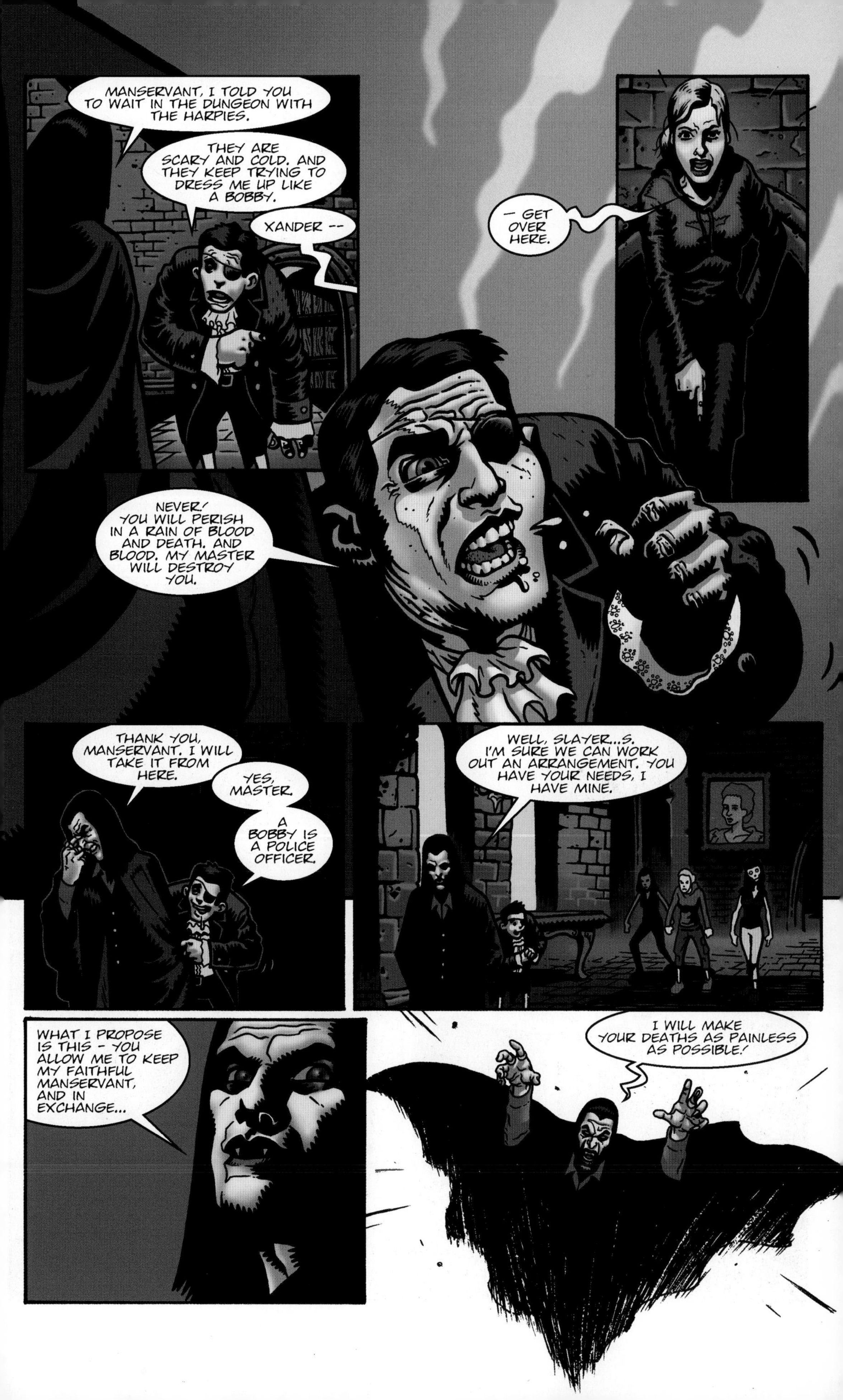
MANSERVANT, I TOLD YOU TO WAIT IN THE DUNGEON WITH THE HARPIES.
THEY ARE SCARY AND COLD. AND THEY KEEP TRYING TO DRESS ME UP LIKE A BOBBY.
XANDER --
— GET OVER HERE.
NEVER! YOU WILL PERISH IN A RAIN OF BLOOD AND DEATH. AND BLOOD. MY MASTER WILL DESTROY YOU.
THANK YOU, MANSERVANT. I WILL TAKE IT FROM HERE.
YES, MASTER.
A BOBBY IS A POLICE OFFICER.
WELL, SLAYER...S. I'M SURE WE CAN WORK OUT AN ARRANGEMENT. YOU HAVE YOUR NEEDS, I HAVE MINE.
WHAT I PROPOSE IS THIS - YOU ALLOW ME TO KEEP MY FAITHFUL MANSERVANT, AND IN EXCHANGE...
I WILL MAKE YOUR DEATHS AS PAINLESS AS POSSIBLE!

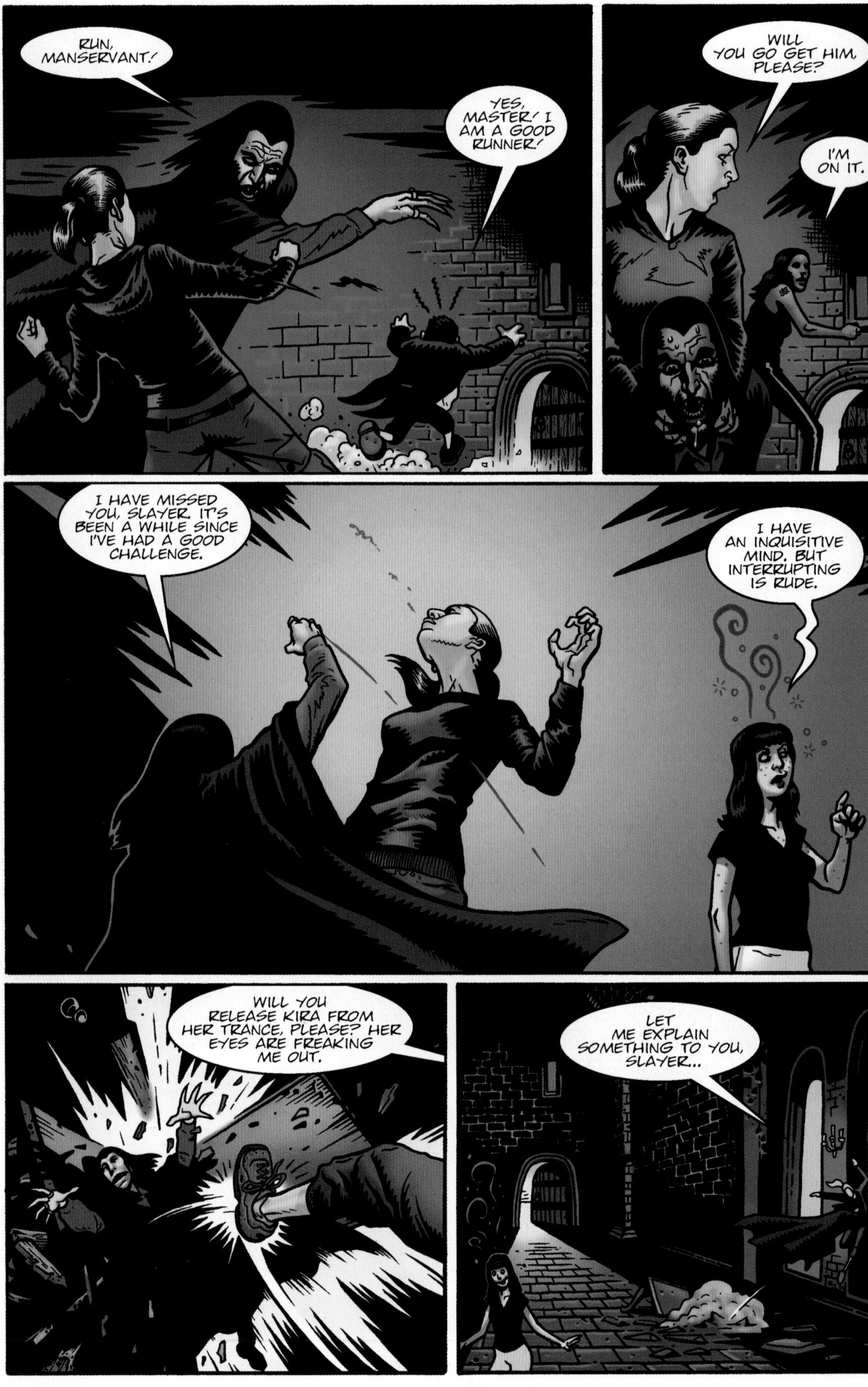
RUN, MANSERVANT!
YES, MASTER! I AM A GOOD RUNNER!
WILL YOU GO GET HIM, PLEASE?
I'M ON IT.
I HAVE MISSED YOU, SLAYER. IT'S BEEN A WHILE SINCE I'VE HAD A GOOD CHALLENGE.
I HAVE AN INQUISITIVE MIND. BUT INTERRUPTING IS RUDE.
WILL YOU RELEASE KIRA FROM HER TRANCE, PLEASE? HER EYES ARE FREAKING ME OUT.
LET ME EXPLAIN SOMETHING TO YOU, SLAYER...

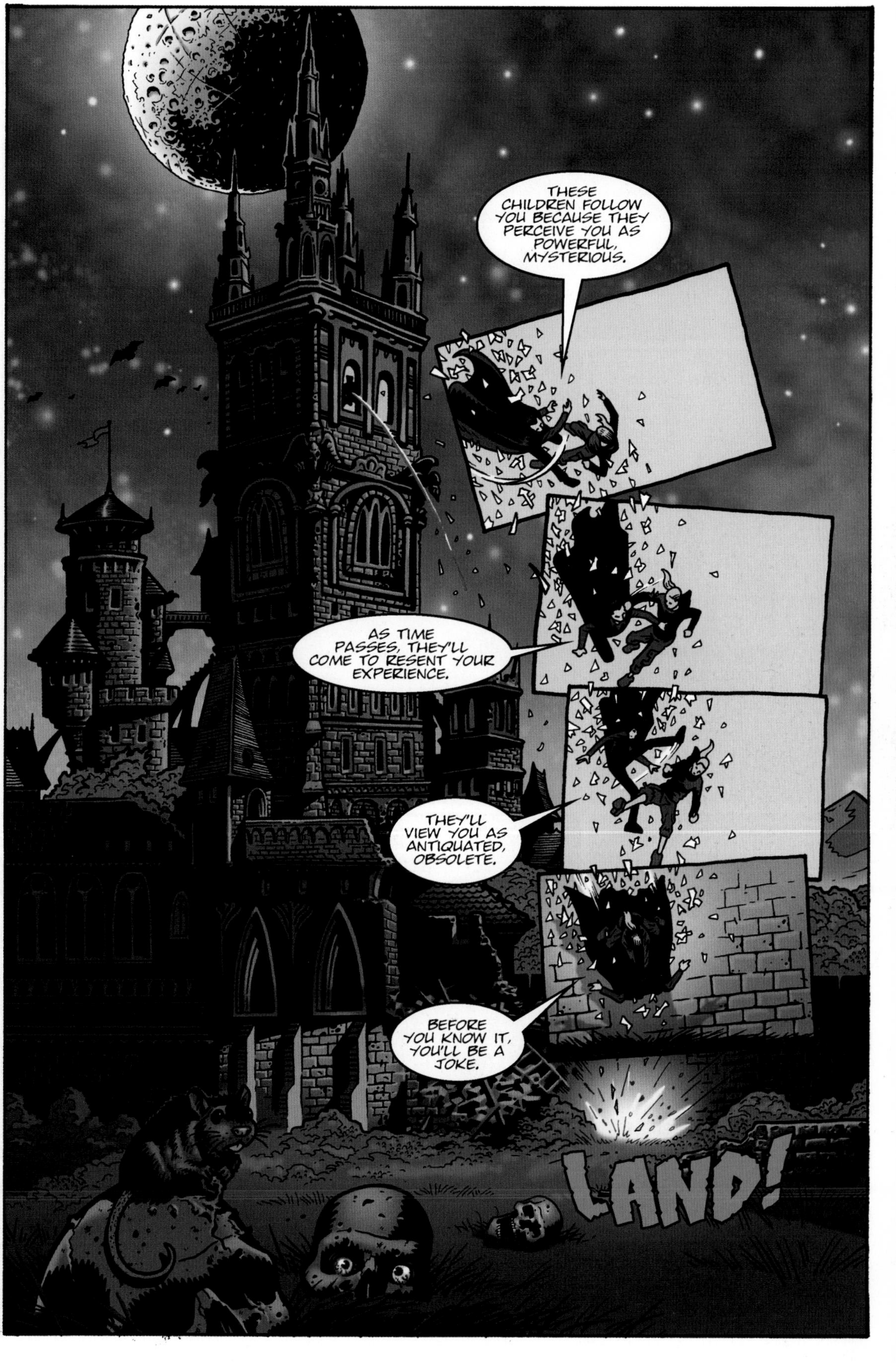
THESE CHILDREN FOLLOW YOU BECAUSE THEY PERCEIVE YOU AS POWERFUL, MYSTERIOUS.
AS TIME PASSES, THEY'LL COME TO RESENT YOUR EXPERIENCE.
THEY'LL VIEW YOU AS ANTIQUATED, OBSOLETE.
BEFORE YOU KNOW IT, YOU'LL BE A JOKE.
LAND!

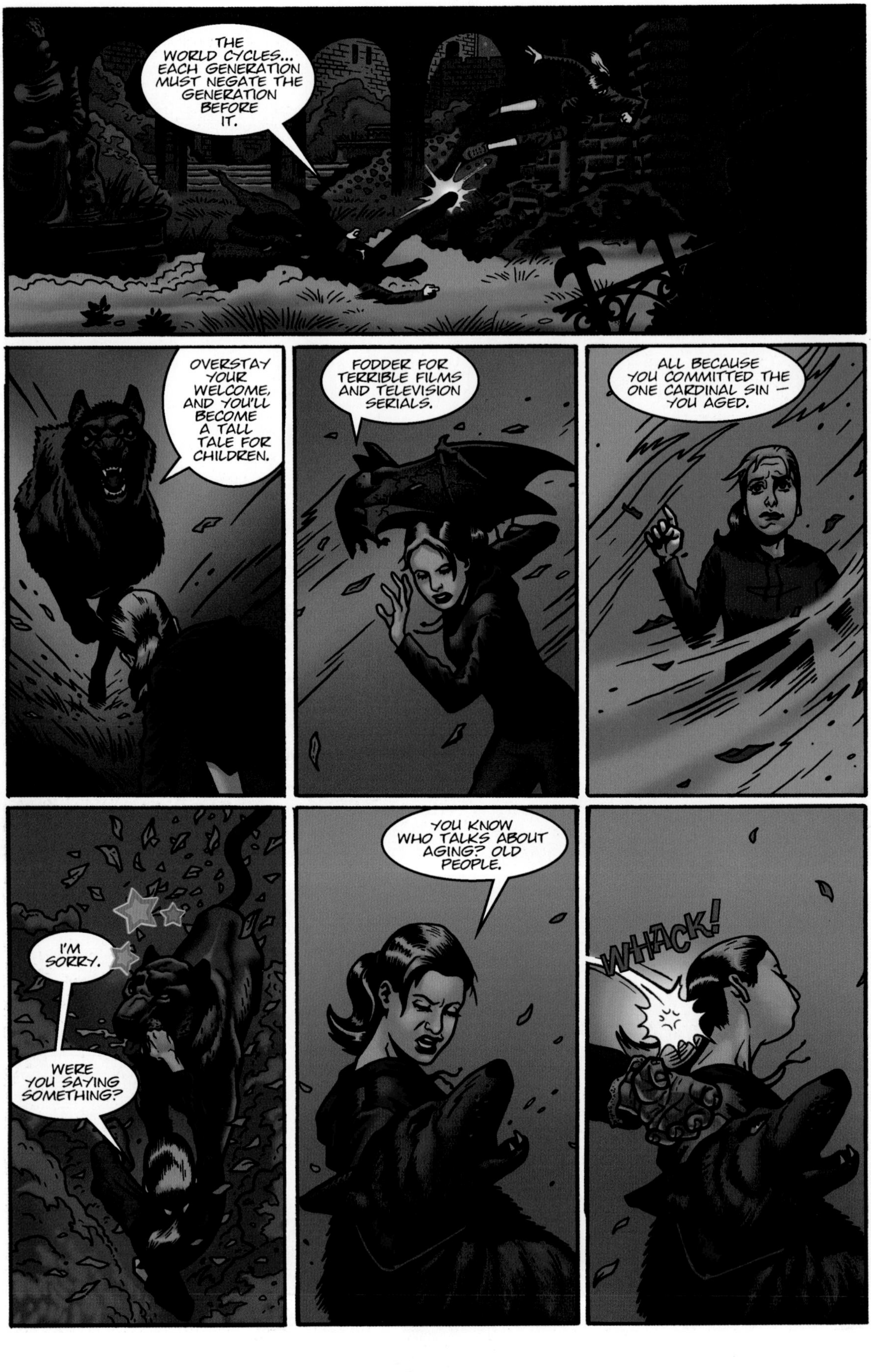
THE WORLD CYCLES... EACH GENERATION MUST NEGATE THE GENERATION BEFORE IT.
OVERSTAY YOUR WELCOME, AND YOU'LL BECOME A TALL TALE FOR CHILDREN.
FODDER FOR TERRIBLE FILMS AND TELEVISION SERIALS.
ALL BECAUSE YOU COMMITTED THE ONE CARDINAL SIN — YOU AGED.
I'M SORRY.
WERE YOU SAYING SOMETHING?
YOU KNOW WHO TALKS ABOUT AGING? OLD PEOPLE.
WHACK!

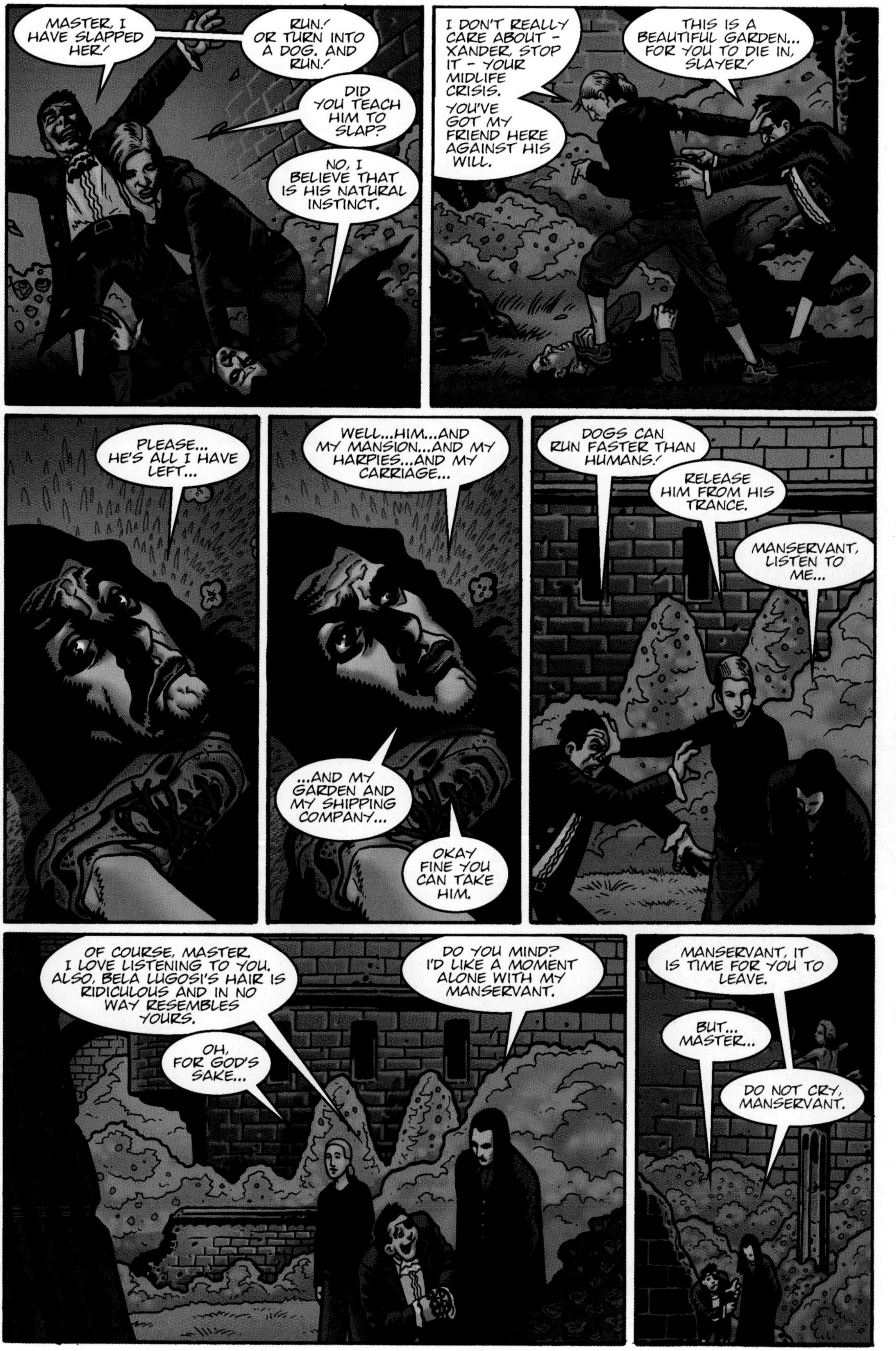

MASTER, I HAVE SLAPPED HER!
RUN! OR TURN INTO A DOG. AND RUN!
DID YOU TEACH HIM TO SLAP?
NO, I BELIEVE THAT IS HIS NATURAL INSTINCT.
I DON'T REALLY CARE ABOUT - XANDER, STOP IT - YOUR MIDLIFE CRISIS.
YOU'VE GOT MY FRIEND HERE AGAINST HIS WILL.
THIS IS A BEAUTIFUL GARDEN... FOR YOU TO DIE IN, SLAYER!
PLEASE... HE'S ALL I HAVE LEFT...
WELL...HIM...AND MY MANSION...AND MY HARPIES...AND MY CARRIAGE...
...AND MY GARDEN AND MY SHIPPING COMPANY...
OKAY FINE YOU CAN TAKE HIM.
DOGS CAN RUN FASTER THAN HUMANS!
RELEASE HIM FROM HIS TRANCE.
MANSERVANT, LISTEN TO ME...
OF COURSE, MASTER. I LOVE LISTENING TO YOU. ALSO, BELA LUGOSI'S HAIR IS RIDICULOUS AND IN NO WAY RESEMBLES YOURS.
OH, FOR GOD'S SAKE...
DO YOU MIND? I'D LIKE A MOMENT ALONE WITH MY MANSERVANT.
MANSERVANT, IT IS TIME FOR YOU TO LEAVE.
BUT... MASTER...
DO NOT CRY, MANSERVANT.

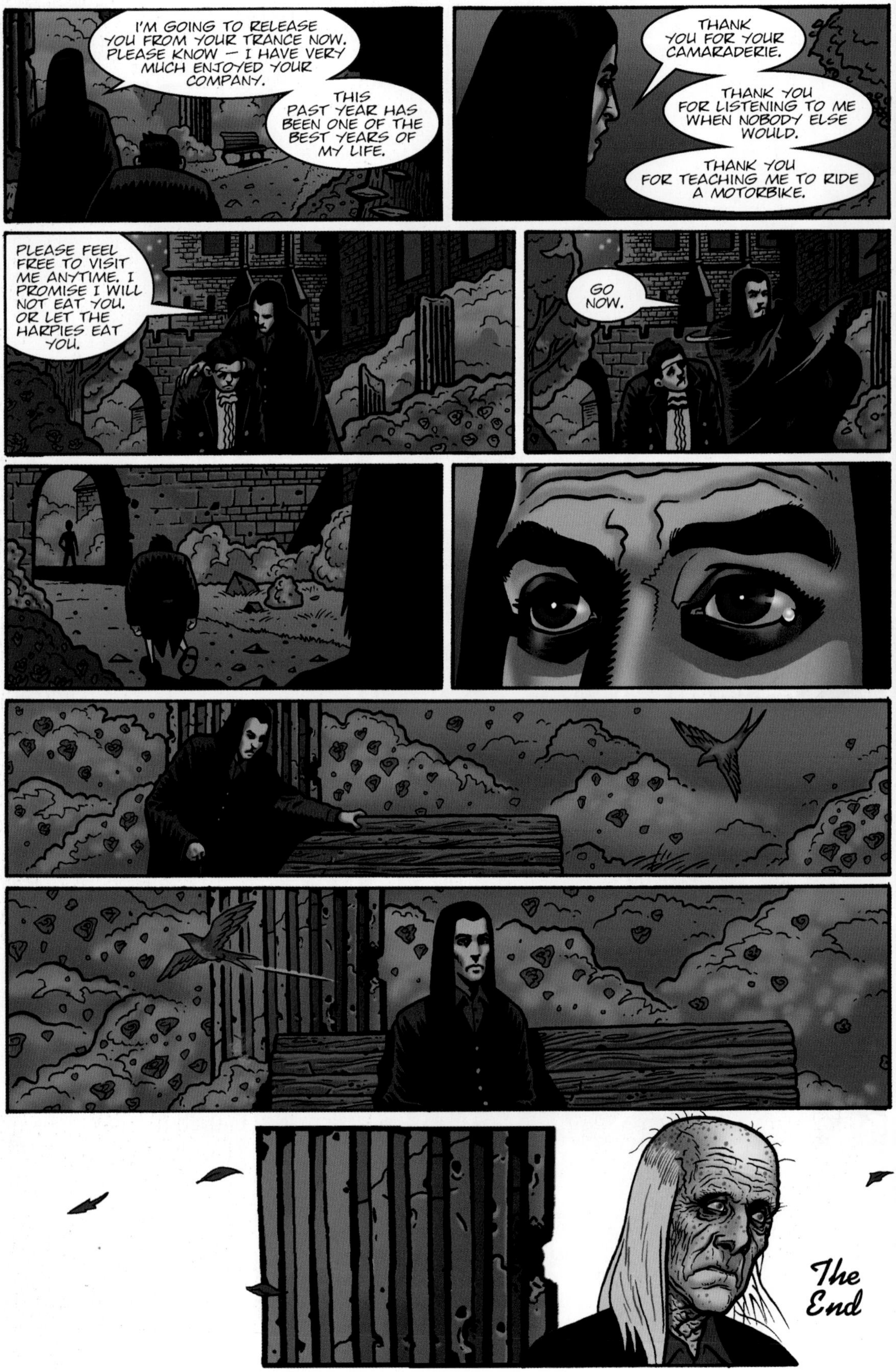
I'M GOING TO RELEASE YOU FROM YOUR TRANCE NOW. PLEASE KNOW — I HAVE VERY MUCH ENJOYED YOUR COMPANY.
THIS PAST YEAR HAS BEEN ONE OF THE BEST YEARS OF MY LIFE.
THANK YOU FOR YOUR CAMARADERIE.
THANK YOU FOR LISTENING TO ME WHEN NOBODY ELSE WOULD.
THANK YOU FOR TEACHING ME TO RIDE A MOTORBIKE.
PLEASE FEEL FREE TO VISIT ME ANYTIME. I PROMISE I WILL NOT EAT YOU. OR LET THE HARPIES EAT YOU.
GO NOW.
The End

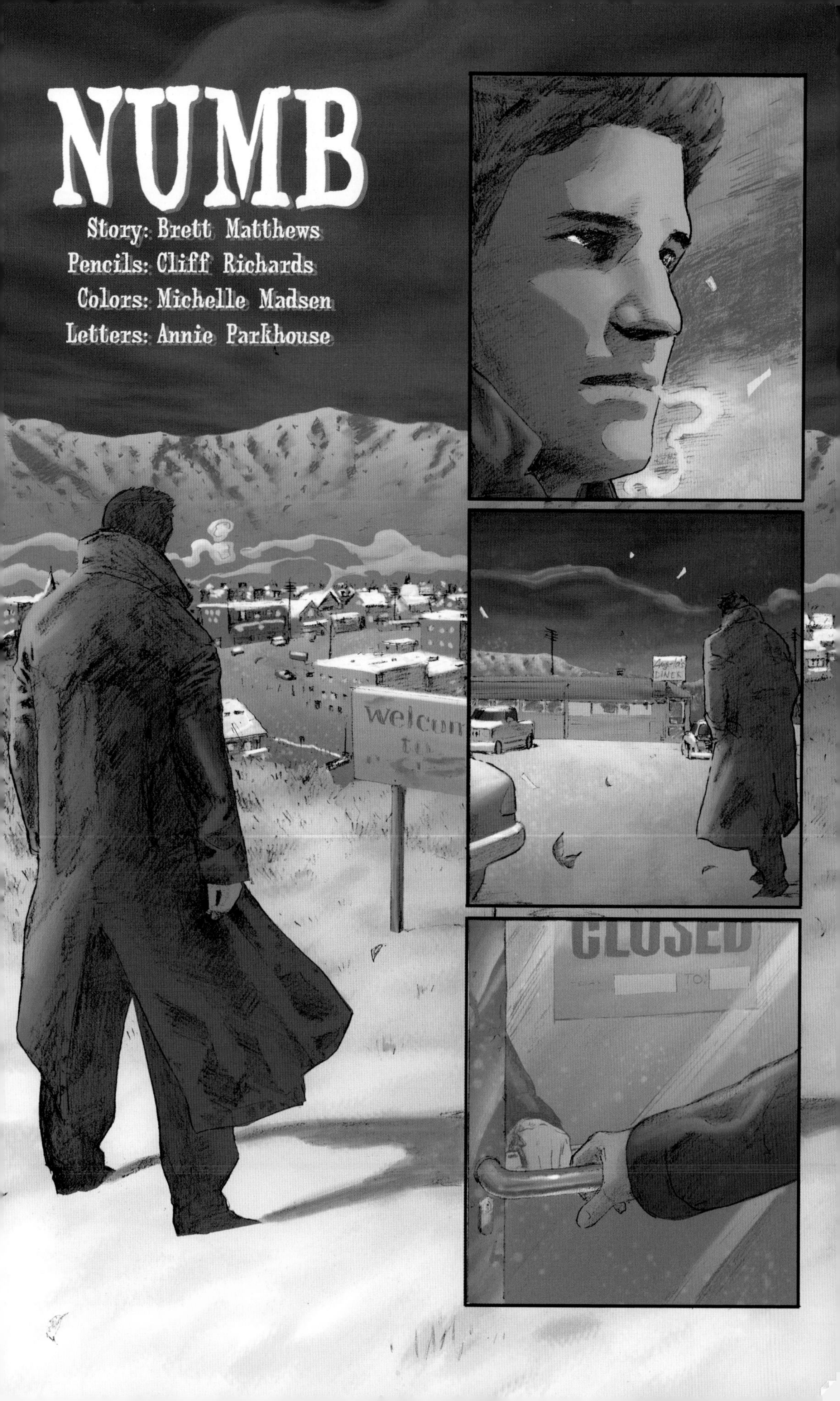
NUMB
Story: Brett Matthews
Pencils: Cliff Richards
Colors: Michelle Madsen
Letters: Annie Parkhouse
welcum
DINER
CLOSED

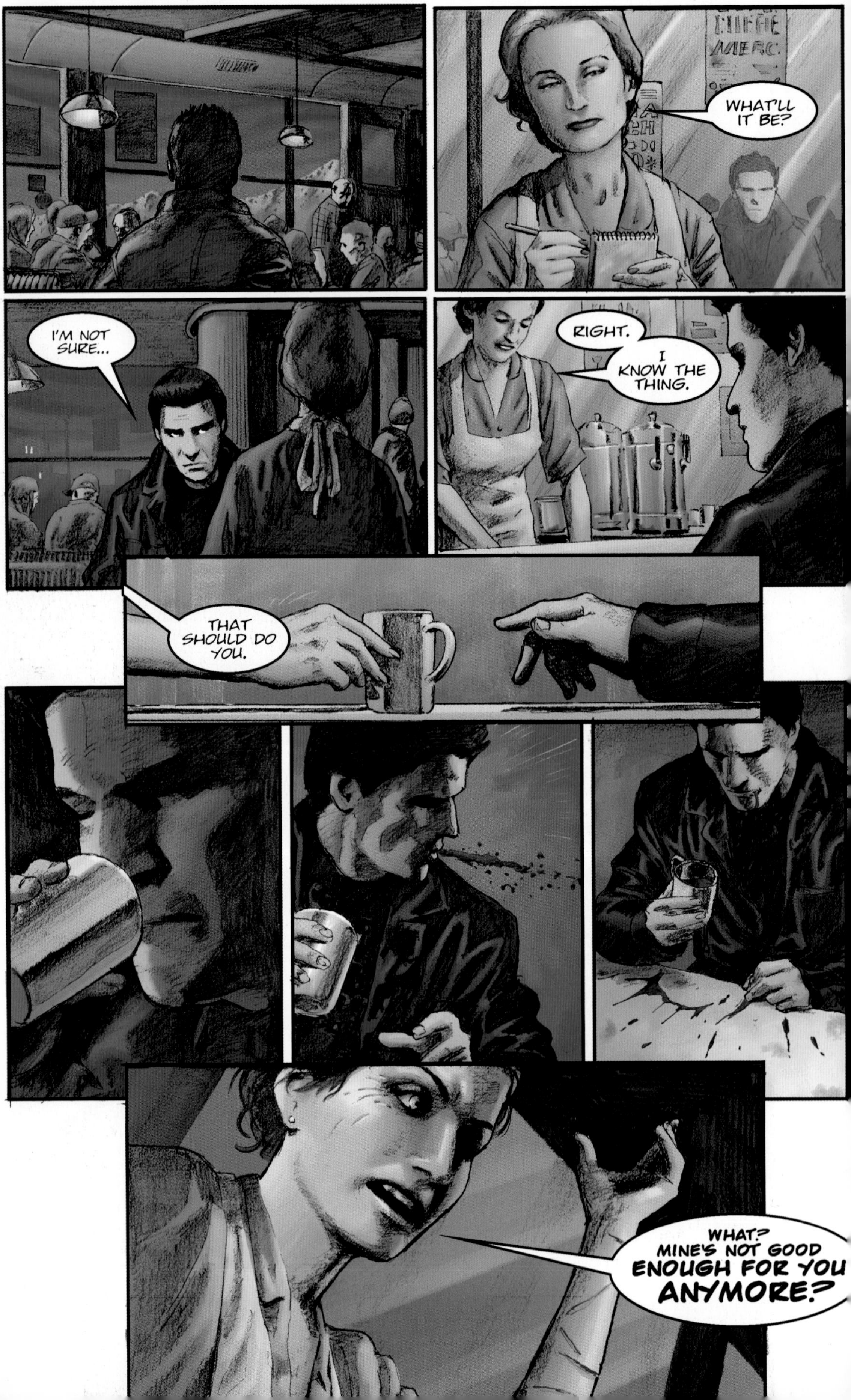
WHAT'LL IT BE?
I'M NOT SURE...
RIGHT.
I KNOW THE THING.
THAT SHOULD DO YOU.
WHAT? MINE'S NOT GOOD ENOUGH FOR YOU ANYMORE?

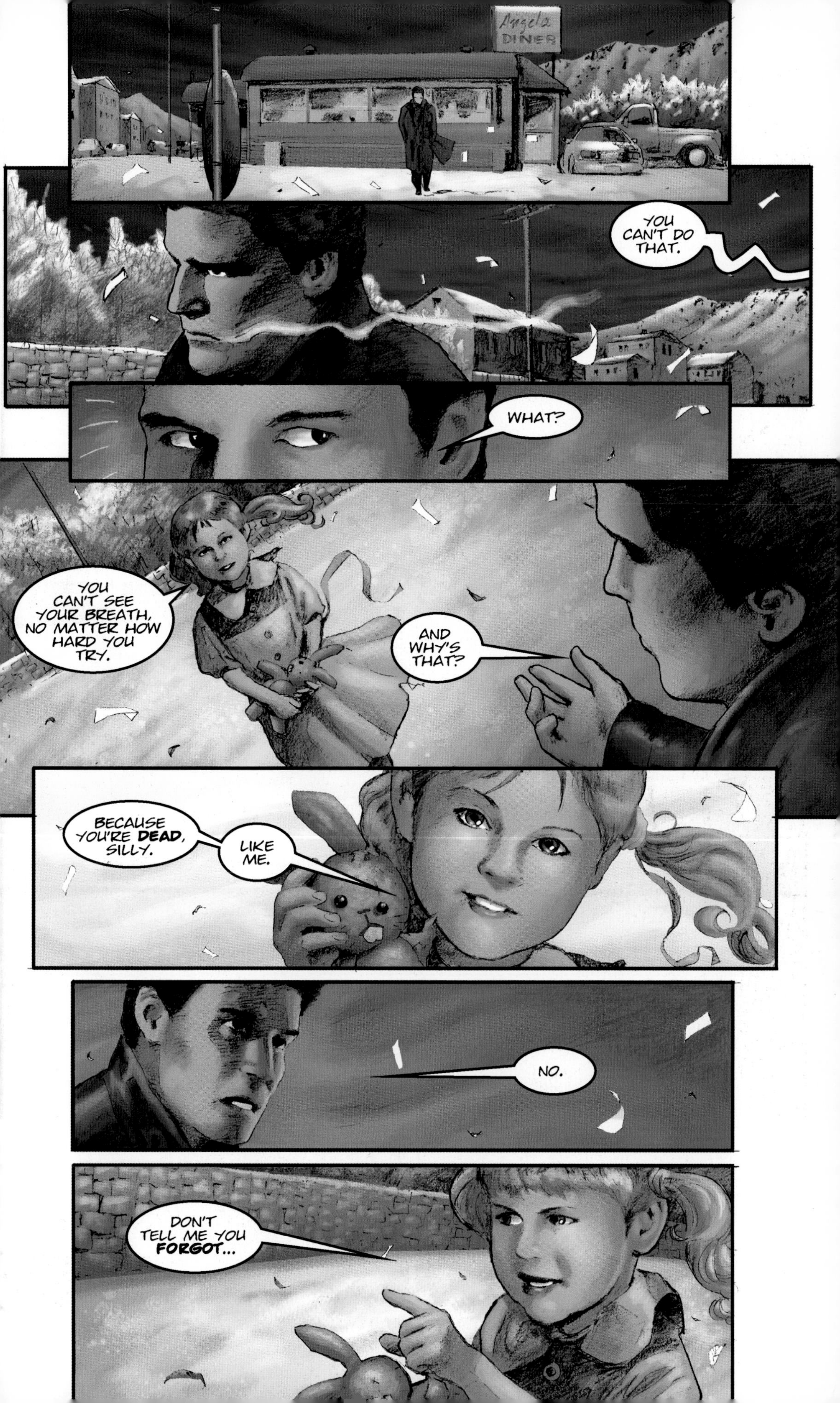
Angela DINER
YOU CAN'T DO THAT.
WHAT?
YOU CAN'T SEE YOUR BREATH, NO MATTER HOW HARD YOU TRY.
AND WHY'S THAT?
BECAUSE YOU'RE **DEAD**, SILLY.
LIKE ME.
NO.
DON'T TELL ME YOU **FORGOT**...

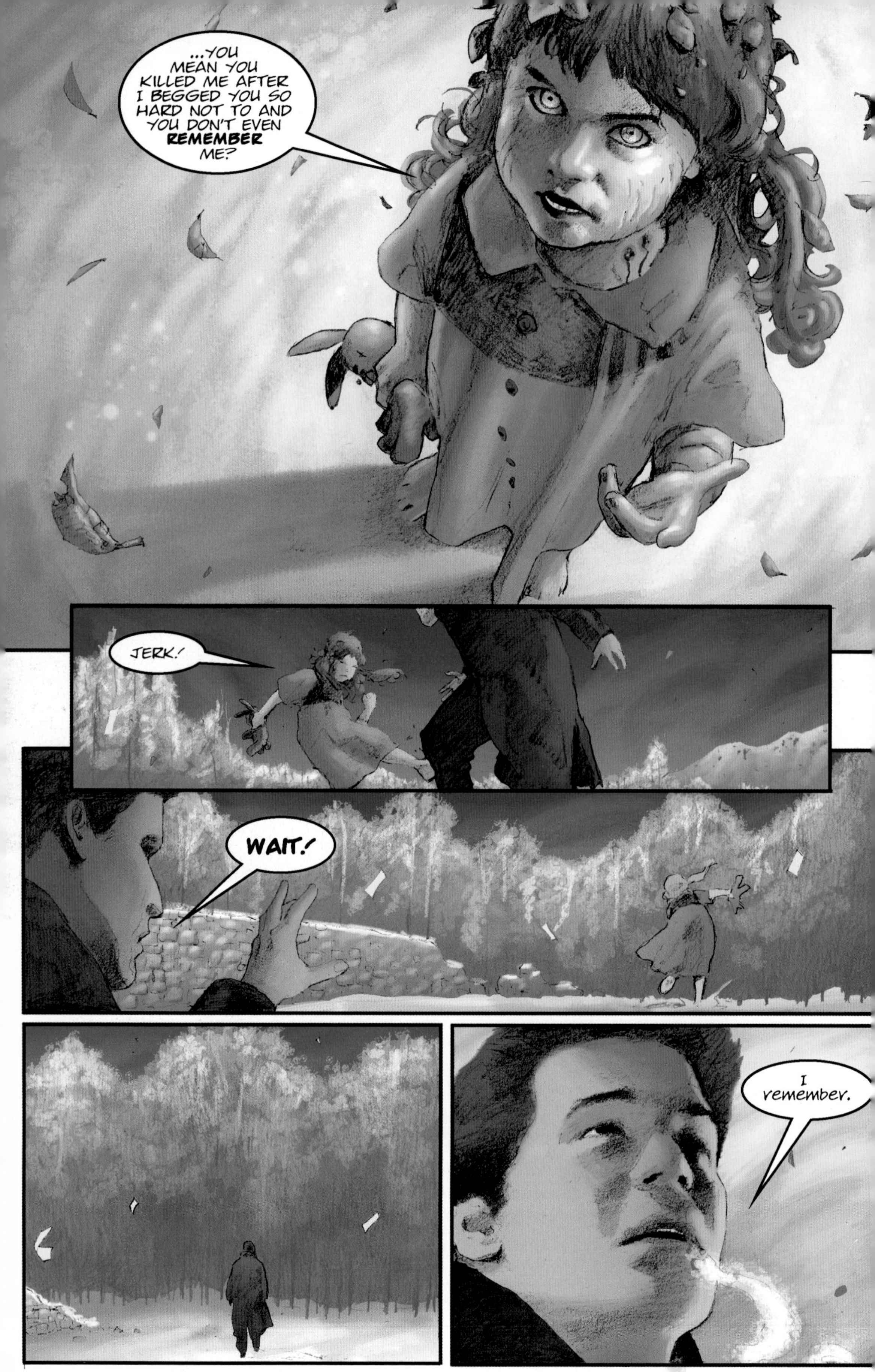
...YOU MEAN YOU KILLED ME AFTER I BEGGED YOU SO HARD NOT TO AND YOU DON'T EVEN REMEMBER ME?
JERK!
WAIT!
I remember.

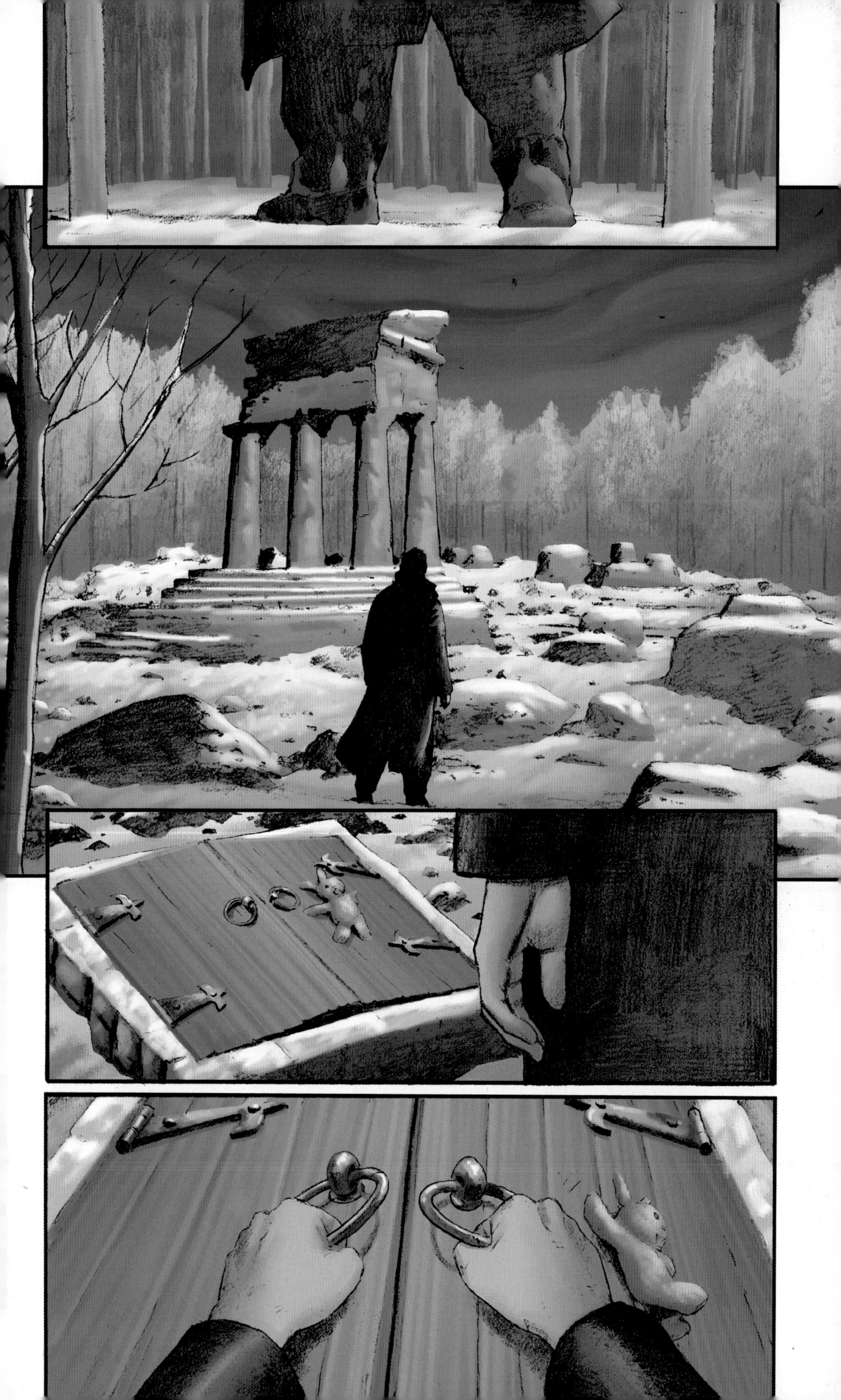

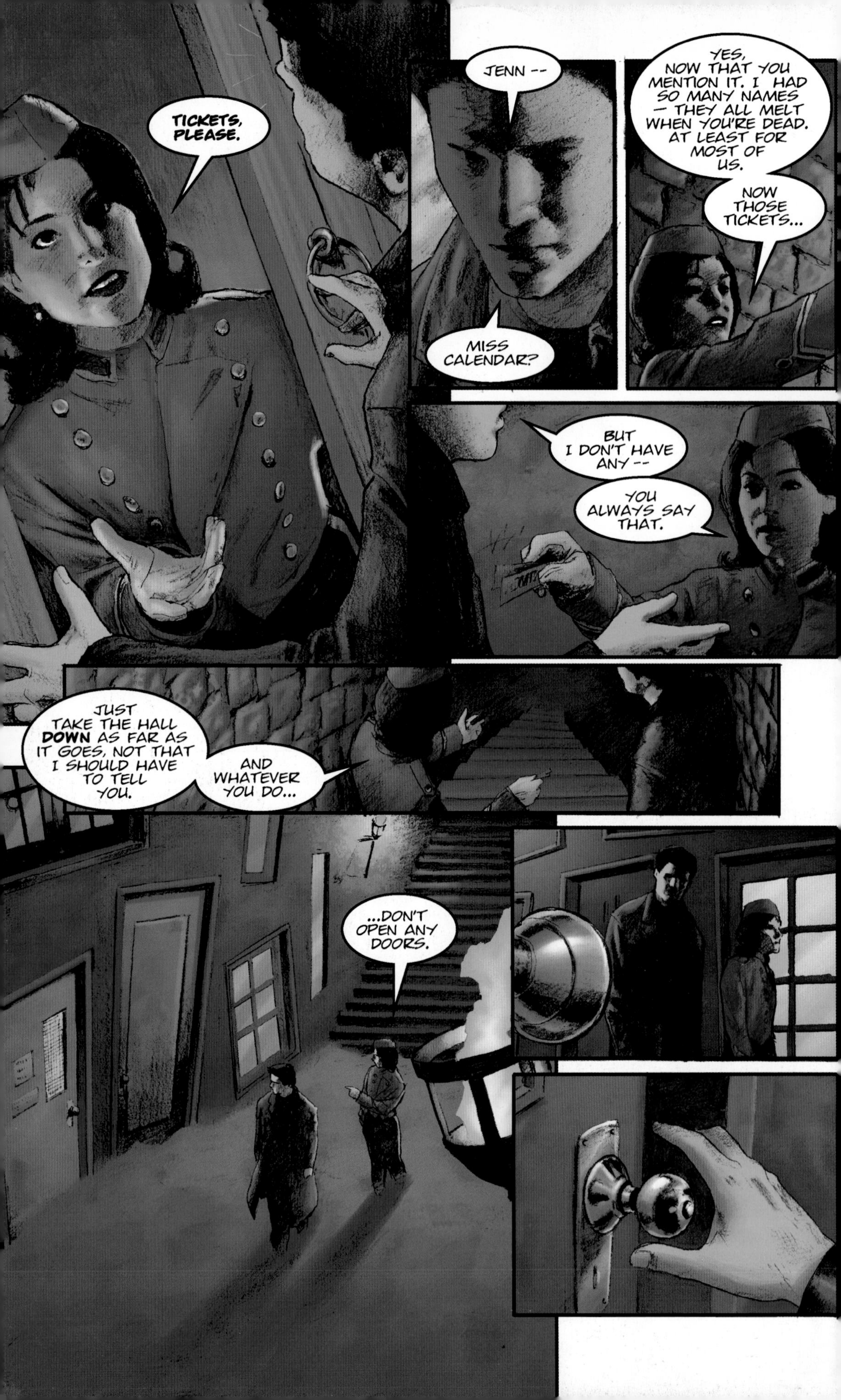

TICKETS, PLEASE.
JENN --
MISS CALENDAR?
YES, NOW THAT YOU MENTION IT. I HAD SO MANY NAMES — THEY ALL MELT WHEN YOU'RE DEAD. AT LEAST FOR MOST OF US.
NOW THOSE TICKETS...
BUT I DON'T HAVE ANY --
YOU ALWAYS SAY THAT.
JUST TAKE THE HALL **DOWN** AS FAR AS IT GOES, NOT THAT I SHOULD HAVE TO TELL YOU.
AND WHATEVER YOU DO...
...DON'T OPEN ANY DOORS.

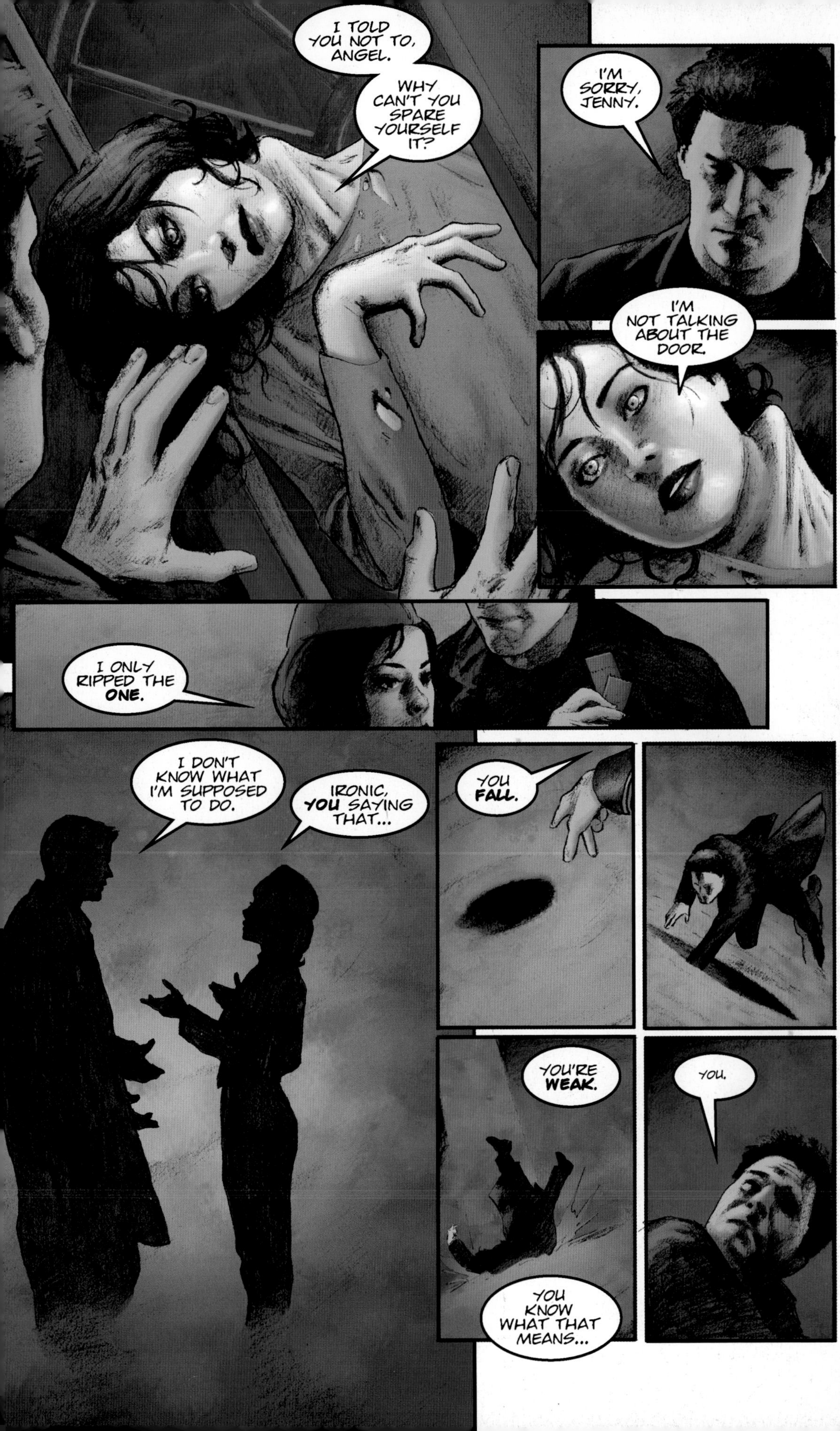
I TOLD YOU NOT TO, ANGEL.
WHY CAN'T YOU SPARE YOURSELF IT?
I'M SORRY, JENNY.
I'M NOT TALKING ABOUT THE DOOR.
I ONLY RIPPED THE ONE.
I DON'T KNOW WHAT I'M SUPPOSED TO DO.
IRONIC, YOU SAYING THAT...
YOU FALL.
YOU'RE WEAK.
YOU.
YOU KNOW WHAT THAT MEANS...

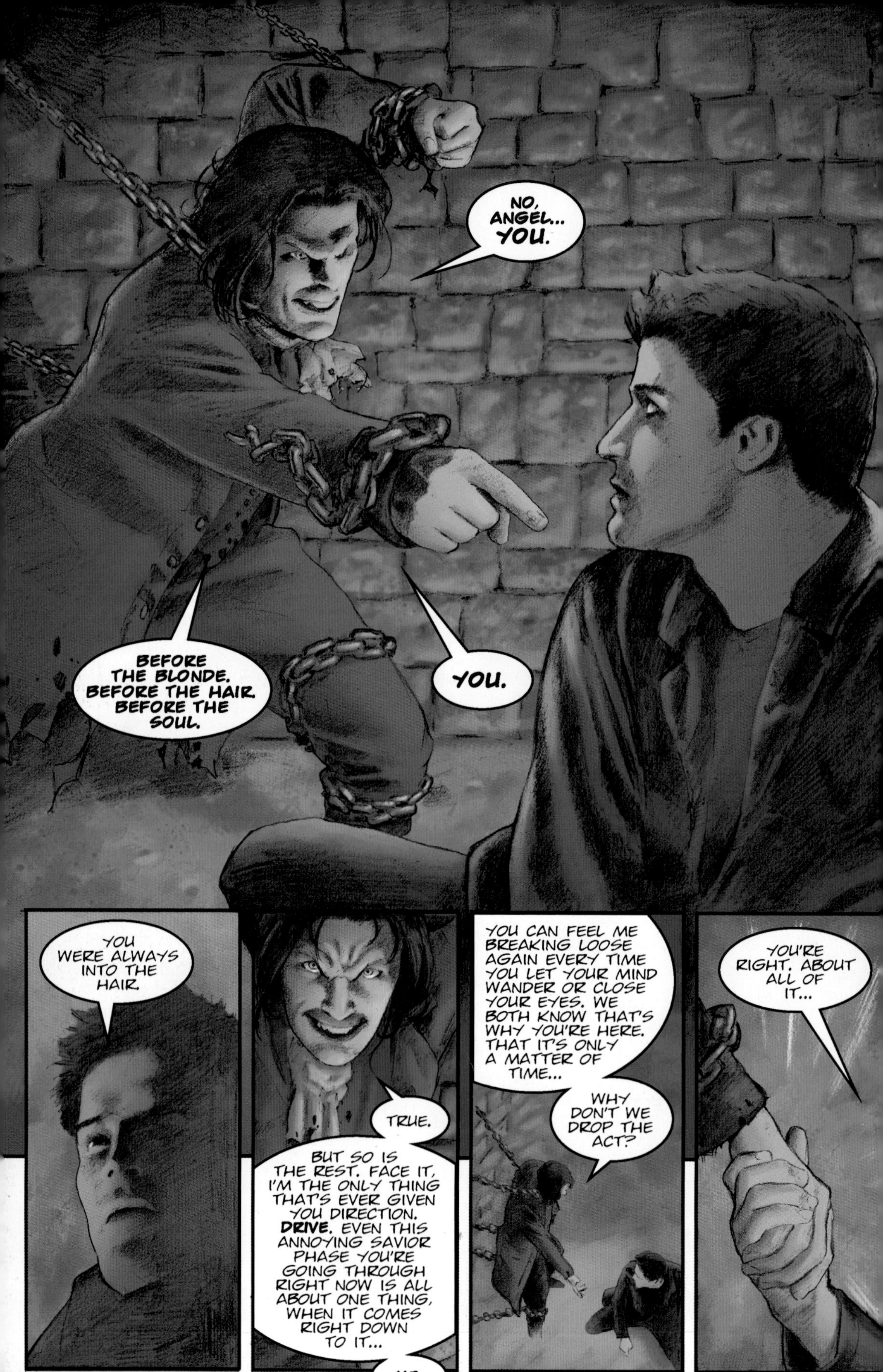
NO, ANGEL... YOU.
BEFORE THE BLONDE. BEFORE THE HAIR. BEFORE THE SOUL.
YOU.
YOU WERE ALWAYS INTO THE HAIR.
TRUE.
BUT SO IS THE REST. FACE IT, I'M THE ONLY THING THAT'S EVER GIVEN YOU DIRECTION. DRIVE. EVEN THIS ANNOYING SAVIOR PHASE YOU'RE GOING THROUGH RIGHT NOW IS ALL ABOUT ONE THING, WHEN IT COMES RIGHT DOWN TO IT...
ME.
YOU CAN FEEL ME BREAKING LOOSE AGAIN EVERY TIME YOU LET YOUR MIND WANDER OR CLOSE YOUR EYES. WE BOTH KNOW THAT'S WHY YOU'RE HERE. THAT IT'S ONLY A MATTER OF TIME...
WHY DON'T WE DROP THE ACT?
YOU'RE RIGHT. ABOUT ALL OF IT...

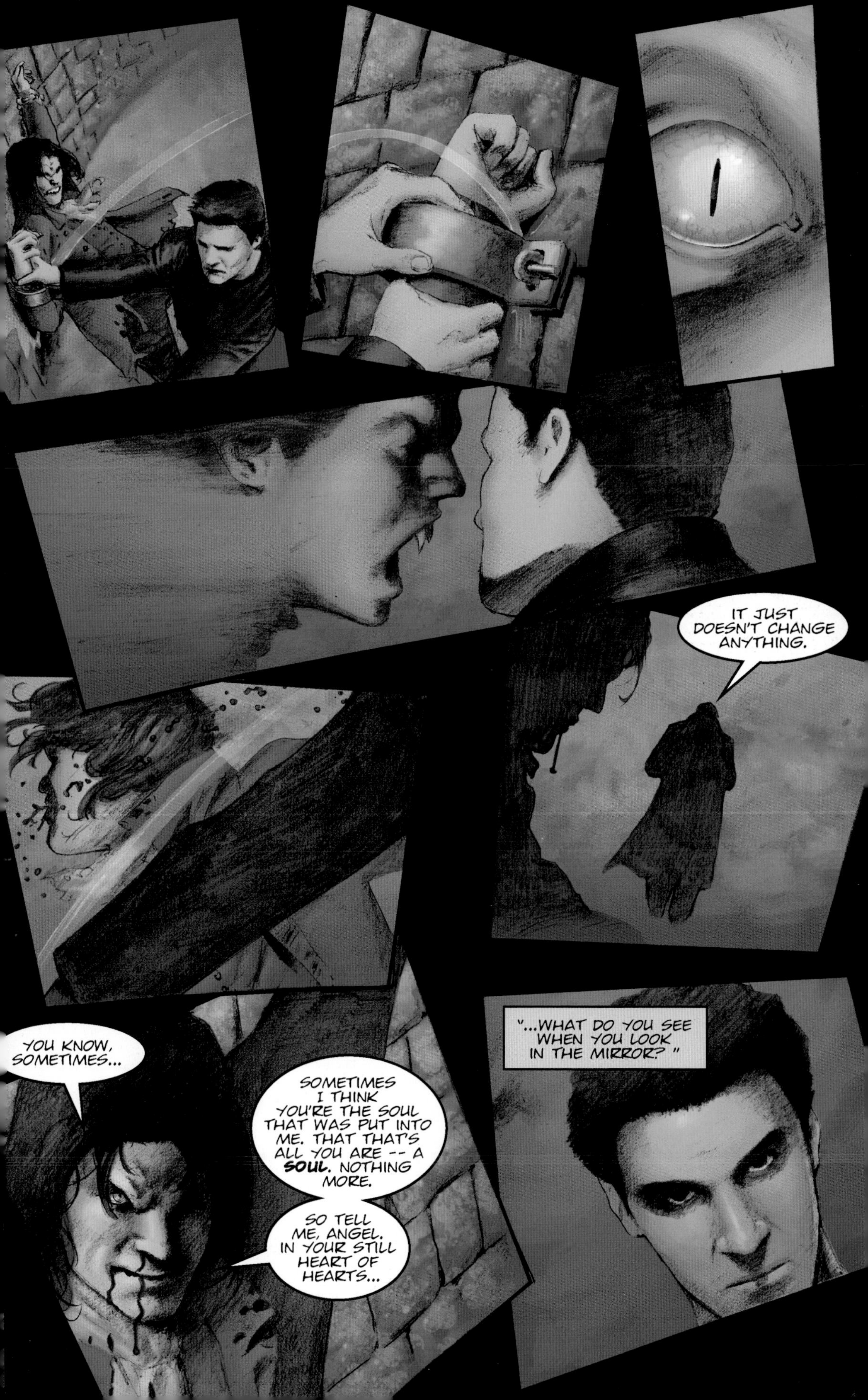
IT JUST DOESN'T CHANGE ANYTHING.
YOU KNOW, SOMETIMES...
SOMETIMES I THINK YOU'RE THE SOUL THAT WAS PUT INTO ME. THAT THAT'S ALL YOU ARE -- A **SOUL**. NOTHING MORE.
SO TELL ME, ANGEL, IN YOUR STILL HEART OF HEARTS...
"...WHAT DO YOU SEE WHEN YOU LOOK IN THE MIRROR?"

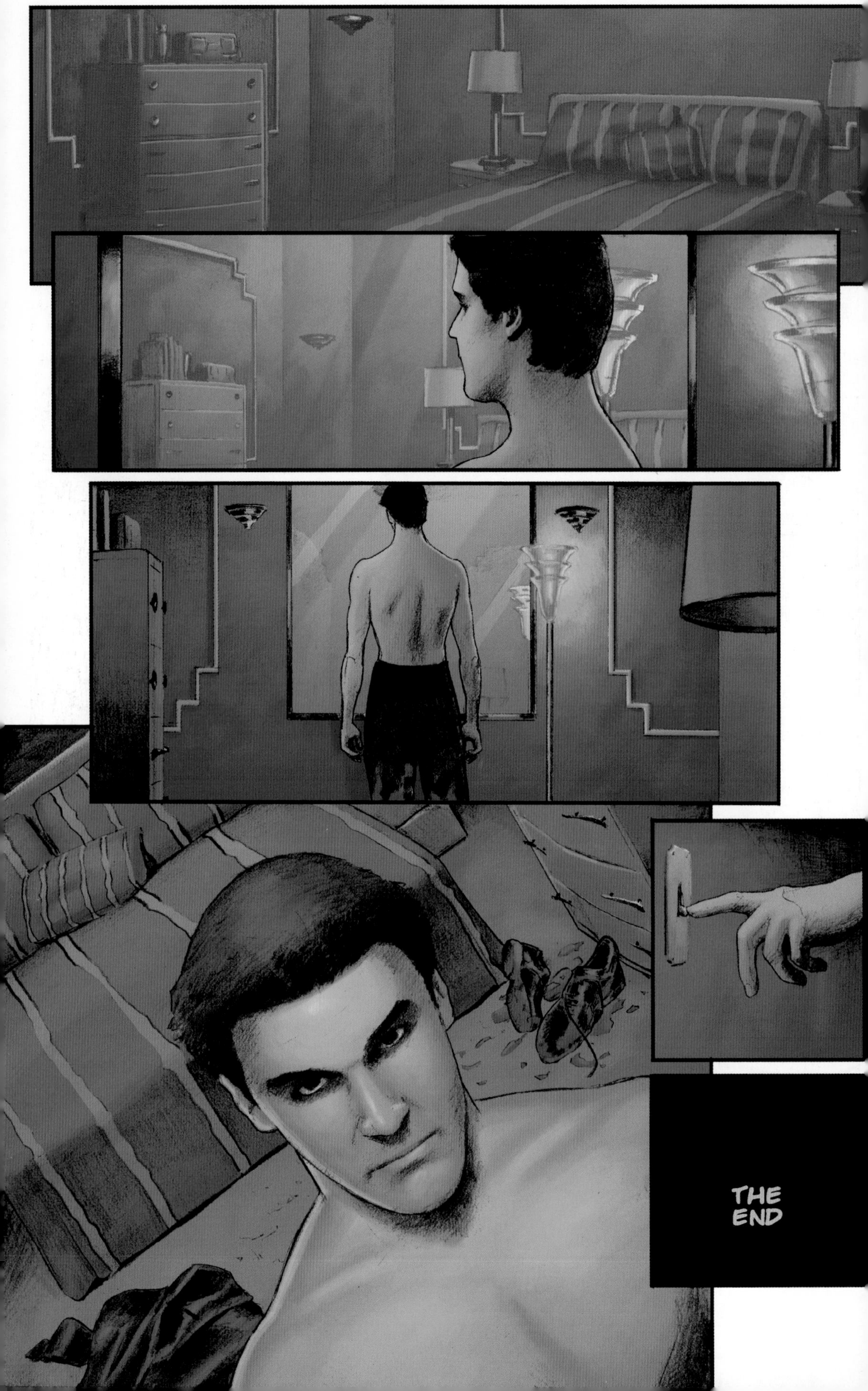
THE
END

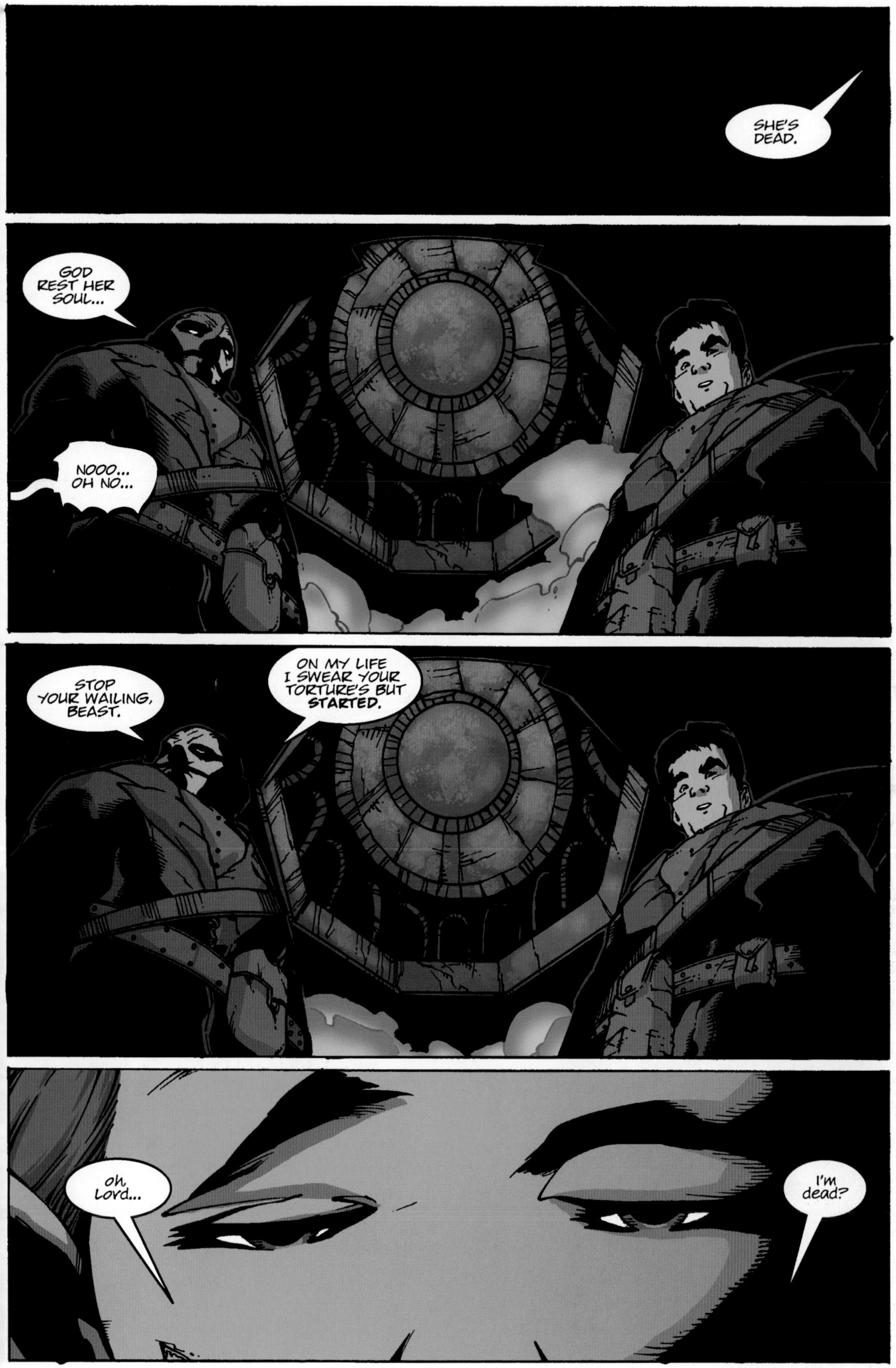
SHE'S DEAD.
GOD REST HER SOUL...
NOOO... OH NO...
STOP YOUR WAILING, BEAST.
ON MY LIFE I SWEAR YOUR TORTURE'S BUT STARTED.
oh Lord...
I'm dead?

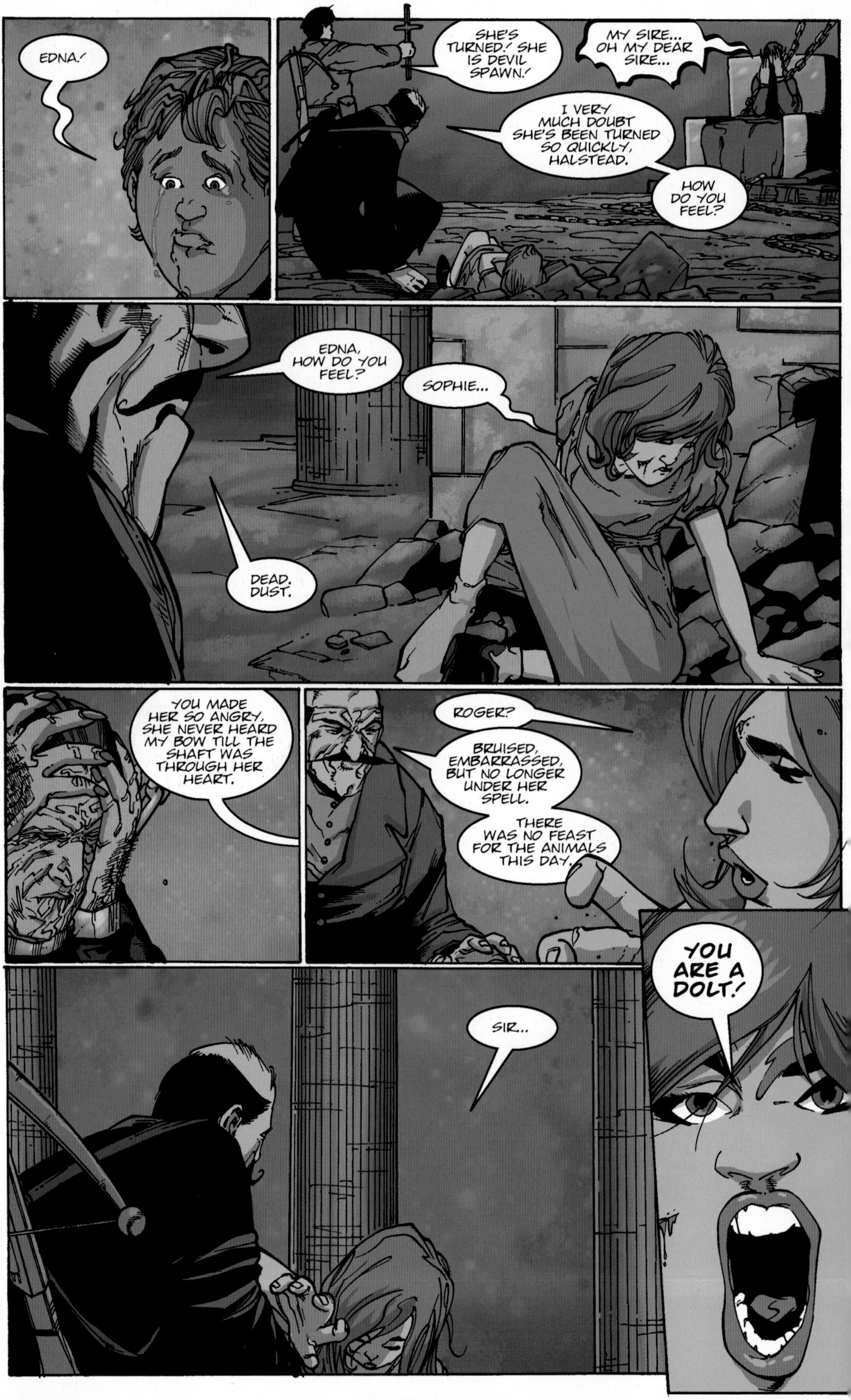
EDNA!
SHE'S TURNED! SHE IS DEVIL SPAWN!
MY SIRE... OH MY DEAR SIRE...
I VERY MUCH DOUBT SHE'S BEEN TURNED SO QUICKLY, HALSTEAD.
HOW DO YOU FEEL?
EDNA, HOW DO YOU FEEL?
SOPHIE...
DEAD. DUST.
YOU MADE HER SO ANGRY, SHE NEVER HEARD MY BOW TILL THE SHAFT WAS THROUGH HER HEART.
ROGER?
BRUISED, EMBARRASSED, BUT NO LONGER UNDER HER SPELL.
THERE WAS NO FEAST FOR THE ANIMALS THIS DAY.
SIR...
YOU ARE A DOLT!

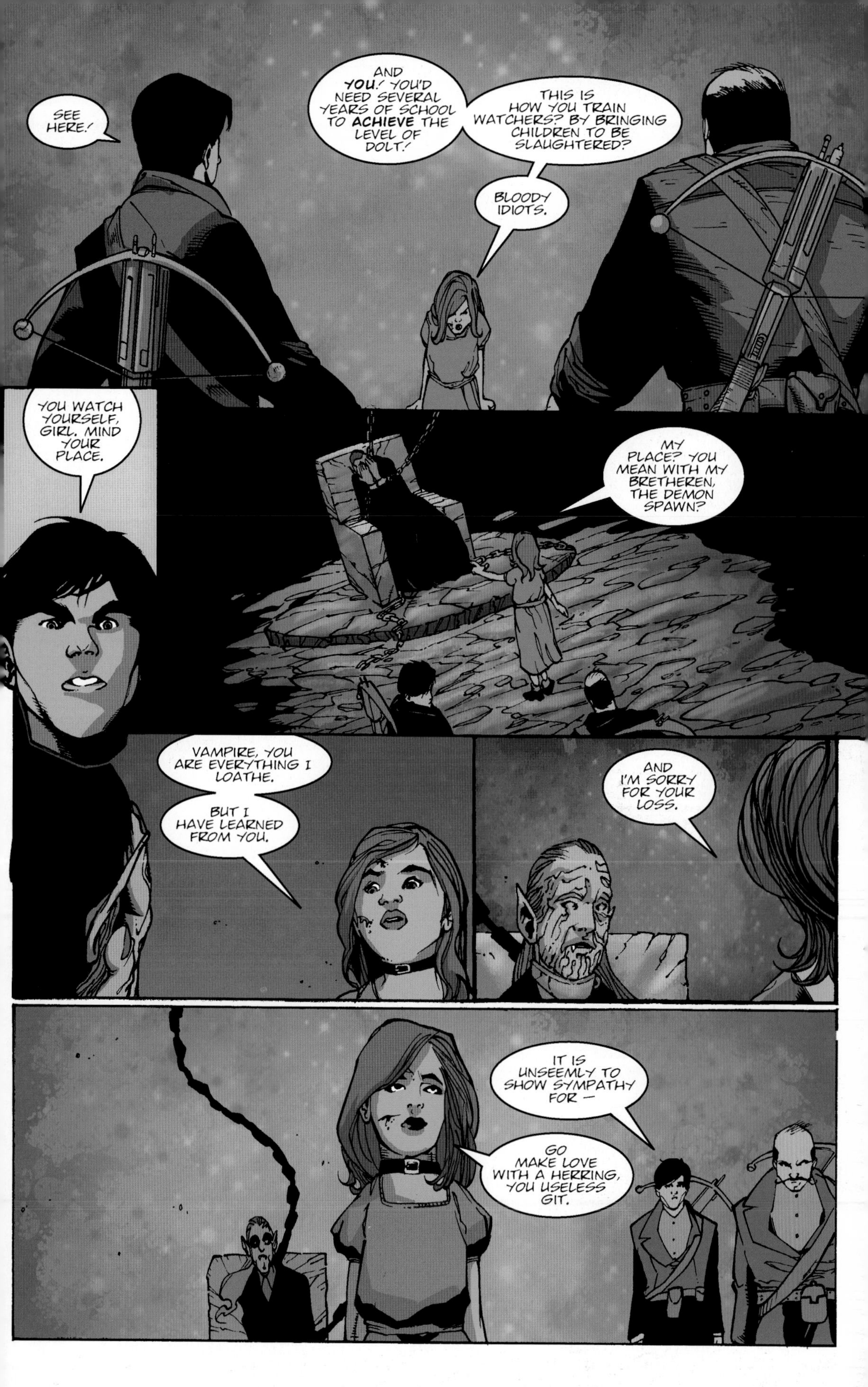
SEE HERE!
AND YOU! YOU'D NEED SEVERAL YEARS OF SCHOOL TO ACHIEVE THE LEVEL OF DOLT!
THIS IS HOW YOU TRAIN WATCHERS? BY BRINGING CHILDREN TO BE SLAUGHTERED?
BLOODY IDIOTS.
YOU WATCH YOURSELF, GIRL. MIND YOUR PLACE.
MY PLACE? YOU MEAN WITH MY BRETHEREN, THE DEMON SPAWN?
VAMPIRE, YOU ARE EVERYTHING I LOATHE.
BUT I HAVE LEARNED FROM YOU.
AND I'M SORRY FOR YOUR LOSS.
IT IS UNSEEMLY TO SHOW SYMPATHY FOR —
GO MAKE LOVE WITH A HERRING, YOU USELESS GIT.

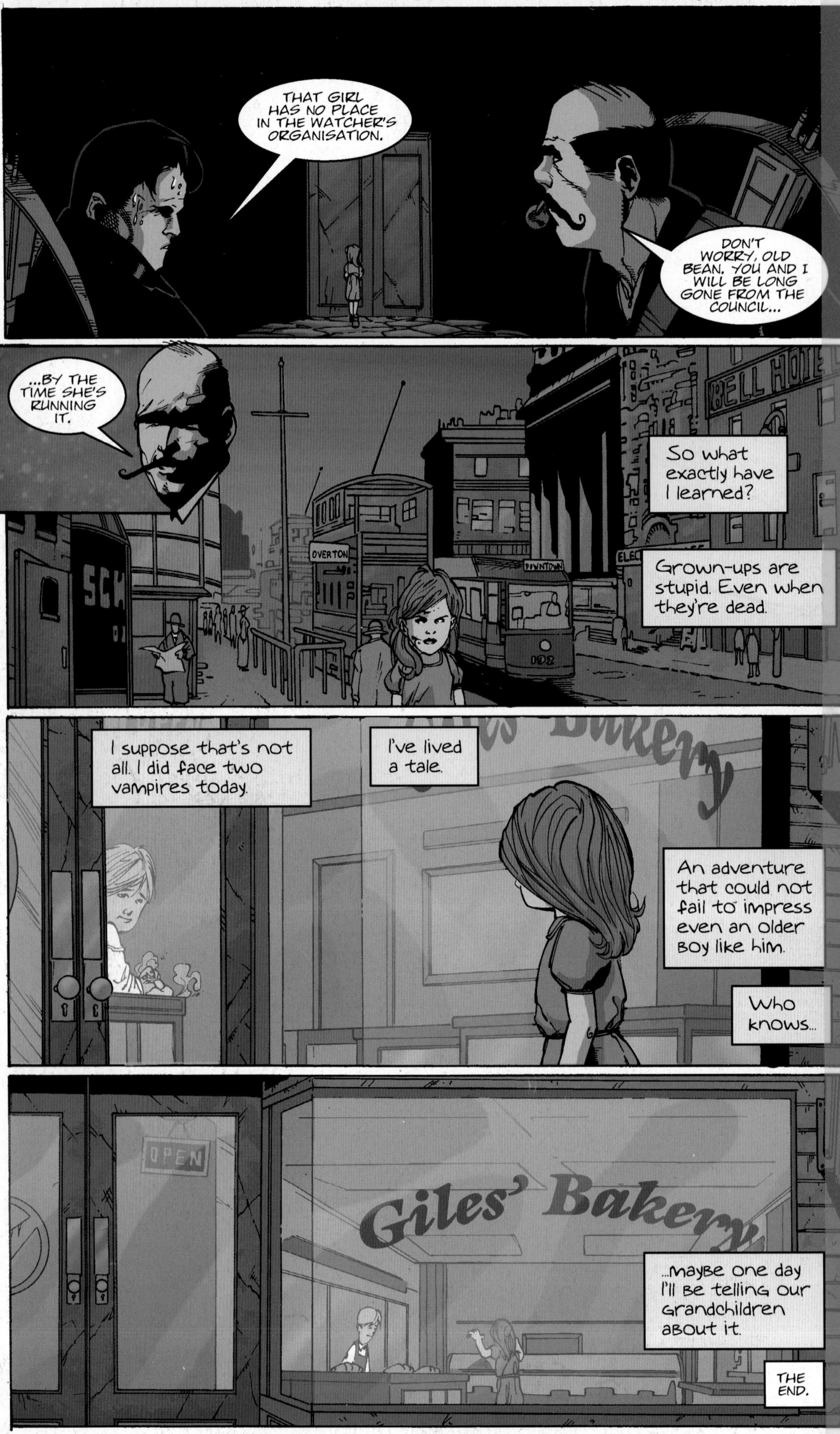

THAT GIRL HAS NO PLACE IN THE WATCHER'S ORGANISATION.
DON'T WORRY, OLD BEAN. YOU AND I WILL BE LONG GONE FROM THE COUNCIL...
...BY THE TIME SHE'S RUNNING IT.
BELL HOTEL
So what exactly have I learned?
OVERTON
DOWNTOWN
192
Grown-ups are stupid. Even when they're dead.
I suppose that's not all. I did face two vampires today.
I've lived a tale.
An adventure that could not fail to impress even an older boy like him.
Who knows...
OPEN
Giles' Bakery
...maybe one day I'll be telling our grandchildren about it.
THE END.

THE GALLERY

featuring

JOHN TOTLEBEN
colors by
DAVE STEWART

BEN TEMPLESMITH

ERIC POWELL

BEN EDLUND
colors by
MICHELLE MADSEN

BRIAN HORTON

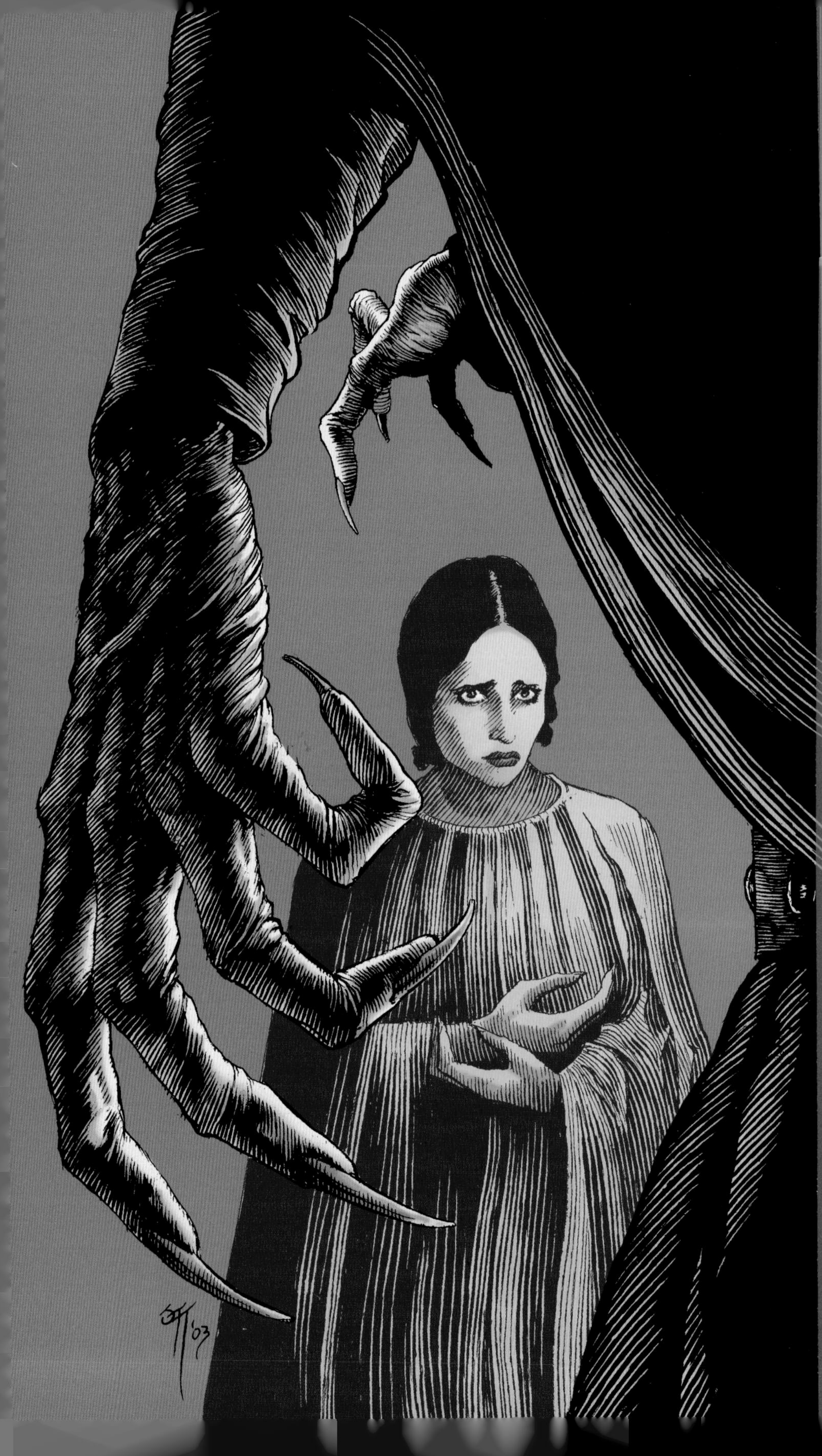

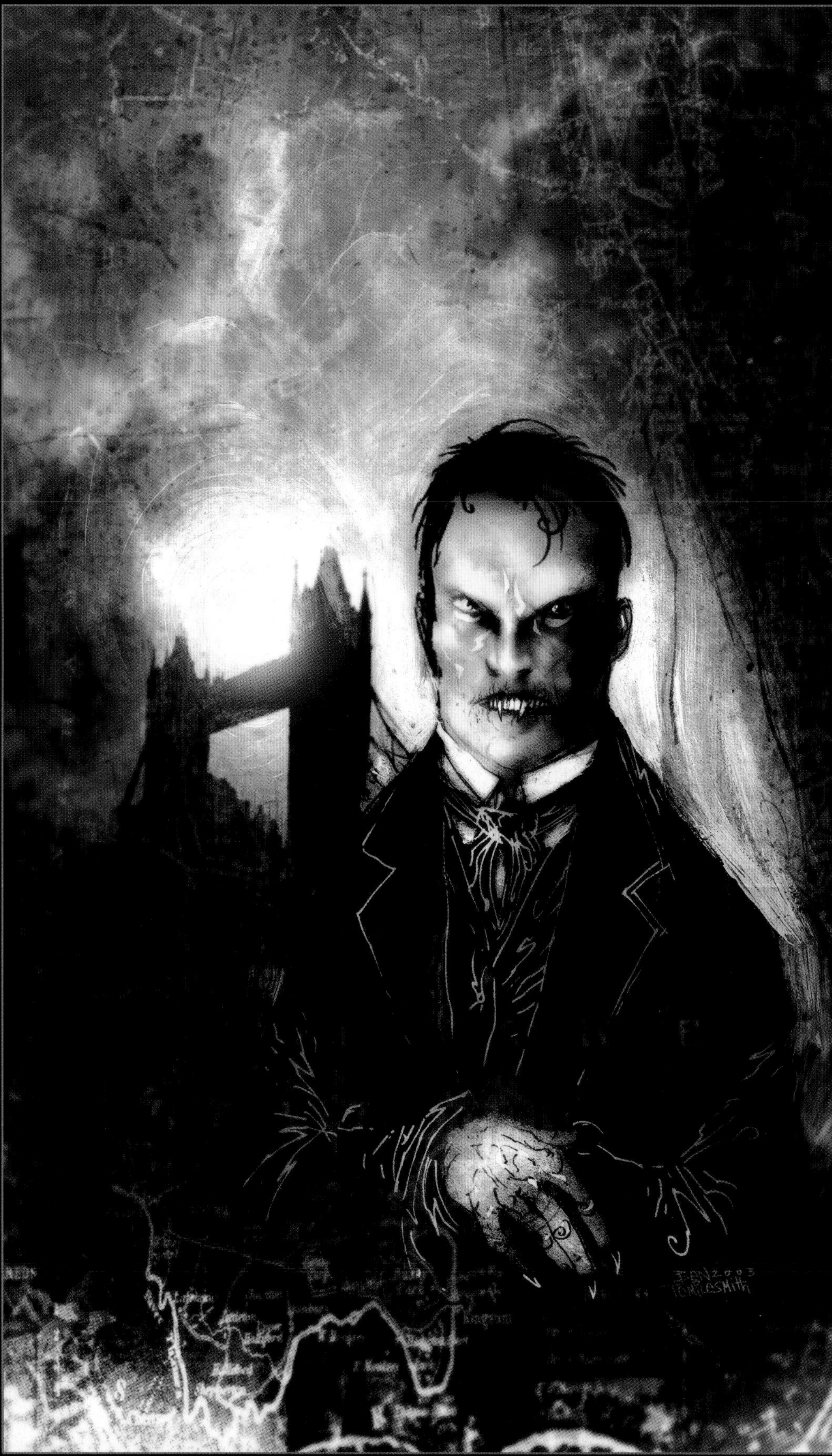
BEN2003
TEMPLESMITH

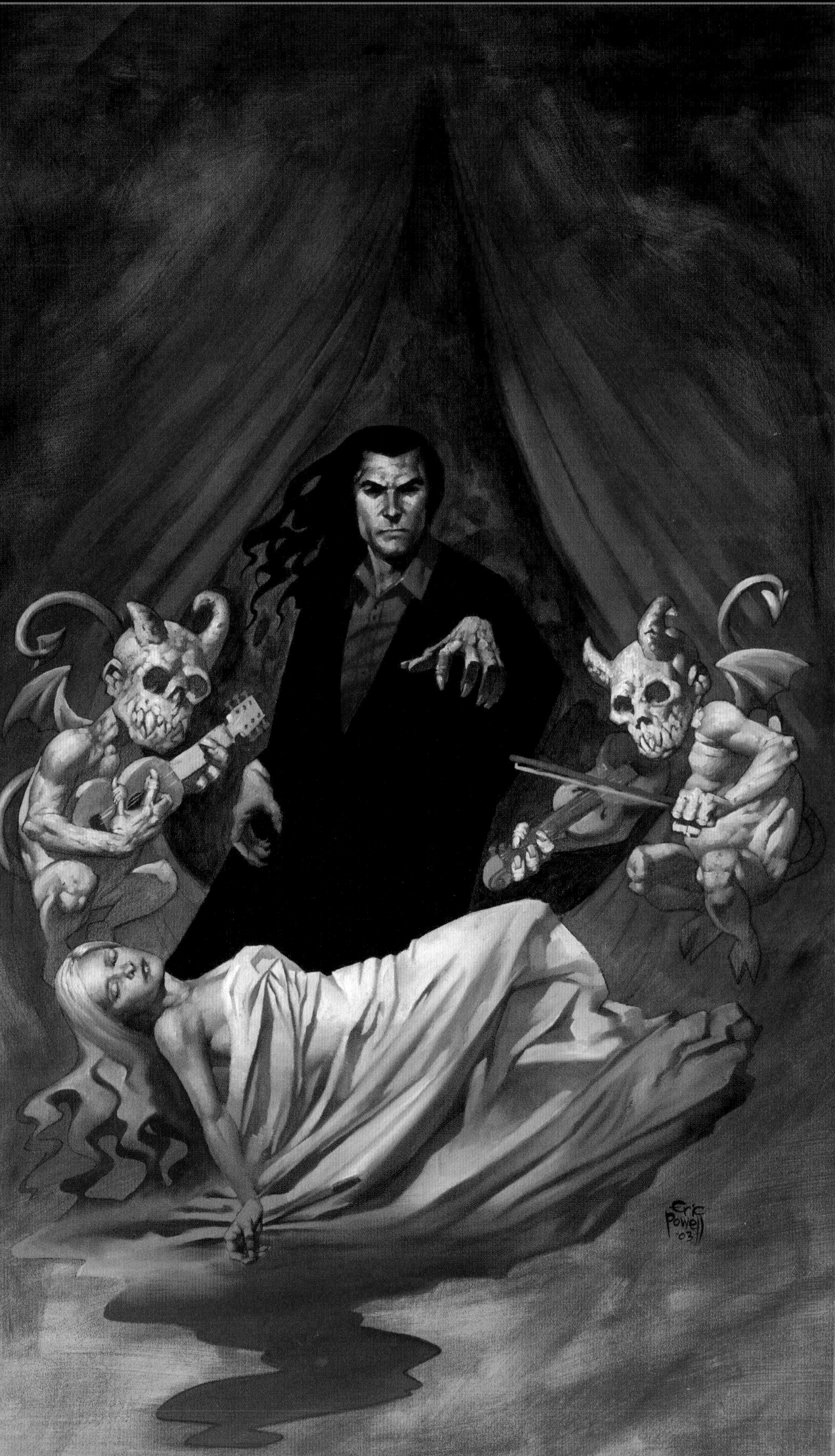
Eric Powell '03

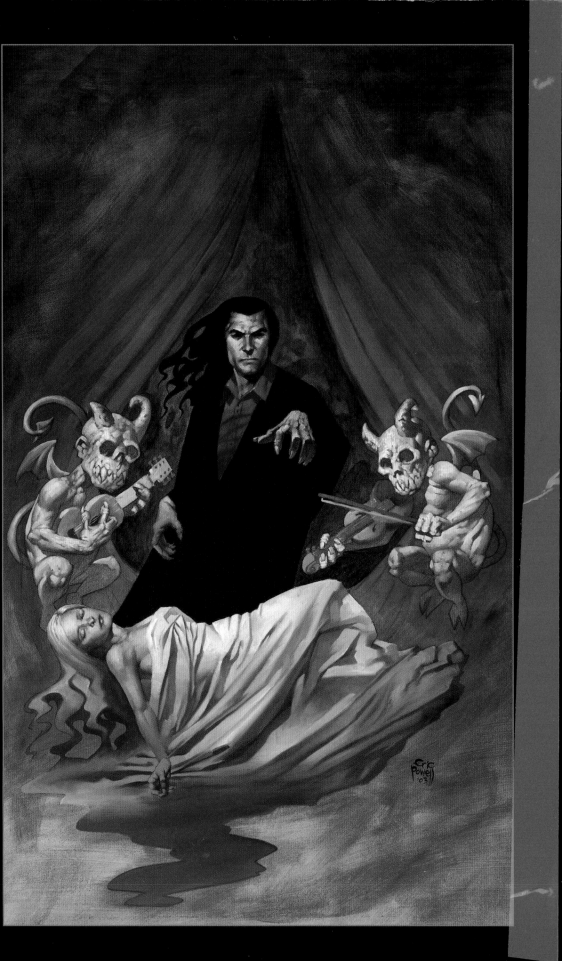

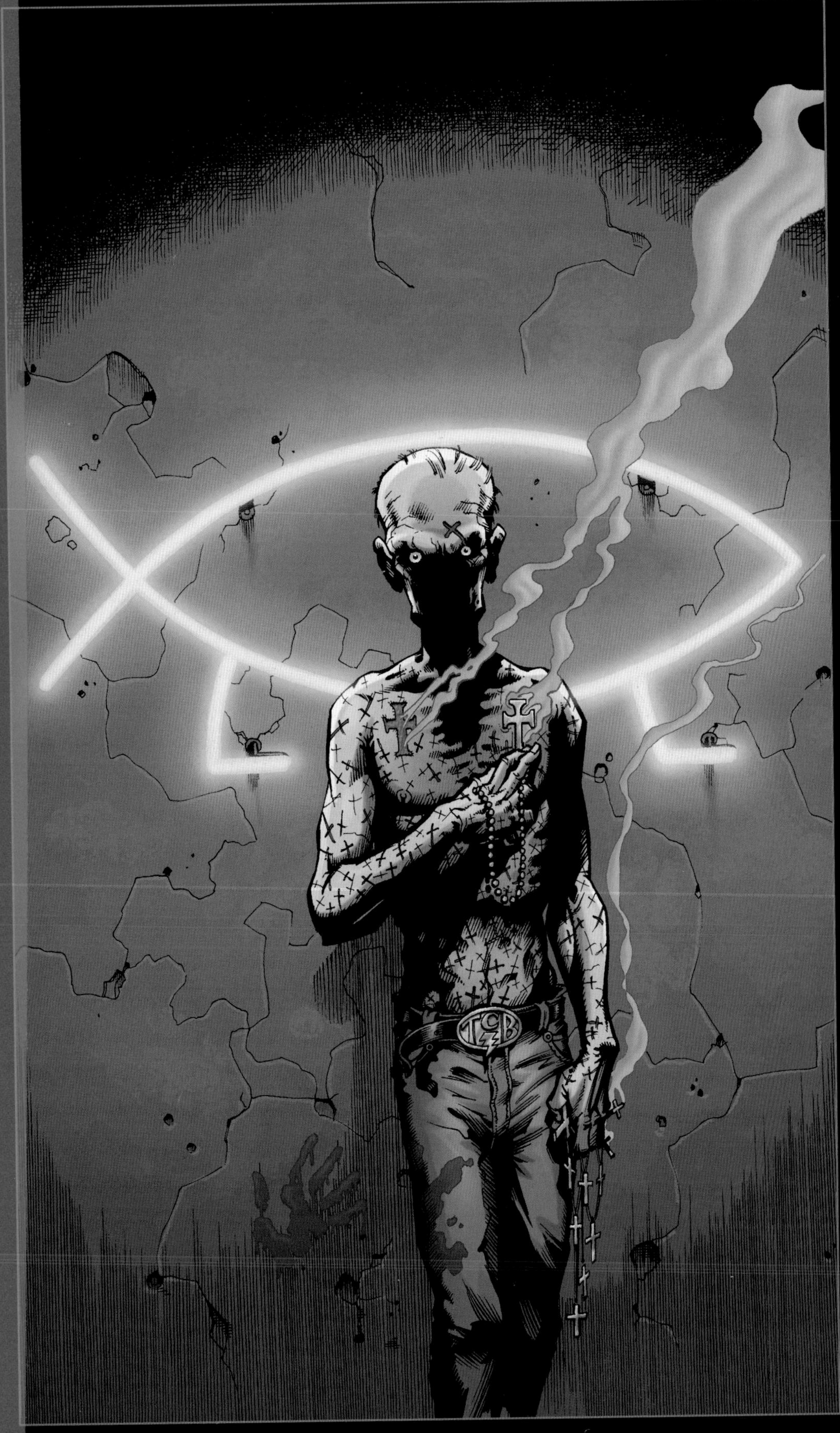
TCB

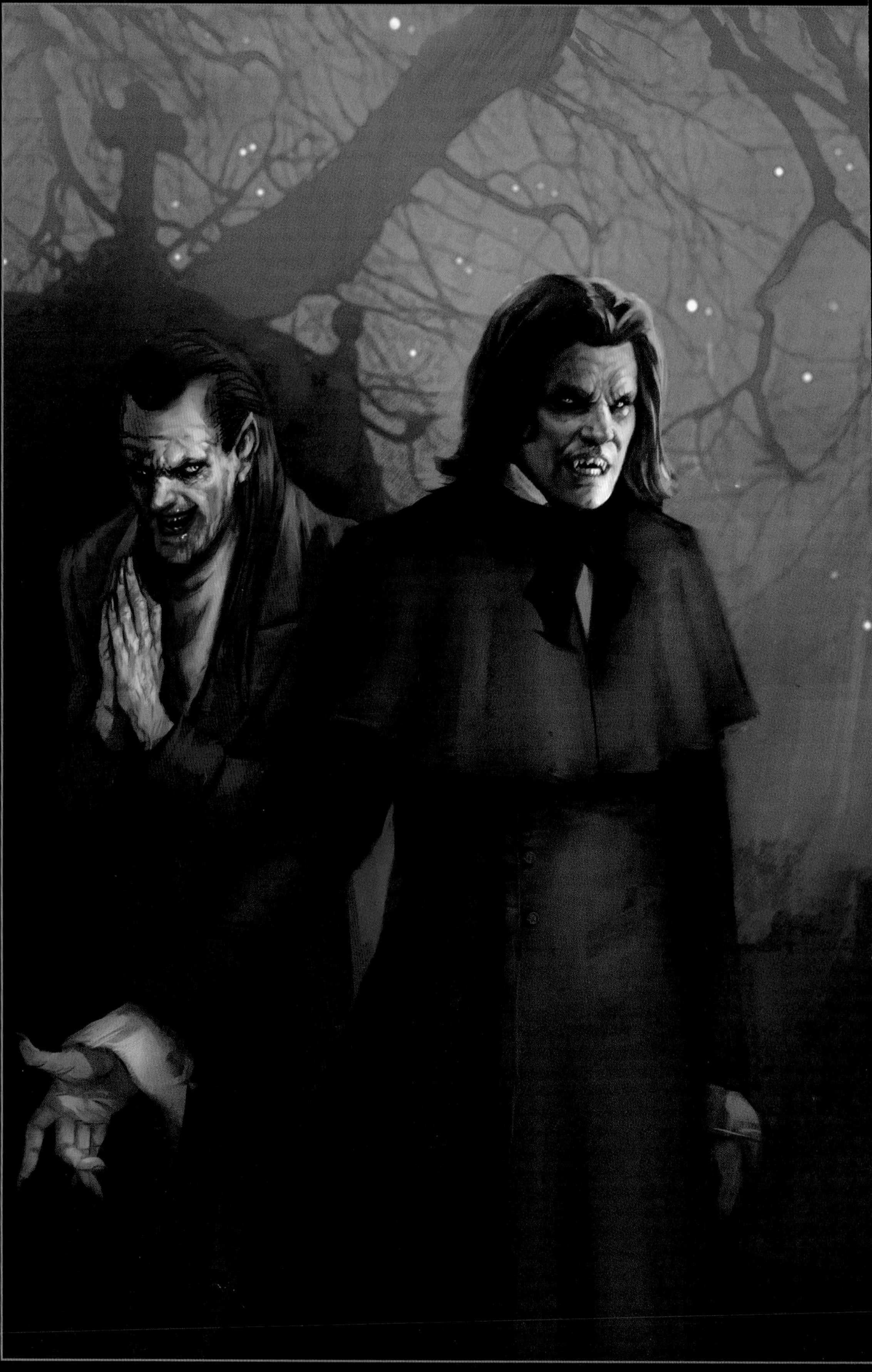

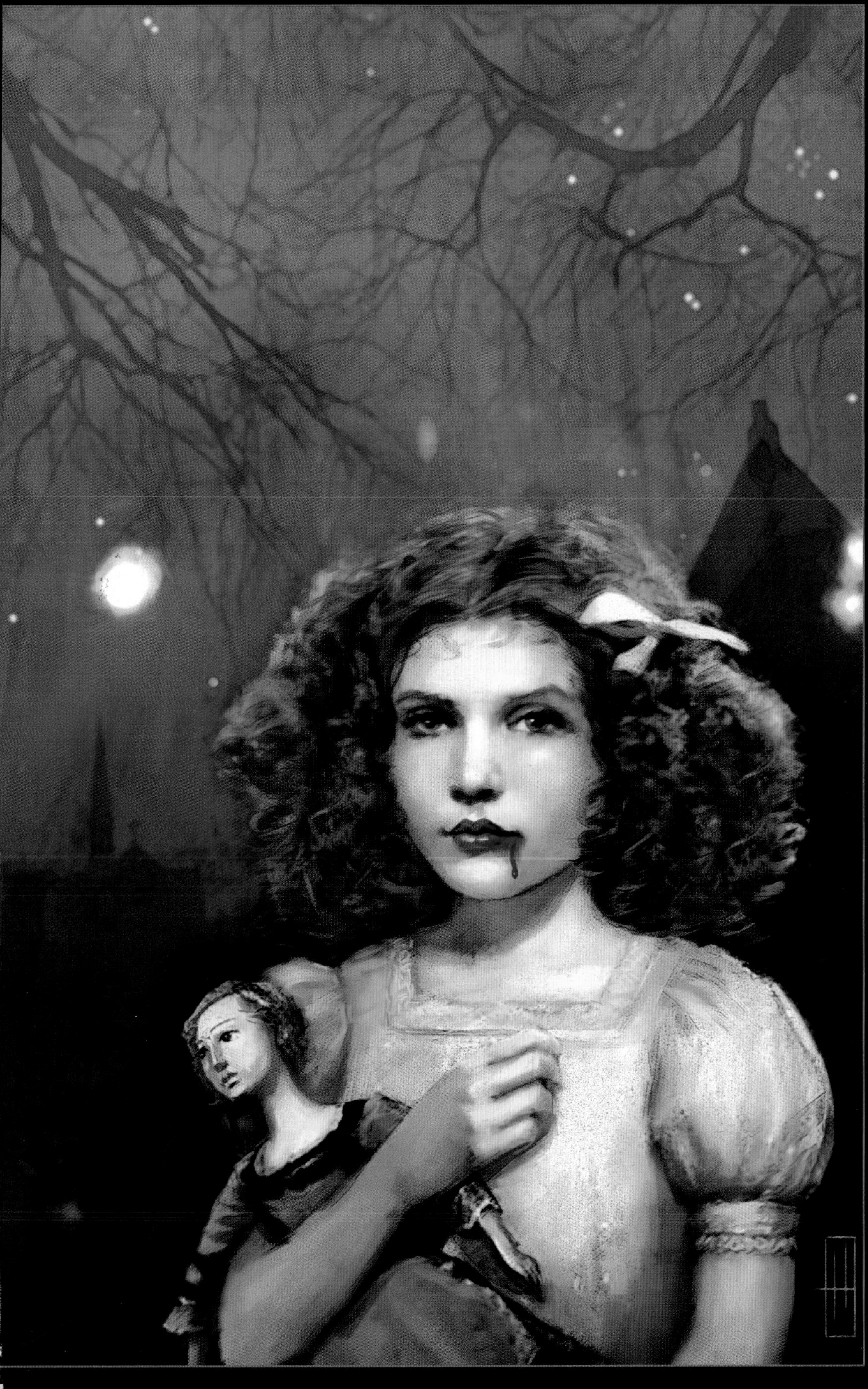

JUST JOSSING...
By Marv Wolfman

More has been written about vampires throughout the world than any other fictional monster. There has been an uncountable number of novels and short stories, movies, anime, video games, television shows, "true" stories, and yes, comic books, too. All exploring the psycho-sexual aspects of these walking undead, all searching desperately to find something new to say about them. For some reason we are endlessly fascinated by this perverse, reverse-Christian monster and can't get enough of it. Thank God for that.

During the 1970s I spent more than eight years sucking at the teat of Bram Stoker with Marvel Comics' award-winning series, *The Tomb of Dracula*, and later on a few more months with *The Curse of Dracula*, published by Dark Horse. To keep things exciting, I created many different characters, the most notable being Blade, the Vampire Hunter, who later starred in two excellent films with a third to come in December of 2004 featuring another of my characters, the vampire detective Hannibal King.

I know how hard it is to keep coming up with new approaches to the old myths, to keep the readers not only interested, but demanding even more.

Which leads us to a most improbably named character, *Buffy the Vampire Slayer*. The original *Buffy* movie was part joke and part horror film. Compared with the TV series to come, the movie is often put down, unfairly I think, because underneath whatever problems it may have had, it also had an abundance of truly original ideas. At any rate, it didn't do too well at the box office, which is all that counts in Hollywood, and within a few weeks it was out of the theaters, consigned to rerunning forever on cable TV.

Yet, like the vampire that won't stay dead, *Buffy* returned, this time to television, and this time she was done right.

Taking his cues from Stoker's Dracula, and perhaps, according to some interviews he's given, even mine, *Buffy* creator Joss Whedon fashioned a brilliant mythology that he and his writers explored week after week, enriching it throughout the seasons, adding characters and ideas, but never losing focus of his main heroes, Buffy, Xander, and Willow. The writers made us care about these fictional people who grew and changed and matured. Joss and company made us care for them so much we didn't even scream in protest when he introduced, seemingly from nowhere, Buffy's non-existent younger sister, surely a shark-jumping character if anyone else had created her. But Joss and his writers made her work, and we accepted her.

Buffy transcended ordinary television because, though the plots dealt with the melodrama of fighting monsters, the stories were actually about people. They told tales that we hadn't seen before on TV, exploring ideas, friendship, growing up, religion, high school, college, and yes, even sex—God, did they explore sex—all in a mature fashion while disguised as something that, in less capable hands, could very well have been called, *Dude, Where's My Monster?*

As with all TV, *Buffy*, and later its spin-off series, *Angel*, finally came to an end. Normally, that would be the end of it; the writers would move on to some other show with little more than a "Bye, Scoobies. Bye, Angel. What's next?"

But the writers, again led by Joss, weren't done. Maybe they wouldn't be writing stories about the vampire hunters, but what about the vampires? Surely there were stories the writers wanted, perhaps needed, to tell? And if they couldn't tell these stories on TV, why not do them in comics?

Except, of course, that comics pay about a hundredth of what writers earn in television. But Joss and company created a Buffyverse that can't easily be walked away from. Which takes us to *Tales of the Vampires*.

The writers of *Buffy* and *Angel* have come together to spin eleven wonderful vampire stories that are surrounded by bridging material written by Joss. Interestingly, for people who work in the very rigid structure of television script writing, they are exploring comics, a very different medium, with eyes wide open and a desire to play with the form.

Tales of the Vampires successfully brings many new ideas to the old myths, enriching an already rich tapestry, but above all, making the reader, myself included, demand more.

Enjoy!
Marv Wolfman
June 22, 2004

TALES OF THE VAMPIRES

story by
JOSS WHEDON
pencils by
ALEX SANCHEZ
inks by
DEREK FRIDOLFS
colors by
MICHELLE MADSEN
letters by
ANNIE PARKHOUSE

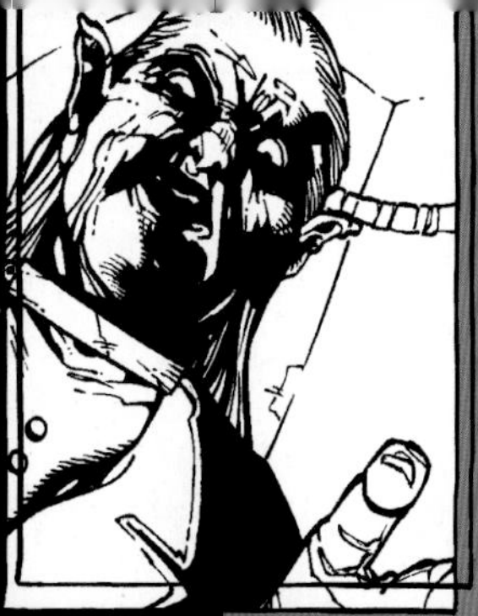

FATHER

story by
JANE ESPENSON
art by
J. ALEXANDER
colors by
MICHELLE MADSEN
letters by
ANNIE PARKHOUSE

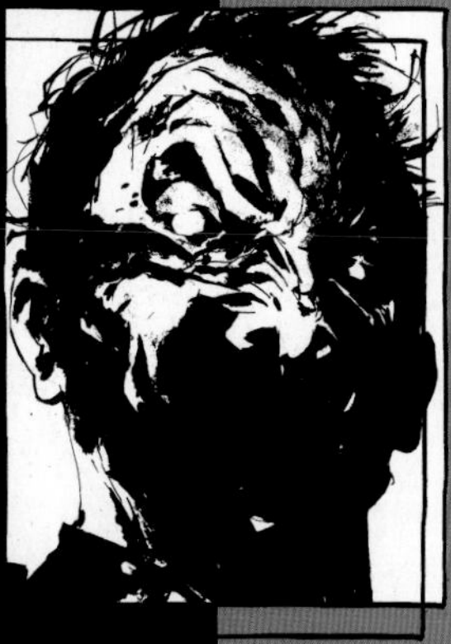

SPOT THE VAMPIRE

story by
JANE ESPENSON
art by
SCOTT MORSE

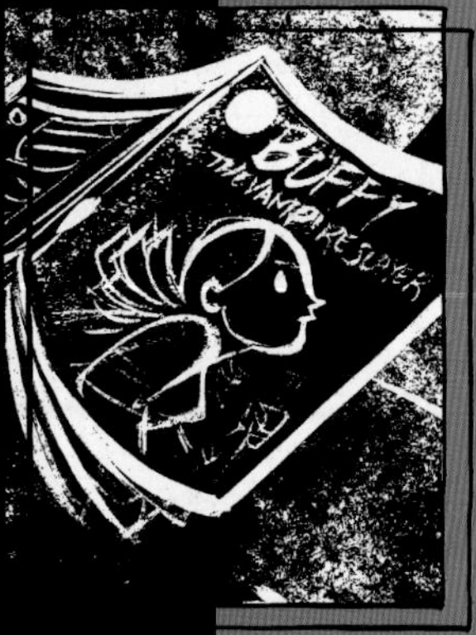
BUFFY
THE VAMPIRE SLAYER

DUST BOWL

story by
JANE ESPENSON
art by
JEFF PARKER

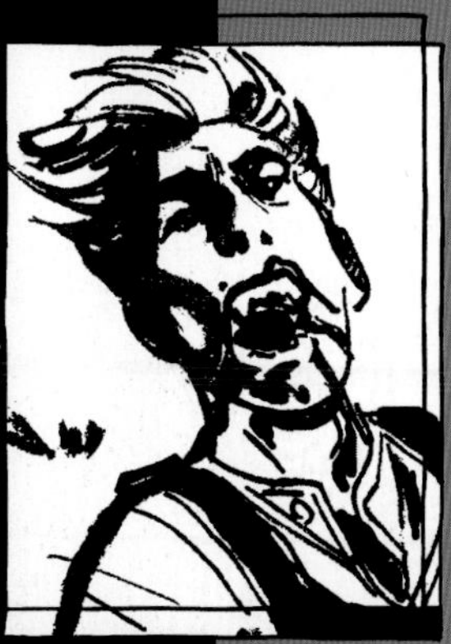

JACK

story by
BRETT MATTHEWS
art by
VATCHE MAVLIAN
colors by
MICHELLE MADSEN
letters by
ANNIE PARKHOUSE

STACY

story by
JOSS WHEDON
art by
CAMERON STEWART
color assists by
CHIP ZDARSKY
letters by
ANNIE PARKHOUSE

SOME LIKE IT HOT

story by
SAM LOEB
art by
TIM SALE
letters by
RICHARD STARKINGS and COMICRAFT

THE PROBLEM WITH VAMPIRES

story by
DREW GODDARD
art by
PAUL LEE
colors by
MICHELLE MADSEN
letters by
ANNIE PARKHOUSE

TAKING CARE OF BUSINESS

story and pencils by
BEN EDLUND
inks by
DEREK FRIDOLFS
colors by
DAVID NESTELLE
letters by
ANNIE PARKHOUSE

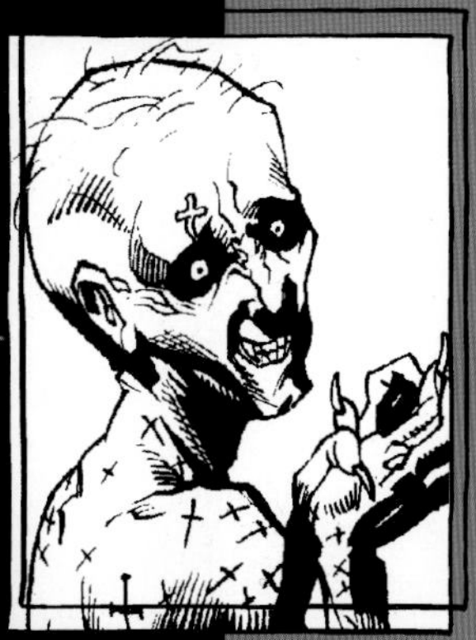

DAMES

story by
BRETT MATTHEWS
art by
SEAN PHILLIPS

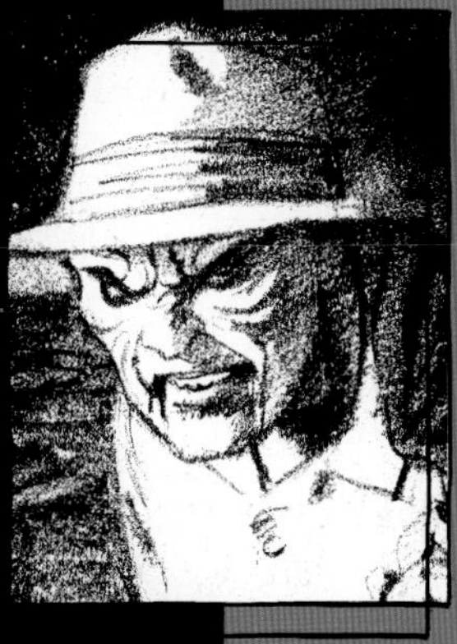

ANTIQUE

story by
DREW GODDARD
art by
BEN STENBECK
letters by
ANNIE PARKHOUSE

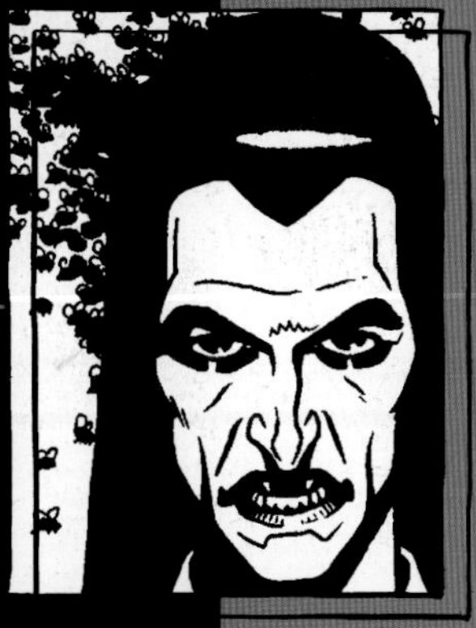

NUMB

story by
BRETT MATTHEWS
art by
CLIFF RICHARDS
color art by
MICHELLE MADSEN
letters by
ANNIE PARKHOUSE

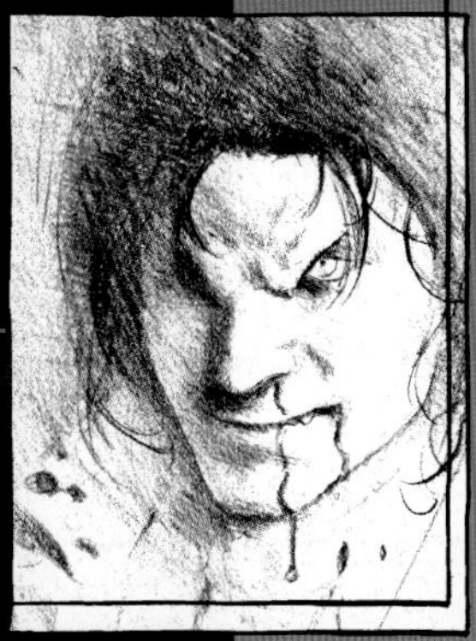

cover art by
MIKE MIGNOLA
cover colors by
DAVE STEWART
edited by
SCOTT ALLIE

publisher
MIKE RICHARDSON
assistant editor
MATT DRYER
book designer
LANI SCHREIBSTEIN
art director
LIA RIBACCHI

Special thanks to
JASON HVAM *at* DARK HORSE COMICS, DEBBIE OLSHAN, CRYSTAL YANG, *and* ALISON WALLACE *at* TWENTIETH CENTURY FOX, *and to* MICHAEL BORETZ *at* MUTANT ENEMY.

Special thanks also to
JEPH LOEB *and* MIKE MIGNOLA.

Buffy the vampire slayer™

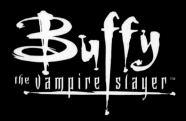

based on the television series BUFFY THE VAMPIRE SLAYER,
created by JOSS WHEDON

PUBLISHED BY
DARK HORSE BOOKS
A DIVISION OF DARK HORSE COMICS, INC.
10956 SE MAIN STREET
MILWAUKIE, OR 97222

FIRST EDITION: NOVEMBER 2004
ISBN: 1-56971-749-4

1 3 5 7 9 10 8 6 4 2

PRINTED IN CHINA

ALSO FROM DARK HORSE COMICS!

joss whedon
karl moline
andy owens
FRAY

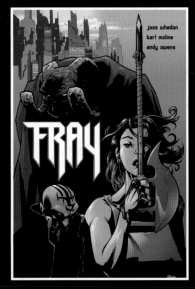

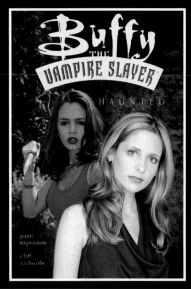

FRAY

By Joss Whedon, Karl Moline, and Andy Owens

In a future Manhattan so poisoned that it doesn't notice the monsters on its streets, it's up to a gutter-punk named Fray to unite a fallen city against a demonic plot to consume mankind. But will this girl who though she had no future embrace her destiny in time?

Full color
$19.95, ISBN: 1-56971-751-6

Buffy THE VAMPIRE SLAYER
HAUNTED
jane espenson
cliff richards

BUFFY THE VAMPIRE SLAYER: HAUNTED

By Jane Espenson and Cliff Richards

A body-snatching, blood-sucking poltergeist stirs amidst the charred rubble of what used to be Sunnydale High and Buffy's left to face it armed only with an enigmatic message from Faith: "You're already dead." Don't miss Jane Espenson, long-time writer for the *Buffy* TV series, bring you the only appearance of Faith in comics.

Full color
$12.95, ISBN: 1-56971-737-0

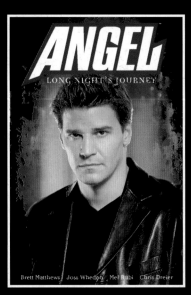

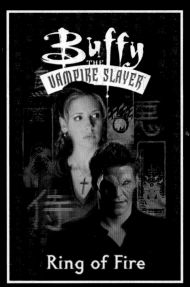

ANGEL
LONG NIGHT'S JOURNEY
Brett Matthews Joss Whedon Mel Rubi Chris Dreier

ANGEL: LONG NIGHT'S JOURNEY

By Brett Matthews, Joss Whedon, Mel Rubi, and Chris Dreier

An enemy from Angel's past has come to L.A. Now, in one catastrophic night, Angel must go toe-to-toe with three of the most unimaginably powerful monsters he has ever faced. Together, Brett Matthews and *Angel* creator Joss Whedon retool and reinvent Angel, crafting a story so big it wouldn't fit on the small screen.

Full color
$12.95, ISBN: 1-56971-752-4

Buffy THE VAMPIRE SLAYER
Ring of Fire

BUFFY THE VAMPIRE SLAYER: RING OF FIRE

By Doug Petrie and Ryan Sook

An apocalypse is brewing over the Hellmouth. Someone has stolen a set of ancient samurai armor from a cargo ship with the hope of reviving its demonic owner. How will Buffy and the crew stand against this unspeakable evil now that Angel has returned to his murderous ways?

Full color
$9.95, ISBN: 1-56971-482-7

HELLBOY VOLUME 1: SEED OF DESTRUCTION
By Mike Mignola and John Byrne

Watch as Hellboy, the world's greatest paranormal investigator, dives fist-first into battle with the most powerful wizard on earth. Witness as he discovers his link to the Nazi occultists who promised Hitler a final solution in the form a demonic avatar. Wonder at the graphic novel that inspired a major motion picture event!

Full color
$17.95, ISBN: 1-59307-094-2

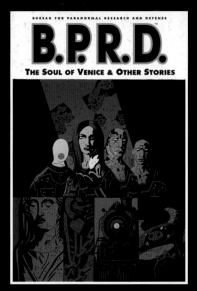

B.P.R.D.: THE SOUL OF VENICE AND OTHER STORIES
Featuring Mike Mignola, Geoff Johns, Michael Avon Oeming, Scott Kolins, Guy Davis, and others. Cover by Mike Mignola

Whether it's a goddess imprisoned beneath a sinking city, a ghost train full of GIs seeking vengeance, or a possessed teddy bear, there's no case too weird for the agents of the B.P.R.D., as proven by this collection of stories, which includes a brand new story by Mike Mignola and Cameron Stewart.

Full color
$17.95, ISBN: 1-59307-132-9

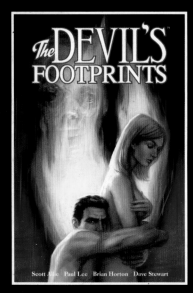

THE DEVIL'S FOOTPRINTS
By Scott Allie, Paul Lee, Brian Horton, and Dave Stewart

Even after death, William Waite's foray into black magic continues to plague his heirs. Now, it's up to his youngest son, Brandon, to protect his loved ones using the only means possible—witchcraft. But supernatural forces are unpredictable and Brandon's good intentions just might destroy everything he's trying to save.

Full color
$14.95, ISBN: 1-56971-933-0

THE DARK HORSE BOOK OF WITCHCRAFT HC
Featuring Mike Mignola, Jill Thompson, Evan Dorkin, Scott Morse, Tony Millionare, and others. Cover by Gary Gianni

Hellboy confronts the nature of monstrosity with a reclusive old woman, a young guitar player taps into the spirit of the blues, and a treacherous reverend leads the people of Salem Village to disaster—only a few of the terrifying tales you'll encounter in this horror anthology featuring the hottest names in comics.

Hard cover, Full color
$14.95, ISBN: 1-59307-108-6

AVAILABLE AT YOUR LOCAL COMICS SHOP OR BOOKSTORE
To find a comics shop in your area, call 1-888-266-4226. For more information or to order direct visit darkhorse.com
or call 1-800-862-0052 • Mon.-Sat. 9 A.M. to 5 P.M. Pacific Time. *Prices and availability subject to change without notice

DARK HORSE BOOKS™ *drawing on your nightmares*
darkhorse.com